THE CLASS OF
NONVIOLENCE

D1604623

designed by Colman McCarthy

ISBN 1440441480   EAN-13 9781440441486
The Class of Nonviolence was developed by Colman McCarthy of the
Center for Teaching Peace
4501 Van Ness Street, NW, Washington, D.C. 20016
202.537.1372

Table of Contents

Introduction

Welcome to class. Your class. Your time. Your future. The literature on nonviolence is rich with powerful prose and trenchant thinking. If peace is what every government of earth says it seeks and if peace is the yearning of every heart, then why aren't we studying it and learning it in schools? All of us are called to be peacemakers. Yet in most schools, the history, methods and successes of creating peace through nonviolence have no place in the curriculum.

The course you are about to take is designed to make modest amends for your peace miseducation. The eight lesson course could really be an eighty lesson course - the literature is there - but since we are all rushing about making sense or making progress, so we think, start with what's here.

Studying peace through nonviolence is as much about getting the bombs out of our world as it is about getting them out of our heart. Many people are avid about creating peace across the ocean but meanwhile there's a war going on across the living room. Every problem we have, every conflict, whether among our family or friends, or internationally among governments, will be addressed through violent force or nonviolent force. No third way exists.

In teaching courses on nonviolence to some 5,000 high school, college and law students since 1982, I have gone into this class the first day knowing I would have a better chance of being understood were I to talk about astro-neo-bio-linear physics and speak Swahili. They would get it sooner than they would nonviolence. Courses on nonviolence should begin in kindergarten and the first grade, and on up, which is how we do with math, science and language. Why not with peacemaking?

Your opportunity with this course is to get involved with remedial learning. In any subject, there are the four As': Awareness, Acceptance, Absorption and Action. This course is meant to place you, at least, in the Awareness stage. If you move on and Accept the truths you have studied, and Absorb them into your heart and soul, then you are ready for Action. Through reflection, possibly prayer, and an openness to risk-taking, it should become clear what kind of Action you are meant for.

Students are hungry to learn nonviolence. They understand it is much more than a noble ideal, it is also a basic survival skill. Learning nonviolence means that we dedicate our hearts, minds, time and money to a commitment that the force of love, the force of truth, the force of justice and the force of organized resistance to corrupt power is always more effective, moral and enduring than the force of fists, guns, armies and bombs.

Yet we still resist. Theodore Roszak explains: "The usual pattern seems to be that people give nonviolence two weeks to solve their problem and then decide it has failed. Then they go on with violence for the next hundred years and it seems never to fail or be rejected."

As a student, you have a right to courses in peace. Let's not only give peace a chance, let's give it a place in the curriculum.

Study hard. Think clearly. Listen well to others. Write forcefully. Be of one peace. And remember this thought of Martin Luther King: "The choice is not between violence and nonviolence, but between nonviolence and nonexistence."

Colman McCarthy

Readings for Lesson One

If We Listen Well
by Edward Guinan

Nonviolent Response to Assault
by Gerald Vanderhaar

Human Nature Isn't Inherently Violent
by Alfie Kohn

Axioms of Nonviolence
by Lanzo del Vasto

Teaching Reverence for Life
by Albert Schweitzer

Students Astutely Aware
by Colman McCarthy

If We Listen Well
By Edward Guinan

For too long we have considered peace as the absence of conflict. We have approached the issue with this limited perspective and have directed our attention to the prevailing conflict of the moment, attempting to discover ways of reducing the destructiveness of the event. This approach is both necessary and desirable, but insufficient as we continue to approach the problem in a fragmented and isolated way. We continue to deal in symptomatic terms as if war and destruction and violence are the extensions and natural outgrowths of malignant attitudes, values, relationships, and beliefs that we continue to embrace.

Peace

Conflict will always be an integral part of human life but our methods of dealing with it need to change. We must be willing to develop and ongoing critical view of our values, operating premises and relationships, and a sensitivity to those about us.

Peace demands that one anticipate the effects of his views and actions on others and the unifying or destructive effects they may have. Most importantly one comes to realize that the "end" does not justify the "means": we get what we do, not what we hope for or intend. You cannot improve a man through punishment, nor can you bring peace through war or brotherhood through brutalization.

Finally one comes to appreciate the reality that there can be not "wes" and "theys" in our lives but only brothers and sisters – all children of God – all sacred and dignified. Destruction of any one of these God-gifts means a certain destruction of oneself, and a mystery that is gone forever from this small, fragile world.

Violence

Violence can be seen as destructive communication. Any adequate definition must include physical, verbal, symbolic, psychological and spiritual displays of hostility and hatred. The definition must include both our acts and our inactions and that which is done directly to people or indirectly to them through what they esteem. Many forms will take on a combination of these characteristics.

Violence should then include physical acts against another (i.e., the range of acts from personal attack to war which violate human autonomy and integrity); verbal attacks that demean and humiliate; symbolic acts that evoke fear and hostility; psychological attitudes that deny one's humanity and equality (legal, institutional, and moral); spiritual postures that communicate racism, inferiority, and worthlessness (i.e., beliefs and values that demean or categorize). Violence then becomes a dynamic rather than merely an act.

Hunger, poverty, squalor, privilege, powerlessness, riches, despair, and vicarious living are forms of violence – forms that a society approves and perpetuates. We have been too willing to discuss violence in terms of ghetto uprisings, student unrest, street thievery, and trashing, and have been unwilling to direct our attention to the more pathological types of violence that are acceptable – the types that daily crush the humanity and life from untold millions of brothers and sisters.

In the sixties we spoke with alarm of the "increase of violence" in our society, which may have been a half-truth; violence became more democratic in the decade of the sixties. Instead of resting exclusively with those who construct and maintain ghettos, keep food from the mouths of children, and coerce the young through educational programming and into war, violence became the tool of a widely divergent group seeking equality, power and redress.

Under the umbrella of violence there reside two distinctively different phenomena. First, there is the violence of men and women who act out of frustration, hopelessness and anger in an attempted grasp at life – the act of the slave breaking the chains, which is understandable and inevitable as long as some humans are in bondage. The other type of violence is the violence of the respectable, the violence of the powerful that seeks personal gain and privilege by maintaining inhuman conditions. It is the violence of the board rooms, legislators and jurists – the white collar violence that puts surplus milk down sewers, robs workers of their wages, maintains prisons of infamy, lies to children, discards the weak and old, and insist that some should half-live while others rape and ravage the earth. This latter type of violence is what we must become aware of and actively dismantle if the future is to hold any possibilities for peace and a world where all men and women have a right to live and develop and participate by reason of their humanity, not by reason of their class, productive ability or shrewdness.

Nonviolence

Nonviolence cannot then be understood as passivity or indifference to the dynamic of life (i.e., communication between men). It is not the posture of removing oneself from conflict that marks the truly nonviolent man, but, quite on the contrary, it is placing oneself at the heart of that dynamic. Nonviolence means taking the responsibility for aiding the direction of human communication and brotherhood. Nonviolence means an active opposition to those acts and attitudes that demean and brutalize another and it means an active support of those values and expressions that foster human solidarity. Nonviolence, in essence, means taking a stand in favor of life and refusing to delegate individual moral responsibility to another person or group; it means taking control of one's life and aiding others in doing likewise. Nonviolence is an attempt to find truth and love even in the midst of hatred, destruction and pride.

As the means cannot be separated from the desired ends, nonviolence cannot be separated from peace, for it is the value system and dynamic that makes peace possible.

The Times

The past has not be given to us; it is not ours to breathe or exhale. We live with the smallest perimeter, which we call today, and into this brief moment, into this small space we beckon and command the future.

These are not good times, but good times do not mold great people. The sins of our excesses and arrogance can destroy us, or these failings can humble us to sainthood. Such are the times.

If the great virtues and teachings of the martyrs, resisters, and saints are relegated to a utopian or future-oriented condition, then indeed, they have little value for us at all. But the great heritage that this "community of liberation" has left us is not some unreal, impossible dream. It is this: Love can, and must, be lived today, despite the pain and difficulty of such life. Tomorrow will carry the tenderness and peace which we live now. Do not compromise today. It is all, dear brothers and sisters, that we have. This assembled community of peacemakers has paid dearly for their belief in such words and their lives form a chronicle of inspiration. They have been demeaned and laughed at; they have been dragged through jails and courtrooms and prisons; a few have paid the price of peace with their lives.

The Themes and People

The first signs of a violent society appear in its basic inability to communicate. Words lose their meaning and become hollow. They are twisted and deformed as tools of manipulation and servitude. Noble words such as truth, goodness, and love may come to mean despotism, obedience and death. Peace becomes another name for multiheaded war missiles, and nonviolence is wrenched to mean silence, or lack of opposition, to thievery, privilege and the status quo.

The Spiritual

A line from a contemporary song pleads" "Help me make it through the night." We find our existence framed in terms of aloneness rather than solidarity, struggles rather than consummations; departures rather than arrivals, questions rather than answers, and most importantly, night rather than daylight.

We cry out for fear the night will absorb us, yet we are unsure of any presence; we sing so as not to be crushed, yet the tones reflect the endless chant of the nightingales; we dance so as not to fall prey to these awesome interludes of emptiness; and most of all we pray so as not to lie. And these are the words we may use: "Help us make it through the night." Yet in the aloneness and struggle, in the departures and questions, in the cries and songs, in the dances and prayers there are imprints of heroic men and women, there are weavings of beauty, there are caresses of God. Traced through the faces of the old are messages of dignity and tenderness. The wail of the newborn is proof of silent breaths conspiring together. Each "forgive me" and "I love you" is prefaced by the warm tides of grace. Saints are born in Harlem in precise rhythm. Young people hurdle concrete mazes to touch and remember. Children weep for lost birds. Monks and mystics pray the sun up in the morning and call the evening dew. There are still wonderment, wishes and dreams.

You must never forget that you are the brother or the sister of a carpenter and the child of a king. You must remember that all life is unfulfilled without you. You must learn that life is mysterious and sacred and that you must never, never destroy it. And if you listen well you will hear the chanting of others, and they are singing to you: "Help us make it through the night."

Nonviolent Response to Assault
By Gerard A. Vanderhaar

I've never been mugged – at least not yet. I have often thought, though, about what I would do if someone jumped out of the shadows with a knife and demanded my wallet. Or if that pair of teenagers on the isolated New York subway platform swaggered over and asked for twenty dollars. Or when I was stalled on an empty freeway a car suddenly pulled in front of me and the driver stepped out pointing a gun.

I don't know what I would do, and I'll never know until something like that happens. But right now, when I can think about it coherently, I know what I would like to do: remain calm. I would like to save my life, of course, and avoid whatever would trigger violence in my assailants. I would want to do whatever would diffuse the confrontation and turn it around.

Like automobile accidents, fires, tornados, and earthquakes, the possibility of personal assault is a fact of life today. We are all potential victims of a sudden attack on our persons, our possessions, our life. Everyone should be prepared to face it.

Conventional wisdom says that if we can't get away, we should either submit or fight back strongly. "Save your skin." Self-preservation is nature's first law, we're told. Get by wit the least damage to ourselves. An empty wallet is better than a slit throat. Losing one's virtue is better than losing one's life.

Or we are advised to use force If possible. A Memphis police lieutenant who runs clinics on how to cope with rape gives this advice: "First, try to escape or scare away the assailant by wrenching free or yelling. If the criminal doesn't let go, then you either have to give in, or hurt him in the most effective and efficient manner possible." This means gouge out an eye. Kick hard at the groin. Shoot, if you have a gun, and shoot to kill. His advice has a point for people not sensitive to nonviolence or not practiced in its ways. Essentially he offers the two traditional modes of survival in time of danger: flight or fight.

If we really believe, however, that active nonviolence is an effective alternative to flight or fight in other areas of life, we need to explore how we can respond nonviolently when an assault occurs. Here are some true stories about people who were not experienced in nonviolence, not committed to ahimsa, but who did just the right nonviolent thing at the right time.

Three events

A women with two children in a disabled car late one night on the New Jersey Turnpike looked up to see a man pointing a gun through her window. He ordered her to let him into the car. Instead of panicking, she looked him in the eye and, like an angry mother, commanded, "You put that gun away and get in you car and push me to the service area. And I mean right now!" He looked startled, put the gun away, went back to his car, and did as ordered, pushed her car to the service area.

A colleague of mine walking late one winter afternoon was jumped by two young men hiding in the bushes under a viaduct. They demanded money. He said he didn't have any.

They began punching him, repeating their demand for money. He felt helpless and didn't know what to do. Then it flashed into his mind to call for the only assistance he could think of. He rolled his eyes and started shouting, "Jesus help me. Jesus help me!" And they stopped hitting him and looked at him as if he were crazy. And they ran away.

A lady drove into the parking garage of Memphis' largest hospital one afternoon to visit a friend. As she eased her car into a space she noticed a strange-looking man lurking nearby. No one else was in sight. She usually kept a gun in her glove compartment, she said later, but that afternoon she had left home without it. She had to think fast. She got out of the car, and as the man came over, she looked squarely at him and said in as firm a voice as she could muster, "I'm so glad there's a man around. Could you walk me to the elevator?" He replied meekly, "Yes, ma'am." She thanked him, got on the elevator alone – and practically collapsed out of fear and relief.

Although none of the three people were committed to nonviolence, they had improvised what we recognize as a true nonviolent response. They did not act like victims. They engaged the potential assailants as human beings, and in two of the incidents managed to evoke a sense of decency that resulted in their being helped rather than hurt.

Since we are faced with the possibility of being subject to assault – I prefer to say "subject to" assault rather than "victim of" – there is much we can do nonviolently to keep ourselves from becoming victims.

Prevention

It is very nonviolent, not to mention practical, to do everything we reasonably can to avoid being attacked in the first place. This includes locking doors, walking with others rather than alone, avoiding high risk areas, and being alert to potential danger wherever we are.

For a person tuned to nonviolence, prevention is not being cowardly, but realistic/ We are not helping ourselves or any potential assailants in the vicinity by naively thinking that everything will be all right all the time. Out of ahimsa, the desire for non-harm, we need to avoid making ourselves easy objects for attack. We should not tempt others to attack us.

If we see an attack coming, we should avoid it or seek cover. A woman in Hungerford, England, who was at the scene when a gunman began firing his rifle at marketplace strollers, killing sixteen people said she survived because she "dove for cover."

Our safety precautions send a strong signal to anyone who would do us harm. It is not that we are scared, but that we are alert and prepared to take care of ourselves. Two strange men entered an aerobics class in which my wife was participating and began talking loudly, distracting the exercisers. No one knew what they wanted, but they seemed capable of creating mischief. One of the exercisers went over to speak to them. He told them quietly how serious the class was, and that anyone who wanted to take part had to sign a waiver form and pay a fee. They were welcome to join if they wanted. He didn't accuse or threaten; he just spoke straightforwardly, matter-of-factly. They listened, saw his seriousness, then turned away and left the room. No trouble. That was an exercise in prevention.

Class of Nonviolence

Restraint

If we are against an attacker who is crazed by drug or drink, or who is schizophrenic, or temporarily insane, nonviolent human interaction is nearly impossible. If we have the opportunity, restraint may be our only recourse.

One man told me about his wife who had been mentally ill. "I looked into her eyes, and she seemed like she wasn't there," he said. She would scream and curse and throw things and was incapable of listening to anyone. She refused to see a doctor or do anything to help herself. Then one night, in one of her fits, she took a knife from the kitchen and started towards their child's bedroom. "That was the end of the line," he said. "I had to stop her." He bounded across the room and, as gently as possible but as firmly as necessary, her wrapped one arm around her from behind, grabbed the wrist of the hand that held the knife and squeezed until she dropped it. Then, still holding her, he dialed the emergency telephone number and waited for the ambulance to take her to the hospital. He said it was the hardest thing he ever had to do in his life.

When I think of restraining somebody, nonviolently, I would like to do it as strongly and effectively - and as lovingly – as that man did his wife.

Self-Possession

As a remote preparation, long before any attack occurs, we can sharpen our ability for an effective nonviolent response by increasing the power of our personhood. We believe that we are important, we are valuable, and we want others to believe it about themselves. We are not victims; we are not cowering and cringing before life's challenges, fearfully looking over our shoulder to see what might be pursuing us. We stand straight, eyes calm, alert, moving ahead. We walk confidently, not with cockiness, which is a way of compensating for insecurity, but in a straightforward and open manner. We are not rash or brash; we don't take unnecessary risks, blind to danger. We are who we are, and we present ourselves to the world that way.

The caricature of the swaggering sheriff with a pistol strapped on one side, a heavy flashlight on the other, a Billy club dangling from his belt, so loaded down that he walks with his elbows pointed outward, is the image of a fearful man, so lacking in self-confidence that he needs all this hardware to protect himself.

If we are so dominated by fear that we arm ourselves to hurt those who would attack us, we have sunk to the level of the assaulter. We have become like the enemy in our desperation to overcome the enemy.

In principle, people committed to nonviolence don't carry weapons. It is because we believe in ahimsa, but it is also because we believe that in a crisis our personal ability is more effective than a gun. Truth, righteousness, and readiness are powerful nonviolent weapons. Armed with these, our personal power increases.

These weapons, more than guns and knives, have a deterrent effect on a would-be attacker. Think of a robber lurking in a doorway late at night watching potential marks approaching down the street. The robber will want to pick out those who look like easy victims: timid, uncertain, fearful, unprotected. Someone who appears in command, confident, will not be as appealing a target. If I am this person, I'm likely to be passed over in favor of an easier target (and I'll probably never know how close I came to being attacked.)

A large-statured friend of mine, a long-time peace activist, wasn't passed over once. In a small town in South Dakota, on a sidewalk in full daylight he was suddenly faced with a much smaller man flashing a knife and demanding money. My friend, who has very little money anyway, said that the first thing he thought of was the incongruity of their sizes. "All I could do was laugh," he said. He didn't feel any fear, although later he said he was surprised he hadn't. His self-confidence was deep. The assailant glanced up at him, looked puzzled, then turned and ran away.

If an attack does occur, this kind of self-possession, this awareness of our personal power, this confidence in our nonviolent armor is the foundation of defense. But it's only the foundation. An understanding of what is likely to happen and some practice in nonviolent techniques can give us a truly effective defense against personal assault.

Human Nature Isn't Inherently Violent
By Alfie Kohn

Peace activists can tell when it's coming. Tipped off by a helpless shrug or a patronizing smile, they brace themselves to hear the phrase once again. "Sure, I'm in favor of stopping the arms race. But aren't you being idealistic? After all, aggression is just" – here it comes – "part of human nature."

Like the animals, ~ "red in tooth and claw," as Tennyson put it – human beings are thought to be unavoidably violent creatures. Surveys of adults, undergraduates, and high school students have found that about 60 percent agree with this statement. "Human nature being what it is, there will always be war." It may be part of our society's folk wisdom, but it sets most of the expert's heads to shaking. Take the belief, popularized by Sigmund Freud and animal researcher Konrad Lorenz, that we have within us, naturally and spontaneously, a reservoir of aggressive energy. This force, which builds by itself, must be periodically drained off – by participating in competitive sports, for instance – lest we explode into violence.

It is an appealing model because it is easy to visualize. It is also false. John Paul Scott, professor emeritus at Bowling Green State University in Bowling Green, Ohio, has written: "All of our present data indicate that fighting behavior among higher mammals, including man, originates in external stimulation and that there is no evidence of spontaneous internal stimulation."

Clearly, many individuals – and whole cultures – manage quite well without behaving aggressively, and there is no evidence of the inexorable buildup of pressure this "hydraulic" model would predict.

The theory also predicts that venting aggressive energy should make us less aggressive – an effect known as "catharsis," which follows Aristotle's idea that we can be purged of unpleasant emotions by watching tragic dramas. But one study after another has shown that we are likely to become more violent after watching or participating in such pastimes.

Although the hydraulic model has been discredited, the more general belief in an innate human propensity for violence has not been so easily shaken. Among the arguments one hears is these: Animals are aggressive and we cannot escape the legacy of our evolutionary ancestors; human history is dominated by takes of war and cruelty, and certain areas of the brain and particular hormones are linked to aggression, proving a biological basis for such behavior.

First, we should be cautious in drawing lessons from other species to explain our own behavior, given the mediating force of culture and our capacity for reflection.

But even animals are not as aggressive as some people think – unless the term "aggression" includes killing to eat. Organized group aggression is rare in other species, and the aggression that does exist is typically a function of the environment in which animals find themselves.

Scientists have discovered that altering animals' environment, or the way they are reared, can have a profound impact on the level of aggression found in virtually all species. Furthermore, animals cooperate both within and among species far more than many of us may assume on the basis of watching nature documentaries.

When we turn to human history, we find an alarming number of aggressive behaviors, but we do not find reason to believe the problem is innate. Here are some of the points made by critics of biological determinism:

• Even if a given behavior is universal, we cannot automatically conclude that it is part of our biological nature. All known cultures may produce pottery, but that does not mean that there is a gene for pottery-making.

• Aggression is no where near universal. Many hunter-gatherer societies in particular are entirely peaceful. And the cultures that are "closer to nature" would be expected to be the most warlike if the proclivity for war were really part of that nature. Just the reverse seems to be true.

• While it is indisputable that wars have been fought, the fact that they seem to dominate our history may say more about how history is presented than about what actually happened.

• Many people have claimed that human nature is aggressive after having lumped together a wide range of emotions and behavior under the label of aggression. While cannibalism, for example, is sometimes perceived as aggression, it might represent a religious ritual rather than an expression of hostility.

It is true that the presence of some hormones or the stimulation of certain sections of the brain has been experimentally linked with aggression. But after describing these mechanisms in some detail, K.E. Moyer, a physiologist at Carnegie-Mellon University in Pittsburgh, emphasizes that "aggressive behavior is stimulus-bound. That is, even though the neural system specific to a particular kind of aggression is well activated, the behavior does not occur unless an appropriate target is available (and even then) it can be inhibited."

Regardless of the evolutionary or neurological factors said to underlie aggression, "biological" simply does not mean "unavoidable." The fact that people voluntarily fast or remain celibate shows that even hunger and sex drives can be overridden.

All this concerns the matter of aggressiveness in general. The idea that war in particular is biologically determined is even more far-fetched.

To begin with, we tend to make generalizations about the whole species on the basis of our own experience. "People in a highly warlike society are likely to overestimate the propensity toward war in human nature," says Donald Greenberg, a sociologist at the University of Missouri.

The historical record, according to the Congressional Research Service, shows the United States is one of the most warlike societies on the planet, having intervened militarily around the world more than 150 times since 1850. Within such a society, not surprisingly, the intellectual traditions supporting the view that aggression is more a function of nature than nurture have found a ready audience. The mass media also play a significant role in perpetuating outdated views on violence, according to Jeffrey Goldstein, a psychologist at Temple University.

Because it is relatively easy to describe and makes for a snappier news story, reporters seem to prefer explanations of aggression that invoke biological necessity, he says. An international conference of experts concluded in 1986 that war is not an inevitable part of human nature. When one member tried to convince reporters that this finding was newsworthy, few news organizations in the United States were interested. One reporter told him, "Call us back when you find a gene for war."

Leonard Eron, a psychologist at the University of Illinois in Chicago, observes, "TV teaches people that aggressive behavior is normative, that the world around you is a jungle when it is actually not so." In fact, research at the University of Pennsylvania's Annenberg School of Communications has shown that the more television an individual watches, the more likely he or she is to believe that "most people would take advantage of you if they got the chance."

The belief that violence in unavoidable, while disturbing at first glance, actually holds a curious attraction for some people. It also allows individuals to excuse their own acts of aggression by suggesting that they have little choice.

"In order to justify, accept, and live with war, we have created a psychology that makes it inevitable," says Dr. Bernard Lown, co-chairman of International Physicians for the Prevention of Nuclear War, which received the Nobel peace Prize in 1985. "It is a rationalization for accepting war as a system of resolving human conflict."

To understand these explanations for the war-is-inevitable belief is to realize its consequences. Treating any behavior as inevitable sets up a self-fulfilling prophecy: By assuming we are bound to be aggressive, we are more likely to act that way and provide evidence for the assumption. People who believe that humans are naturally aggressive may also be unlikely to oppose particular wars.

The evidence suggests, then, that humans do have a choice with respect to aggression and war. To an extent, such destructiveness is due to the mistaken assumption that we are helpless to control an essentially violent nature.

"We live in a time," says Lown, "when accepting this as inevitable is no longer possible without courting extinction."

From: Detroit Free Press, August 21, 1988

Axioms of Nonviolence
By Lanzo del Vasto

"Peace" is a strong word. It has the same root as "pact" and presupposes agreement confirmed by sworn faith and the law. It has the same root as "pay" (pacare means to "appease") and so implies measured compensation. It is an act, an act that costs an effort. It belongs to the same family as "compact" and implies solidity and coherence.

This simple consideration of the meaning of words reveals the oneness of peace with justice which is stability, balance, and the law.

Everyone knows that injustice makes peace impossible, for injustice is a state of violence and disorder which cannot and must not be maintained. It asserts itself through violence, holds sway through violence, and leads to the violence of revolt, which shows that if justice is the reason for peace, it is at the same time the cause of revolution and war, acts that always draw their justification from the defense or conquest of rights and the abolition of injustice.

But we started off from justice as the foundation of peace, and here we come to justice as the cause of all conflict. Are there two justices then?

Yes, the true and the false.

The true, which is one as truth is one. True justice is at one with truth. It is above everything, in everything, inscribed in the order of things, exists by itself and is God.

False justice is double and contradictory and, like mental aberration, engenders illusion and idols. But men cling to these phantoms more tenaciously than to reality, and so are tormented and torn asunder and hurled against each other in the perpetual war called history.

Let no one say of justice what is commonly said of truth: that it is inaccessible. Say rather that it is inevitable, obvious as light to the eye, and all error claims its support.

How does true justice lapse into false?　　By means of these three arguments:

1. That we have the right to render evil for evil and to call the evil rendered true and just.
2. That the end justifies the means and good ends justify bad means.
3. That reason, agreement, and consent do not suffice to maintain justice and that it is just to have recourse to fear, compulsion, and force, not only in exceptional cases, but by means of permanent institutions.

These three arguments are tenets of faith for the common man, for the good as for the wicked. They are never called into doubt, never discussed, and on them people base their civil law and rules of behavior.

It has seldom been noticed that they are self-contradictory and can only lead to endless conflict.

Therefore justice and truth require us to disentangle ourselves from these arguments and their consequences. We must free ourselves from them under penalty of death. For

Class of Nonviolence

the fact is that if today we cannot find other means of solving human conflict, we are all condemned to die.

The good news that must be announced in our time is that these means have been found. They are the arms of justice, or active revolutionary nonviolence.

The nonviolent can be distinguished by their refusal of the three arguments everyone repeats in order to justify violence. Nonviolence says:

1. No, evil is not corrected or arrested by an equal evil, but doubled, and to have recourse to it is to become a link in the chain of evil.

2. No, the end does not justify the means. Evil means spoil the best causes. If the end is just, the means must be so too.

3. No, fear, compulsion, and force can never establish justice, any more than they can teach us truth. They can only twist conscience. Now, the righting of conscience is what is called justice.

The nonviolent directly adhere to and act from the justice that is one, universal, and as simple as two-and-two-make-four. Hunger and thirst for justice are what make them act. They are servants of justice and do not make justice their servant so as to justify acts dictated by the motives mentioned earlier or reactions dictated by the adversary's attitude.

That is why Gandhi names direct nonviolent action "satyagraha," that is to say, an act of fidelity to truth. The victory the nonviolent seek is to convince the enemy and bring about a change of heart, to convert him by fighting him and, in the end, to make a friend of him.

Is the thing possible? How can it be done? Who has ever done it? In what circumstances, and with what results? I shall not answer here. Whole books have been written on the subject.

The first thing to learn and understand what it is; the second, to try it out for oneself. But it cannot be learned like arithmetic or grammar. Learning and understanding nonviolence are done from within. So the first steps are self-recollection, reflection on the principles, and conversion, that is to say, turning back against the common current.

For if the purpose of your action is to make the adversary change his mind without forcing him to, how can you do so unless you yourself are converted? If the purpose is to wrest the enemy from his hatred and his evil by touching his conscience, how can you do so if you have not freed yourself from hatred, evil, and lack of conscience? You want to bring peace into the world, which is very generous of you; peace to the uttermost ends of the earth, for you are great-hearted, but do you know how to bring peace into your own house? Is there peace in your heart? Can one give what one does not possess?

As for justice, can you establish it between yourself and others, even those who are strangers and hostile to you, if you cannot succeed with your nearest and dearest? And what is more, if you cannot establish it between you and yourself?

But do not jump to the discouraging conclusion that in order to enter nonviolent combat one must be a saint, or a wise man, or perfect. This form of combat is for one and for all, and we can enter it as we are, with our indignities (and all the better if we are fully conscious of them.) But we should know that in principle, if not in fact, we must prepare ourselves as for all struggle. Here, however, preparation must be inward.

On the other hand, the struggle itself and the tribulations it involves are exercises that will help our transformation, and self-mastery is a pledge of victory over evil.

Peace and justice are harmonious adjustment which does not come about by itself but is the fruit of effort and work upon oneself, before and during confrontation. That is why Vinoba says, "The training ground for nonviolence is a man's heart."

But drill is not enough, nor courage, nor reason. There must also be music and a sense of harmony.

Let us proceed to the other tenets of every man's faith:

4. All violence, including murder, becomes lawful in the case of self-defense. Another argument that no one call in doubt. Do you? Yes. Because self-defense is legitimate, a right, and a duty, but murder, which is offense, not defense, is not.

Therefore, one should not speak of legitimate defense, but of justified offense, which is self-contradictory.

I have no more right to take someone's life in order to defend mine than I have to take his wife in order to ensure my own happiness.

Let it be called "natural' or "animal" defense. It is of capital importance not to drag the law into this matter.

For if we consider legitimate the exceptional case where one can see no other means of staving off aggression than killing, we shall build upon it a whole system of legislation and institutions whose sole office will be to prepare and perpetuate murder.

And that is what we have done. The army, the police, and criminal law are that and nothing else.

Defense will no longer be natural and for that reason excusable; it will be premeditated and systematic crime, and there will no longer be any moral restraint or limit to killing and cruelty.

5. Murder is not only permissible, but a duty when common welfare requires it. Now the "common welfare" in question is not the welfare of all. It is the welfare of a limited group, even if it includes millions of people (the number involved makes no difference.) Common welfare cannot be achieved at anyone's expense. Common welfare is justice and charity toward every human being.

6. Technology, economy. And politics are morally neutral. They obey their own natural laws. Here is how men build the gigantic machinery in which they are caught and crushed. That efficiency is good and always necessary for doing something goes without saying, but it is senseless to attribute value to it in itself. If efficiency lies in doing evil, then the better it is, the worse it is.

7. Justice is established order. This seventh argument, unlike those that have gone before, is not accepted by everyone. There is no regime which does not have its rebels. But the conviction of the greater number is sure that the ordinary citizen is ready to kill and die through obedience to law and power.

Now the law fixes morals. Morals are the effect of a certain balance of force between tribes and classes, hard-won pacts which make possible civil life and work in common.

By the standards of absolute justice, the law always has lamentable shortcomings, in addition to which holders of power commit errors and abuses, all of which is coated over by habit and ignorance. But should the balance or power shift, conscience awake, and there ensures revolt, which results in the creation of other states of injustice.

There must therefore always be a law to correct the law, and the law is constantly having to be amended and adjusted, as in liberal regimes.

But liberal regimes are unstable and continually shaken by rivalry, so that governments have more to do to stay in power than to govern. Nevertheless, they still have enough strength to abuse their power, and the people, enough passion and blindness to abuse their right of opposition. The liberal regime is no doubt more humane than others, but criticism by the opposition is less pure because it requires less courage. Legal and licit means exist of denouncing injustice in the press and raising questions in parliament, but the rich, the powerful, and the intriguers remain masters of the game.

That is why one must have no fear of resorting to direct nonviolent action if necessary, of breaking the law openly, of seeking legal punishment and undertaking fasts and other sacrifices, so that justice which is above all law may dawn in men's consciences.

This does not mean that direct nonviolent action is impossible in nonliberal regimes. To be sure, it is more difficult and victory less certain.

But whoever does not attempt it at a relatively easy stage deserves to fall into bondage and undergo dictatorship.

The fact is that in order to do, one must first be, and that has been our endeavor. We do not regard spiritual preparation as a means, but as something intrinsically more important than our outer demonstration or victory. Bringing man face to face with God, and face to face with himself is what matters and is desirable for its own sake. When the tree of life has been found again, our acts will fall from it like ripe fruit full of savor.

Much more than going into the street, distributing tracts, speaking to crowds, knocking on doors, leading walks and campaigns, invading bomb factories, undertaking public fasts, braving the police, being beaten and jailed (all of which is good on occasion and which we gladly do), the most efficient action and the most significant testimony in favor of nonviolence and truth is living: living a life that is one, where everything goes in the same sense, from prayer and meditation to laboring for our daily bread, from the teaching of the doctrine to the making of manure, from cooking to singing and dancing around the fire; living a life in which there is no violence or unfairness, nor illegal unfairness. What matters is to show that such a life is possible and even not more difficult than a life of gain, nor more unpleasant than a life of pleasure, nor less natural than an "ordinary" life. What matters is to find the nonviolent answer to all the questions man is faced with today, as at all epochs, to formulate the answer clearly and to do our utmost to carry it into effect. What matters is to discover whether there is such a thing as a nonviolent economy, free of all forms of pressure and closed to all forms of unfairness; whether there is such a thing as nonviolent authority, independent of force and carrying no privileges; whether there is such a thing as nonviolent justice, justice without punishment, and punishment without violence; such things as nonviolent farming, nonviolent medicine, nonviolent psychiatry, nonviolent diet.

And to begin with, what matters is to make sure that all violence, even of speech, even of thought, even hidden and disguised, has been weeded out of our religious life.

From: Warriors of Peace on the Techniques of Nonviolence, Knopf, New York, 1974

Teaching Reverence for Life
By Albert Schweitzer

No human being is ever totally and permanently a stranger to another human being. Man belongs to man. Man is entitled to man. Large an small circumstances break in to dispel the estrangement we impose upon ourselves in daily living, and to bring us close to one another, man to man. We obey a law of proper reserve; but that law is bound to give way at times to the rule of cordiality.

There is much coldness among men because we do not dare to be as cordial as we truly are.

Just as the wave cannot exist for itself but must always participate in the swell of the ocean, so we can never experience our lives by ourselves but must always share the experiencing of life that takes place all around us.

The ethics of reverence for life requires that all of us somehow and in something shall act as men toward other men. Those who in their occupations have nothing to give as men to other men, and who possess nothing else they can give away, must sacrifice some of their time and leisure, no matter how sparse it may be. Choose an avocation, the ethics of reverence for life commands – an inconspicuous, perhaps a secret avocation. Open your eyes and seek another human being in need of a little time, a little friendliness, a little company, a little work. It may be a lonely, an embittered, as sick, or an awkward person for whom you can do something, to whom you can mean something. Perhaps it will be an old person or a child. Or else a good cause needs volunteer workers, people who can give up a free evening or run errands. Who can list all the uses to which that precious working capital called man can be put! Do not lose heart, even if you must wait a bit before finding the right thing, even if you must make several attempts.

Be prepared for disappointments also! But do not abandon your quest for the avocation, for that sideline in which you can act as a man for other men. There is one waiting for you, if only you really want it.

This is the message of true ethics to those who have only a little time and a little humanity to give. Fortunate are those who listen. Their own humanity will be enriched, whereas in moral isolation from their fellow men, their store of humanity would dwindle.

Each of us, no matter what our position and occupation, must try to act in such a way as to further true humanity.

Those who have the opportunity to serve others freely and personally should see this good fortune as grounds for humility. The practice of humility will strengthen their will to be of service.

No one has the right to take for granted his own advantages over others in health, in talents, in ability, in success, in a happy childhood or congenial home conditions. One must pay a price for all these boons. What one owes in return is a special responsibility for other lives.

All through the world, there is a special league of those who have known anxiety and physical suffering. A mysterious bond connects those marked by pain. They know the terrible things that man can undergo; they know the longing to be free of pain. Those who have been liberated from pain must not now think they are now completely free again and can calmly return to life as it was before. With their experience of pain and anxiety, they must help alleviate the pain and anxiety of others, insofar as that lies within human powers. They must bring release to others as they received release.

He who has experienced good in his life must feel the obligation to dedicate some of his own life in order to alleviate suffering.

Technical progress, extension of knowledge, do indeed represent progress, but not in fundamentals. The essential thing is that we become more finely and deeply human.

Doing and suffering, we have the chance to prove our mettle to people who have painfully fought our way to the peace that can never be attained by reason alone.

We are headed right when we trust subjective thinking and look to it to yield the insights and truths we need for living.

Just as white light consists of colored rays, so reverence for life contains all of the components of ethics: love, kindliness, sympathy, empathy, peacefulness, power to forgive.

We must all bid ourselves to be natural and to express our unexpressed gratitude. That will mean more sunlight in the world, and more strength for the good. Let us be careful not to incorporate bitter phrases about the world's ingratitude to our philosophy of life. There is much water flowing underground which does not well up from springs. We can take comfort from that. But we ourselves should try to be water that finds its way to a spring, where people can gratefully quench their thirst.

Thoughtlessness is to blame for the paucity of gratitude in our lives. Resist this thoughtlessness. Tell yourself to feel and express gratitude in a natural way. It will make you happy, and you will make others happy.

The man who has the courage to examine and to judge himself makes progress in kindness.

It is a hard fight for all of us to become truly peaceable.

Right thinking leaves room for the heart to add its word.

Constant kindness can accomplish much. As the sun makes the ice melt, kindness causes misunderstandings, mistrust, and hostility to evaporate.

The kindness man pours out into the world affects the hearts and the minds of men.

Where there is energy, it will have effects. No ray of sunlight is lost; but the green growth that sunlight awakens need time to sprout, and the sower is not always destined to witness the harvest. All worthwhile accomplishment is acting on faith.

The thing that truly matters is that we struggle for light to be within us. Each feels the other's struggle and when a man has light within him it shines out upon others.

The great secret is to go through life as an unspoiled human being. This can be done by one who does not cavil at men and facts, but who in all experiences is thrown back upon himself and looks within himself for the explanation of whatever happens to him.

None of us knows what he accomplishes and what he gives to humanity. That is hidden from us, and should remain so. Sometimes we are allowed to see just a little of it, so we will not be discouraged. The effects of energy are mysterious in all realms.

The epithet "mature," when applied to people, has always struck me as somewhat uncomplimentary. It carries overtones of spiritual impoverishment, stunting, blunting of sensibilities. What we usually call maturity in a person is a form of resigned reasonableness. A man acquires it by modeling himself on others and bit by bit abandoning the ideals and convictions that were precious to him in his youth. He once believed in the victory of truth; now he no longer does. He once believed in humanity; that is over. He believed in the Good; that is over. He eagerly sought justice; that is over. He trusted in the power of kindness and peaceableness; that is over. He could become enthusiastic; that is over. In order to steer more safely through the perils and storms of life, he has lightened his boat. He has thrown overboard goods that he considered dispensable. But the ballast he dumped was actually his food and drink. Now he skims more lightly over the waves, but he is hungry and parched.

Adults are only too partial to the sorry task of warning youth that some day they will view most of the things that now inspire their hearts and minds as mere illusions. But those who have a deeper experience of life take another tone. They exhort youth to try and preserve throughout their lives the ideas that inspire them. In youthful idealism man perceives the truth. In youthful idealism he possesses riches that should not be bartered for anything on earth.

Those who vow to do good should not expect people to clear the stones from their path on this account. They must expect the contrary: that others will roll great boulders down upon them. Such obstacles can be overcome only by the kind of strength gained in the very struggle. Those who merely resent obstacles will waste whatever force they have.

Students Astutely Aware
By Colman McCarthy

Teaching has its heartfelt and resounding moments, and for me one of them came on the morning of January 17 when I was leaving Bethesda-Chevy Chase High School. Some students from my daily 7:40-8:30 a.m. class were taking control of their lives. Independent control.

I had just finished meeting with my class, 40 juniors and seniors in a class called "Alternatives to Violence." On the eastern edge of the school's front lawn about 150 students had gathered around a wide stump of an oak tree. Atop it was a young woman giving a speech. When I moved closer, I recognized her s a student from my class. She was speaking to a rapt audience about the war in the Gulf and the need to give nonviolent sanctions a chance.

The evening before, as U.S. bomber pilots began attacking Iraq, George Bush had announced that the world could "wait no longer." He was wrong. This part of the world could wait, as small and peripheral as it seemed on the lawn fronting the school. All semester, while reading and discussing essays on pacifism by Gandhi, Martin Luther King, Jr., Dorothy Day, Tolstoy, and a long list of other practitioners of nonviolence, the Pentagon's preparation for war hovered over the collective consciousness of the class.

Now that the bombing and killing had begun, as more than three-fourths of the class had predicted it would by a show of hands one morning in October, the time had come for action. I looked among the students at the rally. I knew about 20. Some I would have figured to be there, because I had listened to their anti-war views throughout the semester. Others surprised me – reserved ones who had not said much in class one way or the other about the Gulf.

The senior girl who had been speaking when I came over was in the group. I listened in amazement. Where did all that passion come from? And what inner fires had been burning in the next speaker, a senior boy who spoke knowledgeably about draft resistance. Be aware of your rights, he said, and went on to tell about the national groups that provide counseling on conscientious objection.

When the rally dispersed, four students took a large sign – "Honk for Peace" and stood behind it on the highway in front of the school. A clamor of honks began. The group, joined by others, decided to cut classes and go be educated in democracy by visiting the anti-war protest in front of the White House.

They learned there that they were not alone, that resistance to the Gulf war was spreading daily in their country and in Europe. Mr. Bush has vowed that "this will not be another Vietnam." Wrong again. It took less than a week for America's streets, from San Diego to Boston, to be filled with citizens expressing their opposition and contempt for the same kind of war ethic that dragged the United States into Vietnam.

It is common of late for Vietnam veterans to return to Southeast Asia, in exercises of catharsis and reconciliation, and in many cases to ask forgiveness of the villagers who were bombed and sprayed by American soldiers. In 20 years, it could happen that today's U.S. bomber pilots will be returning to Iraq seeking reconciliation and peace. The anti-war demonstrators are saying rightly: Let's seek it now.

Up against the might of a war-approving Congress and the domination of the media by the Pentagon's version of events, plus television's one-sided reliance on ex-generals turned "military analysts" (why no peace analysts on these programs?), a few high school kids making speeches on a stump and holding peace signs is indeed small. Gandhi, as usual, had a thought: "Nonviolence is the finest quality of the soul, but it is developed by practice. Almost everything you do will seem insignificant but it is important that you do it."

Three of my students, articulate and spunky even at 7:40 a.m., were consistently skeptical about nonviolence, but they were willing to push themselves and the rest of us to think freshly about old problems. Moving beyond patented or conventional boundaries, and seeing life differently and acting in the riskiness of that new vision, is a breakthrough to be celebrated, not minimized. Wherever the newness leads, the students will go into adulthood as discoverers, not imitators and least of all followers.

From the Washington Post, January 24, 1991

Questions for Lesson 1

1. Explain what you think nonviolence means

2. Peter Maurin wrote that "society should be so structured that it is easy for people to be good." Do you think this is an idle dream? If achievable, would it make us more peaceful in our relationships?

3. Many anthropologists point to the violence in the animal kingdom as evidence that human animals are prone innately to violence. Are we really inherently violent or have we "learned" violence from others, from society?

4. Of all the forms of violence - physical, verbal, psychological, spiritual - which have you experienced and how did it impact you?

5. Can a nonviolent lifestyle be attained easily in the face of a government which resorts to violence to resolve its conflicts; is there a carryover effect from top-to-bottom stemming from a powerful example from one's own national government?

Class of Nonviolence

Readings for Lesson Two

Doctrine of the Sword
by Mohandas Gandhi

Gandhi in the 'Postmodern' Age
by Sanford Krolick and Betty Cannon

Family Satyagraha
by Eknath Easwaren

Ahimsa
by Eknath Easwaren

My Faith in Nonviolence
by Mohandas Gandhi

Love
by Mohandas Gandhi

A Pause From Violence
by Colman McCarthy

The Doctrine of the Sword
By Mohandas Gandhi

In this age of the rule of brute force, it is almost impossible for any one to believe that any one else could possibly reject the awe of the final supremacy of brute force. And so I receive anonymous letters advising me that I must not interfere with the progress of noncooperation, even though popular violence may break out. Others come to me and, assuming that secretly I must be plotting violence, inquire when the happy moment for declaring open violence is to arrive. They assure me that the English will never yield to anything but violence, secret or open. Yet others, I am informed, believe that I am the most rascally person living in India, because I never give out my real intention and that they have not a shadow of a doubt that I believe in violence just as much as most people do.

Such being the hold that the doctrine of the sword has on the majority of mankind, and as a success of noncooperation depends principally on the absence of violence during its pendency and as my views in this matter affect the conduct of a large number of people, I am anxious to state them as clearly as possible.

I do believe that, where there is only a choice between cowardice and violence, I would advise violence. Thus when my eldest son asked me what he should have done, had he been present when I was almost fatally assaulted in 1908, whether he should have run away and seen me killed or whether he should have used his physical force, which he could and wanted to use, and defended me, I told him it was his duty to defend me even by using violence Hence it was that I took part in the Boer War, the so-called Zulu Rebellion, and the late war. Hence also do I advocate training in arms for those who believe in the method of violence. I would rather have India resort to arms in order to defend her honor than that she should in a cowardly manner become or remain a helpless witness to her own dishonor.

But I believe that nonviolence is infinitely superior to violence, forgiveness is more manly than punishment. Forgiveness adorns the soldier. But abstinence is forgiveness only when there is power to punish: it is meaningless when it pretends to proceed from a helpless creature. A mouse hardly forgives a cat when it allows itself to be torn to pieces by her. I therefore appreciate the sentiment of those who cry out for the condign punishment of General Dyer and his ilk. They would tear him to pieces if they could. But I do not believe India to be helpless. I do not believe myself to be a helpless creature. Only I want to use India's and my strength for a better purpose.

Let me not be misunderstood. Strength does not come from physical capacity. It comes from an indomitable will. An average Zulu is any way more than a match for an average Englishman in bodily capacity. But he flees from an English boy, because he fears the boy's revolver or those who will use it for him. He fears death and is nerveless in spite of his burly figure. We in India may in a moment realize that 100,000 Englishmen need not frighten 300 million human beings. A definite forgiveness would therefore mean a definite recognition of our strength. With enlightened forgiveness must come a mighty wave of strength in us, which would make it impossible for a Dyer and a Frank Johnson to heap affront upon India's devoted head. It matters little to me that for the moment I do not drive my point home. We feel too downtrodden not to be angry and revengeful. But I must not refrain from saying that India can gain more by waiving the right of punishment. We have better work to do, a better mission to deliver to the world.

I am not a visionary. I claim to be a practical idealist. The religion of nonviolence is not meant merely for the Rishis[1] and saints. It is meant for the common people as well. Nonviolence is the law of our species as violence is the law of the brute. The spirit lies dormant in the brute and he knows no law but that of physical might. The dignity of man requires obedience to a higher law — to the strength of the spirit.

I have therefore ventured to place before India the ancient law of self-sacrifice. For satyagraha and its offshoots, noncooperation and civil resistance, are nothing but new names for the law of suffering. The Rishis, who discovered the law of nonviolence in the midst of violence, were greater geniuses than Newton. They were themselves greater warriors than Wellington. Having themselves known the use of arms, they realized their uselessness and taught a weary world that its salvation lay not through violence but through nonviolence.

Nonviolence in its dynamic condition means conscious suffering. It does not mean meek submission to the will of the evildoer, but it means the putting of one's whole soul against the will of the tyrant. Working under the law of our being, it is possible for a single individual to defy the whole might of an unjust empire to save his honor, his religion, his soul, and lay the foundation for that empire's fall or its regeneration.

And so I am not pleading for India to practice nonviolence, because she is weak. I want her to practice nonviolence being conscious of her strength and power. No training in arms is required for realization of her strength. We seem to need it, because we seem to think that we are but a lump of flesh. I want India to recognize that she has a soul that cannot perish. And that can rise triumphant above every physical weakness and defy the physical combination of a whole world. What is the meaning of Rama[2], a mere human being, with his host of monkeys, pitting himself against the insolent strength of 10-headed Ravan surrounded in supposed safety by the raging waters on all sides of Lanka? Does it not mean the conquest of physical might by spiritual strength? However, being a practical man, I do not wait till India recognizes the practicability of the spiritual life in the political world. India considers herself to be powerless and paralyzed before the machine guns, the tanks and the aeroplanes of the British. And she takes up noncooperation out of her weakness. It must still serve the same purpose, namely, bringing her delivery from the crushing weight of British injustice, if a sufficient number of people practice it.

I isolate this noncooperation from Sinn Feinism[3], for, it is so conceived as to be offered side by side with violence. But I invite even the school of violence to give this peaceful noncooperation a trial. It will not fail through its inherent weakness. It may fail because of poverty of response. Then will be the time for real danger. The high-souled men, who are unable to suffer national humiliation any longer, will want to vent their wrath. They will take to violence. So far as I know, they must perish without delivering themselves or their country from the wrong. If India takes up the doctrine of the sword, she may gain a momentary victory. Then India will cease to be the pride of my heart. I am wedded to India, because I owe my all to her. I believe absolutely that she has a mission for the world. She is not to copy Europe blindly. India's acceptance of the doctrine of the sword will be the hour of my trial. I hope I shall not be found wanting. My religion has no geographical limits. If I have a living faith in it, it will transcend my love for India herself. My life is dedicated to service of India through the religion of nonviolence which I believe to be the root of Hinduism.

Meanwhile, I urge those who distrust me not to disturb the even working of the struggle that has just commenced by inciting to violence in the belief that I want violence. I detest secrecy as sin. Let them give nonviolent noncooperation a trial and they will find that I had no mental reservation whatsoever.

_____

[1] In Hinduism the Rishis are Holy sages, one of those to whom the mantras and hymns of the Vedas (sacred texts) were revealed. In the epic poems and Puranas the Rishis are regarded as a particular class of beings, distinct from gods and men, the patriarchs or 'creators.' The seven great Rishis - Marichi Atri Angiras, Pulaha, Kratu, Pulastya, Vasishtha are associated with the Big Dipper constellation.

[2] It is believed that Vishnu, the protector of the universe, would have 10 incarnations that would come down to earth to help mankind. At one time, there was an evil demon named Ravana, that all the other gods feared so much they asked Vishnu, the protector of the universe, to help them destroy him. Brahma had promised Ravana that none of the gods would be able to destroy him, so Vishnu promised the gods he would descend to the earth in human form. Vishnu was born on this earth as Rama, the son of a powerful king. With his wife, Sita, and the Monkey King, Hanuman, Rama went to Ravana's kingdom of Lanka, and was able to destroy Ravana.

[3] In the 1920s, when Gandhi was writing, Sinn Fein (Ourselves Alone, pronounced shin fane), was a separatist political group in Northern Ireland; the militant Irish Republican Army (IRA) was part of Sinn Fein.

Gandhi in the Postmodem Age
by Sanford Krolick and Betty Cannon

The theory of nonviolence as an offspring of democracy is still in its infancy. Mohandas Gandhi, the master of this philosophy and its methods, was educated in Britain as a lawyer and learned well the principles of democracy. Throughout his years in South Africa and in the campaign for Indian independence, his efforts in dealing with conflict were consistent with the basic beliefs of democracy. While others fought revolutions promising that victory would bring democracy, Gandhi brought about revolutions using democratic principles and techniques; his victories were signified by the acceptance of democracy. Gandhi never tired of talking about the means and ends, claiming that the means used in settling the dispute between the Indian people and the British Government would determine the type of government India would evolve. He was fond of saying that if the right means are used, the ends will take care of themselves.

Gandhi called his philosophy Satyagraha. In the United States it has been called nonviolence, direct action, and civil disobedience. These terms are inadequate because they only denote specific techniques Gandhi used. However, for the purposes of this discussion, we will use nonviolence to designate the philosophy and resisters to designate those who adopt this philosophy and carry out its methods.

The basic principle of nonviolence is to seek negotiations. The goal of a nonviolent movement is to establish an atmosphere that leads to a successfully negotiated agreement and thereby establishes the basis for compromise in the settlement of future conflicts.

The first step in a nonviolent campaign is for the resisters to define the minimum terms that they would accept in negotiations. Their minimum demands must be precisely that; every effort should be made to ensure that all resisters and opponents clearly understand this, because once at the negotiation table, these demands must not be conceded. They should reflect the fundamental principle involved. The price of bus fare was irrelevant to the freedom riders. The right of each individual to choose where he wished to sit was fundamental to the recognition of the principle of equal treatment regardless of race.

There are pragmatic as well as philosophical reasons for demanding the minimum terms. A statement of maximum demands can put the opponent on the defensive, and perhaps make him feel that the resisters have mapped out a master plan for the future that affords little latitude for expressing his ideas and needs. He would then believe that negotiations would result in his being forced to capitulate rather than in his gaining an honorable agreement.

Too many demands may be confusing. Dissatisfaction and disunity can result if serious negotiations reveal that the leaders and participants have different priorities. Furthermore, the opponent might seek a solution to what he believes is the main point but which is only of marginal importance to the resisters, and thus end up disgusted when his efforts do not yield settlement. More important, the opponent must clearly understand that the resisters cannot be "bought off" by minor or irrelevant concessions that do not recognize the fundamental principles involved. Thus the minimum demands must be stated at the beginning, repeated continuously, and upheld throughout the negotiations. The resisters must not accept any settlement that fails to recognize these demands unless they become convinced their position is incorrect. If the resisters are purists, as Gandhi was, they will also refuse to abide by an agreement to which the opponent concedes (possibly out of frustration) if he is not convinced of the validity of the resisters' position.

Publicity about the movement and its objectives is essential for educating the opponent, the participants, and the public. Resisters should pursue publicity with unrelenting enthusiasm, either on their own using a duplicating or copying machine or through newspapers and national television. They must publish the objectives, the strategy, and the tactics of the campaign. Secrecy has no place in a nonviolent campaign; it serves only to destroy communications with the participants and invite suspicion from the public and the opponent.

In a nonviolent campaign the opponent must always be informed ahead of time of the precise course of any action that is planned-for example, the exact route a demonstration intends to follow. This is particularly important if confrontation is likely since it reduces the possibility of violence through panic on either side. Of course, the authorities can thwart action by arresting resisters ahead of time, but plans that have been well publicized can arouse sympathy and attract support.

Publicity should also be understood as a form of communication that lays the groundwork for agreement. Until the opponent agrees to formal negotiations, publicity should be treated as a substitute. Honesty and accuracy are critical, as is the avoidance of any derogatory or slanderous statements. Insults from the opponent are best ignored. The movement will be judged by the honesty and fairness with which its case is presented.

The resisters' communications should indicate that they are listening as well as talking and are willing to admit a mistake or miscalculation. These steps must be continued throughout the movement until final agreement is reached. They are the basic tools for airing differences and settling disputes within a democratic framework.

Such activities may evoke a violent response from authorities who hope to quell the movement quickly. They might also bring a sympathetic offer to negotiate. However, it is most likely they will bring no response at all. Most nonviolent groups are destroyed by neglect, not by action. Finding their proposals are ignored, not even dignified by a response or reaction, resisters become stifled and the movement dissolves. Perhaps this is why pacifism has been considered weak and ineffective in America. It is all too easy for frustration to lead to violence. When this happens the resisters have lost the initiative.

Keeping the Initiative

Gandhi's most important contribution to the theory of nonviolence was his insistence that the resisters must keep the initiative at all times. While the opponent must be given ample opportunity to consider the proposals, he must not be allowed to ignore them. Gandhi fully understood that half the battle, indeed often the most difficult part of the battle, is to convince the opponent that he must deal with resisters. Even in using force the opponent becomes involved in a relationship with the movement and makes a commitment to resolving the issue. .

If the minimum demands of the resisters have been clearly formulated and extensively publicized, and if every avenue to the establishment of negotiations has been tried but the opponent has either refused to negotiate or will not deal with the minimum demands, then nonviolent direct action is necessary if the resisters are to keep the initiative. Direct action should be pursued only when all other alternatives, with the exception of violence, have been tried. The focus of the action must be carefully chosen, for it must both demonstrate the problem and elicit a response from the opponent. The action must leave the opponent latitude for response; above all, it must allow for face saving. While action should be dramatic, it should not be presented in a way that calls for surrender or capitulation of the opponent. A creatively negotiated settlement between equals remains the objective.

No matter what the response of the opponent may be, he must always be treated with the respect and dignity that the resisters are seeking for themselves. In actual practice, there are only a few times during a nonviolent campaign when direct action is truly necessary. During 25 years of almost continuous nonviolent activities, Gandhi used organized direct action fewer than 10 times.

The major techniques of direct action fall under two headings: noncooperation and civil disobedience. The techniques of noncooperation include mass rallies, strikes, picketing, and boycotts. The grape workers' campaign led by Cesar Chavez illustrates these techniques. The aim of the grape workers was honorable negotiations. They wanted to be recognized as a union with the right to bargain collectively with growers for wages, hours, and benefits. The workers established a union hall and held mass meetings throughout the campaign. When the growers were not willing to negotiate, the workers voted to go on strike, refusing to cooperate in harvesting the crop. The growers responded by hiring other migrants and some seasonal workers from Mexico.

The resisters then established picket lines near the farms in hope of gaining the cooperation of the strike breakers. Although this tactic continued daily for many months, it was not successful in preventing the harvest or in gaining negotiations with the growers. Chavez then decided to initiate a nationwide boycott of grapes. He sent the young people who had come to California to offer their support to the movement back to the cities to organize the boycott. This move widened the issue by creating interest and involvement across the nation. The individual shopper's decision about purchasing grapes was less crucial than the involvement of established union members who refused to cross picket lines to ship and handle grapes. In September 1966 the grape workers voted for the union with which the growers agreed to bargain.

The second method of direct action, more suitable to situations that do not involve economic relationships, is civil disobedience. This involves noncooperation with respect to a specific law or set of laws. In using this technique it is essential that all participants disobey only the law or laws specified, while obeying all others. The point is not to bring the opponent to his knees but to the negotiating table. Great care must be taken in selecting the law to be contravened. It can be central to the grievance or symbolic of it. The more important determinant is the involvement of the participants. From the resister's viewpoint, it should be a law that has regularly affected large groups. The number of people affected by the injustice is more important than the injustice done. This was understood by Martin Luther King Jr., in singling out public lunch counters that refused service to black customers as the issue of the Birmingham, Alabama civil disobedience demonstration. Such humiliation had been experienced by many blacks. The issue emphasized the demand for equal treatment, and the action pointed to the local laws that violated the rights of black citizens.

Civil disobedience is serious business. The deliberate violation of law is virtually guaranteed to evoke response from governmental authorities. The strength, determination, and cohesiveness of the resisters will be tested. Typically, arrests will be made. The ability of the movement to continue with disciplined resisters once the leaders are arrested is crucial. The aim is "to fill the jails," thus jamming the courts while retaining public interest and sympathy.

In Birmingham, King initiated the movement with only 20 resisters. Through nightly mass meetings, volunteers came forth in increasing numbers to fill the places of the men who were jailed. King testified that the turning point came when he called upon high school students to join the march to city hall, challenging the police barricades and courting arrest. The news service coverage of the march included a picture of a six-year-old being arrested. On May 7, 1963, the Senior Citizens Committee of 125 business leaders of Birmingham met with King. As they walked out on the street for lunch,

> ... "there were square blocks of Negroes, a veritable sea of black faces. They were committing no violence. They were just present and singing. Downtown Birmingham echoed to the strains of the freedom songs."

King states that when the meeting reconvened. "One of the men who had been in the most determined opposition cleared his throat and said: 'You know, I've been thinking this thing through. We ought to be able to work something out.' "

In their civil disobedience campaigns, both Gandhi and King focused on the ambiguity between the officially stated democratic principles and the clear violation of these principles in practice. "These campaigns compelled the government authorities to choose between ideals and actions. Either they had to renounce their democratic ideals and suppress the resisters by force in order to maintain their dominance, or they had to affirm their ideals, honestly negotiate, and replace dominance with compromise. As the choice became increasingly clear, the response of the authorities to the resisters depended in part on the reaction of the majority of citizens. In this, nonviolence paid tremendous dividends. By 1947 the majority of British citizens were unwilling to support massive repression of India. In 1960 many in the South and North were unwilling to support massive repression of civil rights marchers.

In a direct action campaign it is essential that the resisters avoid using violence in any form. This is not an end in itself; it is a means of breaking the cycle of fear and repression in order to establish a basis for trust and democratic negotiation. An. action cannot be characterized as nonviolent if it is performed out of fear, for that may lead to submission. As Gandhi was fond of saying, the mouse does not exercise nonviolence in allowing the pussycat to eat him. Gandhi also insisted that when one saw no choices except to respond with violence or to submit, violence was the better choice because it afforded more self-respect than did cowardly submission. He emphasized the third alternative, nonviolent resistance, as a conscious choice.

Nonviolence is sterile unless it is coupled with a program to bring about change. A firm commitment to refuse to respond with violence or to submit to fear comes from strength, courage, and self-discipline. Nonviolence is truly the conquest of violence.

Actors and Roles in Nonviolent Confrontation

Perhaps a clearer understanding of nonviolence can be gained if the conflict is viewed in terms of individuals. The average individual approaches a new relationship with mixed feelings. He hopes to gain understanding, respect, and appreciation; he fears that he may suffer rejection, disgrace, or humiliation. Most relationships contain a mixture of these feelings and reactions. The direction in which a relationship develops depends in large part on how conflicts that arise are resolved. If resolution based on understanding, mutual respect, and honesty is found, then a basis of trust is initiated. Each conflict that is resolved by these methods increases the trust and reinforces feelings of respect and understanding.

In contrast, if a conflict is not settled or is settled in a manner that leads one or both parties to believe that his basic rights and self-respect have been damaged, then feelings of misunderstanding and anger jeopardize the basis of trust. If this pattern is repeated in future conflicts, these feelings are reinforced. The ineffective means of resolving one conflict lays the foundation for dealing with the next, and this has a spiraling effect. Distrust, apprehension, and fear that stem from a lack of trust can come to govern the course of the relationship. As tension mounts each person becomes increasingly suspicious of the other's motives. Each then becomes afraid to yield his power and position because he imagines that his opponents will take advantage of him. Each clings to what he has, refusing to make concessions. Each believes any gain by the other is his loss. Each side thus becomes locked into a position, unable to move for fear of giving the advantage to the other.

Yet the strange part of such a relationship is that each becomes increasingly dependent upon the other. The negative feelings of distrust, anger, and fear tie them together like an invisible bond. Each perceives that he could or would change if he could trust the other, each looks to the other to make the first move for compromise, and each sees the possibility of resolving the situation as depending upon the other. The result is that both are deadlocked in a relationship that they find uncomfortable and threatening, yet one in which each has surrendered his own ability to solve the problem by assigning the other the responsibility for making the first move to end the deadlock. Each blames the other for the situation, which is only another way of assigning the opponent the power and responsibility for resolving the dispute. If the opponent has the power to create the problem, then he should have the power to resolve it. The ability to exercise creativity, individuality, and initiative is gone.

If the situation escalates, anger and fear build. Each party in the dispute begins to think of the other in dehumanizing ways. Each begins to imagine that the other is evil, and think and talk of him as sinister, scheming, devoid of human sympathy and honor. These thoughts can give rise to self-fulfilling actions; as each opponent spends considerable time scheming, entertaining uncharitable thoughts, and plotting revenge, he does become sinister and increasingly devoid of charity. Total victory—the ability to force the opponent into complete submission-is seen as the only way out of the situation. The appalling fact is that violence can so dehumanize people that they are willing to sacrifice their own lives in order to destroy an opponent.

Nonviolence is a program for breaking the cycle of fear while, at the same time, achieving the desired social or political ends. But it is not without its own risks. Personal injury, legal sanctions, and social criticism are always possibilities. Resisters have to weigh these costs when deciding whether their protest is worth it. Charles Evers, civil rights leader from Mississippi, weighed his participation this way:

> *"My life would be safe if I shuffled and tommed and said, 'Yassuh, Mr.*
> *Charlie, we niggers is real happy.' But then I'd be dead already. I'd rather die*
> *on my feet than live on my knees."*

In summary, we have presented the basic tenets of nonviolence. Our object has been to describe those tactics that resisters need to follow if they are to engage in nonviolent protest. These include seeking negotiations (where minimum terms have been defined and the objectives of the protest made clear) and keeping the initiative both at the negotiating table and, if necessary, in the streets. Direct action such as noncooperation or civil resistance should be used only if the paths to negotiation are blocked.

These tactics are bound to create tensions in a democratic society. Obviously, if many actions were protested, the society would be in turmoil and the government would probably resort to more and more force to maintain order. Democracy might soon be ended under the guise of protecting it. On the other hand, if governmental decisions and social mores could not be protested, then the system could hardly be called democratic. While majority rule is a fundamental principle, so is the right of a minority to defend itself, its rights, and its interests. Jefferson proclaimed this in 1776. But unlike the tactics that he and his fellow colonists used, the nonviolent resisters of this century have protested within the structure and, for the most part, the rules of the system. For the sake of democracy, it is well that they have done so. Violence threatens the character of the system; nonviolence is a democratic means of conflict resolution.

Family Satyagraha
by Eknath Easwaren

Personal relationships offer fertile ground to learn and use satyagraha. Gandhi called this "domestic satyagraha." We get a clear idea of what he meant when we look at his early life in South Africa —not, interestingly enough, at satyagraha as he was to develop it later, but as it was used against him. Gandhi was a domineering, sometimes petulant husband during those years in Johannesburg, because he believed, as he recounts, that it was his right to impose his will upon his wife. When Kasturbai objected to his unilateral approach, Gandhi only became more adamant. But Kasturbai had an intuitive grasp of the properties of nonviolent love, and during those tumultuous years of domestic strife, she proved to be Gandhi's equal. Her attitude transformed his relationship with her and in the process revealed to him the beauty and the power of nonviolent resistance.

"I learnt the lesson of nonviolence from my wife, when I tried to bend her to my will. Her determined resistance to my will, on the one hand, and her quiet submission to the suffering my stupidity involved, on the other, ultimately made me ashamed of myself and cured me of my stupidity...in the end, she became my teacher in nonviolence."

Without knowing it, Kasturbai had used satyagraha's foremost weapons to win over her husband: a readiness to suffer rather than retaliate, and an implacable will.

Family satyagraha is founded, like all satyagraha, on this delicate balance of patience and determination, in which, when rightly practiced can become a cornerstone for deep personal relations between men and women. The discovery Gandhi made in his own household at the turn of the century in Johannesburg is of critical importance today, when these relationships have become fraught with competition and tension. Few homes today seem able to withstand even the predictable tensions of married life. So that estrangement and alienation have become common ingredients in the modem household. At this low ebb, in family living, Gandhi's way rings especially true: forgive, forbear, support the other person always, and when it becomes necessary to resist, do so lovingly and without rancor. The apex of this ideal is reached when the wife's welfare becomes more important to the husband than his own happiness, and the husband's welfare takes on a similar importance to the wife. This kind of relationship marks one of the highest achievements of true ahimsa.

Between parents and children, satyagraha has a natural place. Here again, patience mingled with firmness frames the approach. The "irreducible minimum" in family satyagraha is that the welfare: of the children comes first; their growth and development take precedence over everything else. It means making minor sacrifices of small pleasures at times or saying no, gently but firmly, more often than one wants to. Most important, in Gandhi's thinking, is that the example set by the parents be true to their ideals. When Gandhi moved to Tolstoy Farm in 1909, it was with a motley group of children whom he immediately took under his fatherly wing. They were an "ill-assorted" lot, but in Gandhi's eyes, he and they were "all one family." "I saw," he writes, "that I must be good and live straight, if only for their sakes." The seeds of family satyagraha were sown by Gandhi in the rich soil of Tolstoy Farm, and years of careful husbandry brought them into full bloom; in time this demanding relationship with children became a natural, almost effortless attitude for him.

During the thirties a woman came to Sevagram asking Gandhi to get her little boy to stop eating sugar, it was doing him harm. Gandhi gave a cryptic reply: "Please come back next week."

The woman left puzzled but returned a week later, dutifully following the Mahatma's instructions. "Please don't eat sugar," Gandhi told the young fellow when he saw him. "It is not good for you." Then he joked with the boy for a while, gave him a hug, and sent him on his way. But the mother, unable to contain her curiosity, lingered behind to ask, "Bapu, why didn't you say this last week when we came? Why did you make us come back again?"

Gandhi smiled. "Last week," he said to her. "I too was eating sugar."

Gandhi was personal in all his relations. Even at the height of the freedom movement in India, he would not allow his campaigns to drift into nonpersonal postures. Regardless of how institutional his opponents might appear behind their marbled corridors and initialed titles, Gandhi's adversaries were always people first, "tarred with the same brush" and akin to him in their common humanity. Personal relationships were neither a luxury nor an imposition to Gandhi, but rather natural and vital expression of ahimsa; at each level of human interaction they build the forum in which satyagraha operates — It is interesting to watch Gandhi's circle of friendships gradually evolve from his immediate family in Porbandar and Johannesburg to his many followers living in his ashrams, until finally it included all India and much of the world.

One of the main features of satyagraha, as we have seen, is its "open-endedness," its capacity to adapt creatively to new contexts while adhering to its irreducible principles of truth and nonviolence. This flexibility has never been more important than today, when the challenges we face are so different from those Gandhi confronted. Merely to imitate the forms of Gandhi's political campaigns, such as strikes and demonstrations, would tragically limit satyagraha to the narrow context of political reform. The crises that threaten our lives today are not so much political as spiritual: personal and social matters of alienation, isolation, and increasing polarization between men and women, old and young. Consequently, our times require a determined movement towards nonviolence and unity in our families and communities.

Ahimsa
by Eknath Easwaran

Ahimsa, nonviolence, was the noblest expression of Truth for Gandhi—or, properly speaking, the way to Truth.

"Ahimsa and Truth are so intertwined that it is practically impossible to disentangle and separate them. They are like the two sides of a coin, or rather a smooth unstamped metallic disc. Who can say which is the obverse and which the reverse? Nevertheless ahimsa is the means; truth is the end."

Ahimsa is the bedrock of Satyagraha, the "irreducible minimum" to which satyagraha adheres and the final measure of its value.

In the traditional lore of India there is a story about an old sannyasi, a Hindu monk, who was sitting on the bank of a river silently repeating his mantram. Nearby a scorpion fell from a tree into the river, and the sannyasi, seeing it struggling in the water, bent over and pulled it out. He placed the scorpion back in the tree, but as he did so, the creature bit him on the hand. He paid no heed to the bite, but went on repeating his mantram. A little while later, the scorpion again fell into the water. As before, the monk pulled him out and set him back in the tree and again was bitten. This little drama was repeated several times, and each time the sannyasi rescued the scorpion, he received a bite.

It happened that a villager, ignorant of the ways of holy men, had come to the river for water and had seen the whole affair. Unable to contain himself any longer, the villager told the sannyasi with some vexation:

"Swamiji, I have seen you save that foolish scorpion several times now and each time he has bitten you. Why not let the rascal go?"

"Brother," replied the sannyasi. "the fellow cannot help himself. It is his nature to bite."

"Agreed," answered the villager. "But knowing this, why don't you avoid him?"

"Ah, brother," replied the monk, "you see, I cannot help myself either. I am a human being; it is my nature to save."

Ahimsa is usually translated as "nonviolence," but as we have seen, its meaning goes much beyond that. Ahimsa is derived from the Sanskrit verb root *san*, which means to kill. The form *hims* means "desirous to kill"; the prefix a- is a negation. So a-himsa means literally "lacking any desire to kill," which is perhaps the central theme upon which Hindu, Jain, and Buddhist morality is built. In the Manu Smriti, the great lawbook of Hinduism, it is written, "Ahimsa paramo dharma": ahimsa is the highest law. It is, as Gandhi puts it, the very essence of human nature.

"Nonviolence is the law of our species as violence is the law of the brute. The spirit lies dormant in the brute and he knows no law but that of physical might. The dignity of man requires obedience to a higher law—to the strength of the spirit."

The word nonviolence connotes a negative, almost passive condition, whereas the Sanskrit term ahimsa suggests a dynamic state of mind in which power is released. "Strength,"

Gandhi said, "does not come from physical capacity. It comes from an indomitable will." Therein he found his own strength, and there he exhorted others to look for theirs. Latent in the depths of human consciousness, this inner strength can be cultivated by the observance of complete ahimsa. Whereas violence checks this energy within, and is ultimately disruptive in its consequences, ahimsa. properly understood, is invincible. "With satya combined with ahimsa, "Gandhi writes, "you can bring the world to your feet."

When Gandhi speaks of ahimsa as a law, we should take him at his word. Indeed, it was a law for him like gravity; and could be demonstrated in the midst of human affairs. Gandhi even characterized his practice of ahimsa as a science, and said once, "I have been practicing with scientific precision nonviolence and its possibilities for an unbroken period of over 50 years." He was a precise man, meticulous and exacting, fond of quoting a Marathi hymn that goes, "Give me love, give me peace, O Lord, but don't deny me common sense." He valued experience as the test of truth, and the nonviolence he pursued and called "true nonviolence" had to conform to experience in all levels of human affairs. "I have applied it," he declares, "in every walk of life: domestic, institutional, economic, political. And I know of no single case in which it has failed." Anything short of this total application did not interest Gandhi, because ahimsa sprang from and worked in the same continuum as his religion, politics, and personal life. Daily practice could determine its value, "when it acts in the midst of and in spite of opposition," and he advised critics to observe the results of his experiments rather than dissect his theories.

> "nonviolence is not a cloistered virtue to be practiced by the individual for his peace and final salvation, but it is a rule of conduct for society. To practice nonviolence in mundane matters is to know its true value. It is to bring heaven upon earth. I hold it therefore to be wrong to limit the use of nonviolence to cave dwellers [hermits] and for acquiring merit for a favored position in the otherworld. All virtue ceases to have use if it serves no purpose in every walk of life. "

Gandhi's adherence to nonviolence grew from his experience that it was the only way to resolve the problem of conflict personally. Violence, he felt, only made the pretense of a solution, and sowed seeds of bitterness and enmity that would ultimately disrupt the situation.

One needs to practice ahimsa to understand it. To profess nonviolence with sincerity or even to write a book about it was, for Gandhi, not adequate. "If one does not practice nonviolence in one's personal relationships with others. one is vastly mistaken. Nonviolence, like charity, must begin at home." The practice of nonviolence is by no means a simple matter, and Gandhi never intimated that it was. As a discipline, a "code of conduct," true nonviolence demands endless vigilance over one's entire way of life because it includes words and thought as well as actions.

"Ahimsa is not the crude thing it has been made to appear. Not to hurt any living thing is no doubt a part of ahimsa. But it is its least expression. The principle of ahimsa is hurt by every evil thought, by undue haste, by lying, by hatred, by wishing ill to anybody. It is also violated by our holding on to what the world needs."

Class of Nonviolence

My Faith in Nonviolence
by Mohandas Gandhi

I have found that life persists in the midst of destruction and, therefore, there must be a higher law than that of destruction. Only under that law would a well ordered society be intelligible and life worth living. And if that is the law of life, we have to work it out in daily life. Wherever there are jars, wherever you are confronted with an opponent, conquer him with love. In a crude manner I have worked it out in my life. That does not mean that all my difficulties are solved. I have found, however, that this law of love has answered as the law of destruction has never done. In India we have had an ocular demonstration of the operation of this law on the widest scale possible. I do not claim therefore that nonviolence has necessarily penetrated the 300 million, but I do claim that it has penetrated deeper than any other message, and in an incredibly short time. We have not been all uniformly nonviolent; and with the vast majority, nonviolence has been a matter of policy. Even so, I want you to find out if the country has not made phenomenal progress under the protecting power of nonviolence.

It takes a fairly strenuous course of training to attain to a mental state of nonviolence. In daily life it has to be a course of discipline though one may not like it, like, for instance, the life of a soldier. But I agree that, unless there is a hearty cooperation of the mind, the mere outward observance will be simply a mask, harmful both to the man himself and to others. The perfect state is reached only when mind and body and speech are in proper coordination. But it is always a case of intense mental struggle. It is not that I am incapable of anger, for instance, but I succeed on almost all occasions to keep my feelings under control. Whatever may be the result, there is always in me a conscious struggle for following the law of nonviolence deliberately and ceaselessly. Such a struggle leaves one stronger for it. Nonviolence is a weapon of the strong. With the weak it might easily be hypocrisy. Fear and love are contradictory terms. Love is reckless in giving away, oblivious as to what it gets in return. Love wrestles with the world as with the self and ultimately gains mastery over all other feelings. My daily experience, as of those who are working with me, is that every problem lends itself to solution if we are determined to make the law of truth and nonviolence the law of life. For truth and nonviolence are, to me, faces of the same coin.

The law of love will work, just as the law of gravitation will work, whether we accept it or not. Just as a scientist will work wonders out of various applications of the law of nature, even so a man who applies the law of love with scientific precision can work greater wonders. For the force of nonviolence is infinitely more wonderful and subtle than the material forces of nature, like, for instance, electricity. The men who discovered for us the law of love were greater scientists than any of our modem scientists. Only our explorations have not gone far enough and so it is not possible for everyone to see all its workings. Such, at any rate, is the hallucination, if it is one, under which I am laboring. The more I work at this law the more I feel the delight in life, the delight in the scheme of this universe. It gives me a peace and a meaning of the mysteries of nature that I have no power to describe.

Practically speaking there will be probably no greater loss in men than if forcible resistance was offered; there will be no expenditure in armaments and fortifications. The nonviolent training received by the people will add inconceivably to their moral height. Such men and women will have shown personal bravery of a type far superior to that shown in armed warfare. In each case the bravery consists in dying, not in killing. Lastly, there is no such thing as defeat in nonviolent resistance. That such a thing has not happened before is no answer to my speculation. I have drawn no impossible picture. History is replete with instances of individual nonviolence of the type I have mentioned. There is no warrant for saying or thinking that a group of men and women cannot by sufficient training act nonviolently as a group or nation. Indeed the sum total of the experience of mankind is that men somehow or other live on. From which fact I infer that it is the law of love that rules mankind. Had violence, i.e., hate, ruled us, we should have become extinct long ago. And yet the tragedy of it is that the so-called civilized men and nations conduct themselves as if the basis of society was violence. It gives me ineffable joy to make experiments proving that love is the supreme and only law of life. Much evidence to the contrary cannot shake my faith. Even the mixed nonviolence of India has supported it. But if it is not enough to convince an unbeliever, it is enough to incline a friendly critic to view it with favor.

From Nonviolent Resistance, Schocken Books, 1961

Class of Nonviolence

Love
by Mohandas Gandhi

I accept the interpretation of ahimsa, namely, that it is not merely a negative state of harmlessness but it is a positive state of love, of doing good even to the evildoer. But it does not mean helping the evildoer to continue the wrong or tolerating it by passive acquiescence. On the contrary, love, the active state of ahimsa, requires you to resist the wrongdoer by dissociating yourself from him even though it may offend him or injure him physically. Thus if my son lives a life of shame, I may not help him to do so by continuing to support him; on the contrary, my love for him requires me to withdraw all support from him although it may mean even his death. And the same love imposes on me the obligation of welcoming him to my bosom when he repents. But I may not by physical force compel my son to become good. That in my opinion is the moral of the story of the Prodigal Son.

Noncooperation is not a passive state; it is an intensely active state—more active than physical resistance or violence. Passive resistance is a misnomer. Noncooperation in the sense used by me must be nonviolent and, therefore, neither punitive nor vindictive nor based on malice, ill-will, or hatred. It follows therefore that it would be sin for me to serve General Dyer and cooperate with him to shoot innocent men. But it will be an exercise of forgiveness or love for me to nurse him back to life, if he was suffering from a physical malady. I would cooperate a thousand times with this government to wean it from its career of crime, but I will not for a single moment cooperate with it to continue that career. And I would be guilty of wrongdoing if I retained a tide from it or "a service under it or supported its law courts or schools." Better for me a beggar's bowl than the richest possession from hands stained with the blood of the innocents of Jalianwala[1]. Better by far a warrant of imprisonment than honeyed words from those who have wantonly wounded the religious sentiment of my 70 million brothers.

Noncooperation and civil disobedience are but different branches of the same tree called Satyagraha. It is my Kalpadruma—my Jam-i-Jam—the Universal Provider. Satyagraha is search for Truth; and God is Truth. Ahimsa or nonviolence is the light that reveals that Truth to me. Swaraj[2] for me is part of that truth. This Satyagraha did not fail me in South Africa, Kheda, or Champaran and in a host of other - cases I could mention. It excludes all violence or hate. Therefore, I cannot and will not hate Englishmen. Nor will I bear their yoke. I must fight unto death the unholy attempt to impose British methods and British institutions on India. But I combat the attempt with nonviolence.

In theory, if there is sufficient nonviolence developed in any single person, he should be able to discover the means of combating violence, no matter how widespread or severe, within his jurisdiction. I have repeatedly admitted my imperfections. I am no example of perfect ahimsa. I am evolving.

From Nonviolent Resistance, New York, Schocken Books, 1961

[1] Jalianwala Bagh is a park in Amritsar where some 2,000 Indians—most of them Sikhs—were slaughtered by soldiers of the British colonial army on April 13, 1919. The massacre marked a turning point in India's struggle for self-rule: until then, many Indians might have been content with a high degree of autonomy under British rule; after Jalianwala, they would settle for nothing short of full independence.

[2] The word Swaraj is a sacred Vedic word meaning self-rule and self-restraint. By Swaraj Gandhi meant the government of India by the consent of the people.

A Pause from Violence
by Colman McCarthy

In a memorable, joyous ceremony last week at Crosslands, Pennsylvania, the government of India bestowed its highest civilian honor on Horace Alexander, a 95-year-old British philosopher and peacemaker who was a friend, student, and biographer of Gandhi. Alexander, a Quaker and a conscientious objector in World War I, first involved himself in Indian affairs in 1926, when he spent a week with Gandhi at the Mahatma's ashram in Sabarmati.

His most recent involvement was a 1983 preface to the second edition of "Gandhi Through Western Eves," Alexander's 1969 classic book in which the Gandhian way—the nonviolent, courageous way—is explained as the world's only rational option for peace.

The Indian government's honoring of Alexander — he received the "Decorated Lotus" award —comes late in this lovely man's long and inspiring life. But the honor breaks into the news when a pause from violence is desperately needed. .

India itself in past weeks has seen a bloody revival of Sikh-Hindu hatred in the Punjab. In the United States, the Reagan administration has sent 400 Stinger antiaircraft missiles to Saudi Arabia. This latest arms shipment ensures that America's role as the world's leading weapons dealer will continue. In 1983, according to the Congressional Research Service, our share of the global arms market rose from 32 percent to 39 percent. The Soviet Union's declined from 26 percent to 16 percent.

Crosslands, Pennsylvania. 30 miles west of Philadelphia, is a Quaker retirement community. Horace Alexander has lived there for the past six years with his American wife. Except for a slight hearing problem, his health is fine and his wit is sharp. Over the phone the other afternoon he said, "I never expected to live to this age—it's ridiculous!" On such current events as the shipment of missiles to Saudi Arabia, he sighed: "I think we're very good at wasting our money. We must change our whole attitude."

Alexander's memories of Gandhi are sharp. The two men were faithful letter-writers to each other. Their correspondence supplemented Alexander's regular visits to Gandhi from the 1920s to the 1940s. A photograph of the two peacemakers shows them crossing a field together near Gandhi's ashram. Alexander. tall and angular, is wearing a suit and tie and holds with his left hand a pair of bird-watching binoculars looped over his neck. Gandhi, barefoot and dressed in a white loincloth, carries a walking stick.

The two appear to be locked in conversation. It is easy to imagine them doing what only true friends can do for each other: disagreeing with gentleness. Alexander wrote of Gandhi that "to gain his respect it was essential that you should show yourself to be at some point sharply critical of him."

During World War II Alexander traveled to India as a staff member of the Friends (Quaker) Ambulance Unit. In 1943 he visited Gandhi during one of Gandhi's prison fasts. The two shared a high moment in Calcutta on Independence Day in 1947. "I remained in

India for some years after Gandhi's death." Alexander recalled, "and at one time considered making my home there. But I concluded that I really belonged in the West and that my job in old age must be to help. In interpreting India or at least Gandhi's India to Western people."

Few callings could be higher. Or more difficult. Schools in India offer no systematic teaching of Gandhi's philosophy of nonviolence and organized resistance. Honored, yes; studied, no. It is the same in the United States with Martin Luther King, Jr.. whose life was turned around by the reading of Gandhi.

In the epilogue to "Gandhi Through Western Eyes," Alexander describes Gandhi as a varicolored thinker. He was a conservative whose beliefs were "held together by a tradition of family interdependence and of village self-government. "He was a liberal who saw his adversaries not as enemies to be defeated but as possible friends to be persuaded: "I am a born cooperator," Gandhi said repeatedly. He was a radical: "Unless the world accepts nonviolence, it will spell certain suicide for mankind."

Horace Alexander is also a conservative-liberal-radical. At 95, and deservedly honored, he has seen and heard it all. Nothing, though, has come into his mind that has made as much sense as the teaching from his Quaker parents and Gandhi that the peaceable kingdom is eminently possible.

From the Washington Post, June 9, 1984

Questions for Lesson Two

1. What do you think Gandhi would say or do if he showed up in the United States at this time?

2. Gandhi believed that "poverty was the worst form of violence." What do you think he meant?

3. Why did Gandhi totally reject the notion of making anyone an "enemy"? Who was the "enemy" in Gandhi's mind?

4. Do you think the U.S. government in El Salvador mirrored the treatment of India by the British during Gandhi's time? The book, "Salvador Witness" by Ann Carrigan, on the life and death of Jean Donovan, will help you answer this relevant question.

5. Describe what Gandhi meant by ahimsa and satyagraha. Do these Gandhian doctrines jibe with his notion that it is better to resort to violence than cowardly retreat from nonviolently confronting unjust aggression?

Readings for Lesson Three

Love is the Measure
by Dorothy Day

Poverty and Precarity
by Dorothy Day

Undeclared War to Declared War
by Dorothy Day

This Money is Not Ours
by Dorothy Day

The Scandal of the Works of Mercy
by Dorothy Day

Dorothy Day
by Colman McCarthy

Love Is the Measure
By Dorothy Day

We confess to being fools and wish that we were more so. In the face of the approaching atom bomb test (and discussion of widespread radioactivity is giving people more and more of an excuse to get away from the philosophy of personalism and the doctrine of free will); in the face of an approaching maritime strike; in the face of bread shortages and housing shortages; in the face of the passing of the draft extension, teenagers included, we face the situation that there is nothing we can do for people except to love them. If the maritime strike goes on there will be no shipping of food or medicine or clothes to Europe or the Far East, so there is nothing to do again but to love. We continue in our 14th year of feeding our brothers and sisters, clothing them and sheltering them, and the more we do it, the more we realize that the most important thing is to love. There are several families with us, destitute families, destitute to an unbelievable extent, and there, too, is nothing to do but to love. What I mean is that there is no chance of rehabilitation, no chance, so far as we see, of changing them; certainly no chance of adjusting them to this abominable world about them, ~ and who wants them adjusted, anyway?

What we would like to do is change the world-make it a little simpler for people to feed, clothe, and shelter themselves as God intended them to do. And to a certain extent, by fighting for better conditions, by crying out unceasingly for the rights of the workers, and the poor, of the destitute-the rights of the worthy and the unworthy poor, in other words-we can to a certain extent change the world; we can work for the oasis, the little cell of joy and peace in a harried world. We can throw our pebble in the pond and be confident that its ever-widening circle will reach around the world.

We repeat, there is nothing that we can do but love, and dear God-please enlarge our hearts to love each other, to love our neighbor, to love our enemy as well as our friend. Whenever I groan within myself and think how hard it is to keep writing about love in these times of tension and strife which may, at any moment, become for us all a time of terror, I think to myself: what else is the world interested in? What else do we all want, each one of us, except to love and be loved, in our families, in our work, in all our relationships? God is Love. Love casts out fear. Even the most ardent revolutionist, seeking to change the world, to overturn the tables of the money changers, is trying to make a world where it is easier for people to love, to stand in that relationship to each other. We want with all our hearts to love, to be loved. And not just in the family, but to look upon all as our mothers, sisters, brothers, children. It is when we love the most intensely and most humanly that we can recognize how tepid is our love for others. The keenness and intensity of love brings with it suffering, of course, but joy, too, because it is a foretaste of heaven.

When you love people, you see all the good in them. There can never be enough thinking about it. St. John of the Cross said that where there was no love, put love and you would draw love out. The principle certainly works. I've seen my friend Sister Peter Claver with that warm friendliness of hers which is partly natural, but is intensified and made enduring by grace, come into a place which is cold with tension and conflict, and warm the house with her love.

And this is not easy. Everyone will try to kill that love in you, even your nearest and dearest; at least, they will try to prune it. "Don't you know this, that, and the other thing about this person? He or she did this. If you don't want to hear it, you must hear. It is for your good to hear it. It is my duty to tell you, and it is your duty to take recognition of it. You must stop loving, modify your loving, show your disapproval. You cannot possibly love-if you pretend you do, you are a hypocrite and the truth is not in you. You are contributing to the delinquency of that person by your sentimental blindness. It is such people as you who add to the sum total of confusion and wickedness and soft appeasement and compromise and the policy of expediency in this world. You are to blame for Communism, for industrial capitalism, and finally for hell on earth!'

To see only the good, the Christ, in others! Perhaps if we thought of how Karl Marx was called "Papa Marx" by all the children on the street, if we knew and remembered how he told fairy stories to his children, how he suffered hunger and poverty and pain, how he sat by the body of his dead child and had no money for coffin or funeral, perhaps such thoughts as these would make us love him and his followers. Dear God, for the memory of that dead child, or that faithful wife, grant his stormy spirit "a place of refreshment, light, and peace." And then there was Lenin. He hungered and thirsted and at times he had no fixed abode. Mme. Krupskaya, his widow, said that he loved to go into the peace of the pine woods and hunt mushrooms. He lived one time in the slums of Paris and ate horsemeat. He started schools for the poor and workers. "He went about doing good." Is this blasphemy? How many people are dying and going to God their Father and saying sadly, "We have not so much as heard that there is a Holy Spirit." And how will they hear if none preaches to them? And what kind of shepherds have many of them had? Ezekiel said in his day, "Woe to the shepherds that feed themselves and not their sheep!"

from By Little and By Little: The Selected Writings of Dorothy Day, Knopf, New York

Poverty and Precarity
by Dorothy Day

It is hard to write about poverty.

We live in a slum neighborhood. It is becoming ever more crowded with Puerto Ricans, those who have the lowest wages in the city, who do the hardest work, who are small and undernourished from generations of privation and exploitation.

It is hard to write about poverty when the backyard at Chrystie Street still has the furniture piled to one side that was put out on the street in an eviction in a next-door tenement.

How can we say to these people, "Rejoice and be exceedingly glad, for great is your reward in heaven," when we are living comfortable in a warm house, sitting down to a good table, decently clothed? Maybe not so decently. I had occasion to visit the city shelter last month where homeless families are cared for. I sat there for a couple of hours, contemplating poverty and destitution - a family with two of the children asleep in the parents' arms and four others sprawled against them; another young couple, the mother pregnant. I made myself known to a young man in charge. (I did not want to appear to spring on them when all I wanted to know was the latest on the apartment situation for homeless families.) He apologized for making me wait, explaining that he had thought I was one of the clients.

We need always to be thinking and writing about poverty, for if we are not among its victims its reality fades from us. We must talk about poverty, because people insulated by their own comfort lose sight of it. So many decent people come in to visit and tell us how their families were brought up in poverty, and how through hard work and cooperation, they managed to educate all the children-even raise up priests and nuns to the Church. They contend that healthful habits and a stable family situation enable people to escape from the poverty class, no matter how mean the slum they may once have been forced to live in. So why can't everybody do it? No, these people don't know about the poor. Their conception of poverty is not what poverty is.

And maybe no one can be told; maybe they will have to experience it. Or maybe it is a grace which they must pray for. We usually get what we pray for, and maybe we are afraid to pray for it. And yet I am convinced that it is the grace we most need in this age of crisis, this time when expenditures reach into the billions to defend "our American way of life." Maybe this defense itself will bring down upon us the poverty we are afraid to pray for.

I well remember our first efforts when we started publishing our paper. We had no office, no equipment but a typewriter which was pawned the first month. We wrote the paper on park benches and the kitchen table. In an effort to achieve a little of the destitution of our neighbors, we gave away our furniture and sat on boxes. But as fast as we gave things away people brought more. We gave blankets to needy families and when we started our first House of Hospitality people gathered together what blankets we needed. We gave away food and more food came in-exotic food, some of it: a haunch of venison from the Canadian

Northwest, a can of oysters from Maryland, a container of honey from Illinois. Even now it comes in, a salmon from Seattle, flown across the continent; nothing is too good for the poor.

No one working with The Catholic Worker gets a salary, so our readers feel called upon to give and help us keep the work going. And then we experience a poverty of another kind, a poverty of reputation. It is said often and with some scorn, "Why don't they get jobs and help the poor that way? Why are they living off others, begging?"

I can only explain to such critics that it would complicate things to give a salary to Roger for his work of 14 hours a day in the kitchen, clothes room, and office; to pay Jane a salary for running the women's house and Beth and Annabelle for giving out clothes, for making stencils all day and helping with the sick and the poor, and then have them all turn the money right back in to support the work. Or to make it more complicated, they might all go out and get jobs, and bring the money home to pay their board and room and the salaries of others to run the house. It is simpler just to be poor. It is simpler to beg. The main thing is not to hold on to anything.

But the tragedy is that we do, we all do hold on to our books, our tools, such as typewriters, our clothes and instead of rejoicing when they are taken from us we lament. We protest when people take our time or privacy. We are holding on to these "goods" too.

Occasionally, as we start thinking of poverty—often after reading the life of such a saint as Benedict Joseph Labre—we dream of going out on our own, living with the destitute, sleeping on park benches or in the city shelter, living in churches, sitting before the Blessed Sacrament as we see so many doing from the Municipal Lodging House around the corner. And when such thoughts come on warm spring days when the children are playing in the park, and it is good to be out on the city streets, we are only dreaming of a form of luxury. What we want is the warm sun, and rest, and time to think and read, and freedom from the people who press in on us from early morning until late at night. No, it is not simple, this business of poverty.

"Precarity," or precariousness, is an essential element in true voluntary poverty, a saintly priest from Martinique has written us. "True poverty is rare," he writes. "Nowadays religious communities are good, I am sure, but they are mistaken about poverty. They accept, admit poverty on principle, but everything must be good and strong, buildings must be fireproof. Precarity is everywhere rejected and precarity is an essential element of poverty. This has been forgotten. Here in our monastery we want precarity in everything except the church. These last days our refectory was near collapsing. We have put several supplementary beams in place and thus it will last maybe two or three years more. Someday it will fall on our heads and that will be funny. Precarity enables us better to help the poor. When a community is always building, enlarging, and embellishing, there is nothing left over for the poor. We have no right to do so as long as there are slums and breadlines somewhere."

from By Little and By Little, the Selected Writings of Dorothy Day, Knopf, New York

Undeclared War to Declared War
By Dorothy Day

Dear Fellow Workers in Christ:

Lord God, merciful God, our Father, shall we keep silent, or shall we speak? And if we speak, what shall we say?

I am sitting here in the church on Mott Street writing this in your presence. Out on the streets it is quiet, but you are there too, in the Chinese, in the Italians, these neighbors we love. We love them because they are our brothers, as Christ is our Brother and God our Father.

But we have forgotten so much. We have all forgotten. And how can we know unless you tell us. For whoever calls upon the name of the Lord shall be saved. How then are they to call upon Him in whom they have not believed? But how are they to believe Him whom they have not heard? And how are they to hear, if no one preaches? And how are men to preach unless they be sent? As it is written, "How beautiful are the feet of those who preach the gospel of peace." (Romans X)

Seventy-five thousand Catholic Workers go out every month. What shall we print? We can print still what the Holy Father is saying, when he speaks of total war, of mitigating the horrors of war, when he speaks of cities of refuge, of feeding Europe.

We will print the words of Christ who is with us always, even to the end of the world. "Love your enemies, do good to those who hate you, and pray for those who persecute and calumniate you, so that you may be children of your Father in heaven, who makes His sun to rise on the good and the evil, and sends rain on the just and unjust."

We are at war, a declared war, with Japan, Germany, and Italy. But still we can repeat Christ's words, each day, holding them close in our hearts, each month printing them in the paper. In times past, Europe has been a battlefield. But let us remember St. Francis, who spoke of peace and we will remind our readers of him, too, so they will not forget.

In The Catholic Worker we will quote our Pope, our saints, our priests. We will go on printing the articles which remind us today that we are all called to be saints," that we are other Christs, reminding us of the priesthood of the laity.

We are still pacifists. Our manifest is the Sermon on the Mount, which means that we will try to be peacemakers. Speaking for many of our conscientious objectors, we will not participate in armed warfare or in making munitions, or by buying government bonds to prosecute the war, or in urging others to these efforts.

But neither will we be carping in our criticism. We love our country and we love our President. We have been the only country in the world where men of all nations have taken refuge from oppression. We recognize that while in the order of intention we have tried to stand for peace, for love of our brother, in the order of execution we have failed as Americans in living up to our principles.

We will try daily, hourly, to pray for an end to the war, such an end, to quote Father Orchard, "as would manifest to all the world, that it was brought about by divine action, rather than by military might or diplomatic negotiation, which men and nations would then only attribute to their power or sagacity."

"Despite all calls to prayer," Father Orchard concludes, "there is at present all too little indication anywhere that the tragedy of humanity and the desperate need of the world have moved the faithful, still less stirred the thoughtless masses, to turn to prayer as the only hope for mankind this dreadful hour.

"We shall never pray until we feel more deeply. And we shall never feel deeply enough until we envisage what is actually happening in the world, and understand what is possible in the will of God; and that means until sufficient numbers realize that we have brought things to a pass which is beyond human power to help or save.

"Those who do feel and see, however inadequately, should not hesitate to begin to pray, or fail to persevere, however dark the prospects remain.

"Let them urge others to do likewise; and then, first small groups, and then the Church as a whole and at last the world, may turn and cry for forgiveness, mercy, and deliverance for all.

"Then we may be sure God will answer, and effectually; for the Lord's hand is not shortened that it cannot save, nor His ear heavy that it cannot hear."

Let us add, that unless we combine this prayer with almsgiving, in giving to the least of God's children, and fasting in order that we may help feed the hungry, and penance in recognition of our share in the guilt, our prayer may become empty words.

Our works of mercy may take us into the midst of war. As editor of The Catholic Worker, I would urge our friends and associates to care for the sick and the wounded, to the growing of food for the hungry, to the continuance of all our works of mercy in our houses and on our farms. We understand, of course, that there is and that there will be great differences of opinion even among our own groups as to how much collaboration we can have with the government in times like these. There are differences more profound and there will be many continuing to work with us from necessity, or from choice, who do not agree with us as to our position on war, conscientious objection, etc. But we beg that there will be mutual charity and forbearance among us all.

This letter, sent to all our Houses of Hospitality and to all our farms, and being printed in the January issue of the paper, is to state our position in this most difficult time. Because of our refusal to assist in the prosecution of war and our insistence that our collaboration be one for peace, we may find ourselves in difficulties. But we trust in the generosity and understanding of our government and our friends, to permit us to continue, to use our paper to preach Christ crucified."

May the Blessed Mary, Mother of love, of faith, of knowledge and of hope, pray for us.

from By Little and By Little, the Selected Writings of Dorothy Day. Knopf, New York

This Money is Not Ours
By Dorothy Day

Editor's note:
A principle, Dorothy Day believed, remains abstract until it costs us something. In 1961, she welcomed the opportunity to see the value of one of her convictions in a gesture of disarming originality. The cost was $3,579.39.

For years the Catholic Worker had repeated Peter Maurin's defense of the medieval ban on usury. The acceptance of the belief that value resides in the currency rather than labor, he believed, was a turning point in the transition from a functional to an acquisitive society. The Catholic Worker could not single-handedly reverse this process, but it could at least issue a solitary protest, and make what Peter would call a Point."

The Catholic Worker
39 Spring Street
New York 12, NY

July, 1960
Treasurer,
City of New York

Dear Sir:
We are returning to you a check for $3,579.39 which represents interest on the $68,700 which we were awarded by the city as a payment for the property at 223 Chrystie Street which we owned and lived for almost 10 years, and used as a community for the poor. We did not voluntarily give up the property – it was taken from us by the right of eminent domain for the extension of the subway which the city deemed necessary. We had to wait almost a year and a half for the money owed us, although the city permitted us to receive two-thirds of the assessed valuation of the property in advance so that we could relocate. Property owning having been made impossible for us by city regulations, we are now renting and continuing our work.

We are returning the interest on the money we have recently received because we do not believe in "money lending" at interest. As Catholics we are acquainted with the early teaching of the Church. All the early councils forbade it, declaring it reprehensible to make money by lending it out at interest. Canon law of the Middle Ages forbade it and in various decrees ordered that profit so obtained was to be restored. In the Christian emphasis on the duty of charity, we are commanded to lend gratuitously, to give freely, even in the case of confiscation, as in our own case – not to resist but to accept cheerfully.

We do not believe in the profit system, and so we cannot take profit or interest on our money. People who take a materialistic view of human service wish to make a profit but we are trying to do our duty by our service without wages to our brothers as Jesus commended in the Gospel (Matthew 25.) Loaning money at interest is deemed by one Franciscan as the principle scourge of civilization. Eric Gill, the English artist and writer, calls usury and war the two great problems of our time.

Since we have dealt with these problems in every issue of The Catholic Worker since 1933 – man's freedom, war and peace, man and the state, man and his work – and since Scripture says that the love of money is the root of all evil, we are taking this opportunity to live in practice of this belief, and make a gesture of overcoming that love of money by returning to you the interest.

Insofar as our money paid for services for the common good, and aid to the poor, we should be very happy to allow you to use not only our money without interest, but also our work, the Works of Mercy which we all perform here at the headquarters of The Catholic Worker without other salary or recompense than our daily food and lodging, clothes and incidental expenses.

Insofar as the use of our money paid for the time being for salaries for judges who have condemned us and others to jail, and for the politicians who appointed them, and for prisons, and the execution chamber at Sing Sing, and for the executioner's salary, we can only protest the use of our money and turn with utter horror from taking interest on it.

Please also be assured that we are not judging individuals, but are trying to make a judgment on the system under which we live and with which we admit that we ourselves compromise daily in many small ways, but which we try and wish to withdraw from as much as possible.

Sincerely yours,
Dorothy Day, Editor

It is not easy, having acted upon principle, to explain it in ways acceptable and understood by others. An instance is our recent sending back of the interest on the money given us for St. Joseph's House on Chrystie Street.

During the course of the month we have received a few letters, not very many, of criticism of our act. One letter, from a generous benefactor who had given us a large sum when her father died, pointed out that if her parent had not invested his money wisely she and her mother would not have had anything left to live on; also that we probably received many donations which came from dividends, interest, etc.

I only try to answer as best I can. But sometimes one confuses others the more by trying to answer objections. When we wrote our letter to the city, and published it in the paper, we also printed some excerpts for the teaching of St. Thomas Aquinas on interest and money lending. We use some of Peter Maurin's easy essays on the subject, and an article by Arthur Sheehan on credit unions which, however, ask for a small interest on their loans. How can this be reconciled with the "gesture" we made of returning to the city the large check which represented the interest for a year and a half on the money paid us for our property on Chrystie Street? First of all, we asked with Chesterton: Whose money is this interest which the city was paying us? Where did it come from? Money does not breed money; it is sterile.

To answer our correspondent: Of course we are involved, the same as everyone else, in living off interest. We are all caught up in this same money economy. Just as "God writes straight with crooked lines," so we too waver, struggle on our devious path – always aiming at God, even though we are conditioned by habits and ancestry, etc. We have free will, which is our greatest gift. We are free to choose, and as we see more clearly, our choice is more direct and easier to make. Be we all see through a glass darkly. It would be heaven to see Truth face to face.

We are publishing a paper in which ideas are discussed and clarified, and illustrated by act. So we are not just a newspaper. We are a revolution, a movement, as Peter Maurin used to say. We are propagandists of the faith. We are the Church. We are members of the Mystical Body. We all must try to function healthily. We do not all have the same function, but we all have a vocation, a calling. Ours is a "prophetic" one, as many priests have said to us. Pope John recently cited the courage of John the Baptist as an example for today. Prophets made great gestures, did things to call attention to whatever they were talking about. That was what we did; we made a gesture, when we returned the money to the city. It was calling attention to a great unsolved problem in which we are all involved, Church, State, corporation, institution, individual.

There is no simple solution. Let the priests and the economists get to work on it. It is a moral and an ethical problem. We can work on the lowest level, the credit union in the parish, for instance. Through the credit union families have been taught to resist the skillful seductions of the advertising men and by doing without many things, to attain ownership, homes, workshops, tools, small factories, and so on. These things have happened in Nova Scotia, in missions throughout the world, and is one way to combat what the bishops call the all-encroaching state. It is the beginning of the decentralist society.

So, primarily, our sending back the money was a gesture. It was the first time we had to do so with so large a sum of money. We were being reimbursed by the city – and generously, as far as money went – for the house and our improvements on it. (They had taken over the property by the right of eminent domain because a subway extension was going through.) One can argue that the value of the property went up, that the city had 18 months' use of our money, that money purchases less now, and so on. The fact remains that the city was doing what it could to pay off each and every tenant in the two tenement houses from which they were being evicted, giving bonuses, trying to find other lodgings, though these were usually unacceptable, being in other neighborhoods or boroughs.

We agree that slums need to be eliminated, but that an entire neighborhood, which is like a village made up of many nationalities, should be scattered, displaced – this is wanton cruelty, and one of the causes of the juvenile delinquency of our cities. Also, it is terribly bad and ruthless management on the part of the city fathers.

Is Robert Moses responsible? He is the planner. But he deals recklessly with inanimate brick and cement at the expense of flesh and blood. He is walking ruthlessly over brokenhearted families to make a great outward show of a destroyed and rebuilt city. He has been doing what blockbusters and obliteration bombing did in European and British cities. Right now an entire neighborhood just south of Tomkins Square where some of our poor friends live is being demolished and the widows and fatherless are crying to heaven. The city fathers try to recompense them, try to give them bonuses to get out quickly. But what good does the money do them when there is no place to go? They do not want to go to another neighborhood or even to another block. Actually, as piled-up furniture on the street testifies, many cling to their poor homes until the last moment, and probably forfeit the 200 or 300 dollars that they are offered, rather than be exiled. That money means as much to them as the 2,000 or 3,000 did to us.

There is talk about doing things economically, yet money is poured out like water in all directions and scandals are always being unearthed of cheating and graft in high places. This extends down to the smallest citizen, too, trying to get in on the big deal and get his – from the building inspector who expects to be tipped, to the little veteran around the corner who is speculating in the real estate by buying and improving and renting and then selling back his property to the city at exorbitant prices. "It doesn't matter if it is going to be torn down in a year or so," he assures us. "Rent out all the apartments and stores and then you can ask more from the city." Big deal! Everyone is trying to get in on the Moses big deal.

So to put it on the natural but often most emotional plane of simple patriotism, love of country or city, this feeling too, prompted us to send back the interest. We do not want to participate in this big deal. "Why are there wars and contentions among you? Because each one seeketh his own."

We considered this a gesture, too, toward peace, a spiritual weapon which is translated into action. We cannot talk about these ideas without trying to put them into practice, though we do it clumsily and are often misunderstood.

We are not trying to be superior, holier than thou. Of course we are involved in paying taxes, in living on money which comes from our industrial capitalist way of life. But we can try, by voluntary poverty and labor, to earn our living, and not to be any more involved than we can help. We, all of us, partake in a way in the sin of Sapphira and Ananias, by holding back our time, our love, our material resources even, after making great protestations of "absolutism." May God and you, our readers, forgive us. We are, in spite of all we try to do, unprofitable servants.

From By Little and By Little: the selected writings of Dorothy Day, Knopf, New York.

The Scandal of the Works of Mercy
By Dorothy Day

One of the peculiar enjoyments I got out of jail was in being on the other side for a change. I was the one working in a laundry, ironing uniforms of jailers. I was the one sitting in the sewing room turning the collar and mending the uniform of an officer. It gave me a chance to tell the other prisoners about Tolstoy, and how he said the first move toward reform was to do one's own work. Everyone regarded the officers as members of the parasite class, though they would not use that word. How much more respect they would have had for the officers, and for the work they themselves had to do, if they had seen the officers sitting mending their own clothes, if they had seen them working to help their fellows. Perhaps it would have meant a beginning of the philosophy of work which Peter Maurin used to say was so sadly lacking today. If prisoners and officers had worked together to make the prison a happier place, what a change there might have been in the hearts of those confined.

The officers sat all day at their desks, watching, directing, always expecting the worst, always looking for some small infraction, always seeing the women as criminals. They did not see that which is of God in every person, as the Friends put it. St. John of the Cross said, "Where there is no love, put love, and you will find love," The officers looked for the criminal and found the criminal.

The women got away with what they could. They fought, they lied, they stole when they could. While working in the laundry I saw a girl put a folded dress, which she wanted for herself, up between her legs, under her skirt. When she spoke of it afterward to some of the other prisoners on our corridor, they jeered. "That's nothing," one said, "I've seen girls who worked in the kitchen get away with a turkey or a ham." Judith made us all hilarious by immediately getting up and trying to impersonate a girl walking out of the kitchen with a turkey or a ham held thus. Looking back on these last paragraphs, I see that I have gone from the sublime to the ridiculous, even to the vulgar and, for some, the revolting. But beauty and joy often spring from the dungheap.

I have said that I enjoyed being on the other side for a time. People come into the Catholic Worker in such numbers: 800 a day for food; hundreds of men, women, and children coming in for clothes. When all the beds in the house are full we often give out "flop" money, the fifty cents a night it costs to sleep on the Bowery. All that we give is given to us to give. Nothing is ours. All we have to give is our time and patient love. In the movie Monsieur Vincent, the saint tells a young nun that she has to love the poor very much for them to forgive her the bread she gives them. How often we have failed in love, how often we have been brusque, cold, and indifferent. "Roger takes care of the clothes; you'll have to come back at ten o'clock." Or "Just sit in the library and wait." "Wait your turn, I'm busy." So it often goes. And now I was getting pushed here and there, told what I could or could not do, hemmed in by rules and regulations and red tape and bureaucracy. It made me see my faults, but it also made me see how much more we accomplish at the Catholic Worker in our own direct way, by not asking questions or doing any investigating, but by cultivating a spirit of trust. The whole experience of jail was good for my soul. I realized again how much ordinary kindness can do. Graciousness is an old-fashioned word but it has a beautiful religious tradition. "Grace is participation in the divine life," according to St. Peter.

Most of the time we were treated like dumb beasts-worse, because it was with indifference and contempt. "You'll be back," was the common farewell to the prisoner. It was, in effect, wishing her not to fare well. There was no goodbye, "God be with you," because there was not enough faith or hope or charity to conceive of a forgiving and loving God being with anyone so lost in vice and crime as prostitutes, drug addicts, and other criminals are supposed to be.

One great indignity is the examination given all women for drugs. There is certainly no recognition of the fact of political imprisonment. All of us were stripped and searched in the crudest way-even to the tearing of tissues so that bleeding resulted. Then there is the matter of clothing--the scanty garments, the crude wrappers which scarcely wrap around one, the floppy cloth slippers which are impossible to keep on! In Russia, in Germany, and even in our own country, to strip the prisoner, to humiliate him, is a definite part and purpose of a jail experience, Even in the Army, making a man stand naked before his examiners is to treat him like a dumb beast or a slave. A great courtesy accorded us was a visit from the warden himself. Never had anything like that happened before, one of the girls assured us. He wanted to know about our demonstration, why we had done it. He was a Hungarian Catholic; so perhaps it was easy to understand his confusion about our pacifism. What man does not wish to resist a foreign aggressor, to defend his home and family? But the problem of the means to an end had never occurred to him. Nowadays it is pretty generally accepted that the end justifies the means. To his mind, one just could not be a pacifist today. It was an "impossible" position.

As to our attitude toward the prison, and the prisoners, he could not understand our love for them, our not judging them. The idea of hating the sin and loving the sinner seemed foreign to him. Of course, he did not hate the sinner but he had to look upon them as evil; otherwise his job would be meaningless. When we talked of the good we found there, in spite of perversion, prostitution, and drugs, he looked at us strangely and wanted to know if we were Christian Scientists. At least he did not call us Communists. He was too intelligent for that. But we seemed to be denying the reality of evil, because we were upholding the prisoners. The evil, was there, all right, frank and unabashed. It was inside and also outside the jail.

One of the greatest evils of the day is the sense of futility. Young people say, "What can one person do? What is the sense of our small effort?" They cannot see that we can only lay one brick at a time, take one step at a time; we can be responsible only for the one action of the present moment. But we can beg for an increase of love in our hearts that will vitalize and transform these actions, and know that God will take them and multiply them, as Jesus multiplied the loves and fishes.

Next year, perhaps, God willing, we will again go to jail; and perhaps conditions will be the same. To be charitable we can only say that the prison officials do the best they can, according to their understanding. In a public institution they are not paid to love the inmates; they are paid to guard them. They admit that the quarters are totally inadequate, that what was built for a House of Detention for women awaiting trial is now being used for a workhouse and penitentiary.

from By Little and By Little, the Selected Writings of Dorothy Day. Knopf, New York.

Dorothy Day (1890-1980)
by Colman McCarthy

NEW YORK – The funeral procession of Dorothy Day, her body in a pinewood coffin, moved out of Maryhouse on Third Street on the way to a requiem mass at Nativity Catholic Church, a half-block away. Someone wondered aloud why more of the poor were not present. The street, as mean as any in this cloister of harshness on the edge of the Bowery, was certainly not overflowing with homeless souls come to mourn the woman who had served them in a personal ministry for half a century. A few men and even fewer women – blank-eyed, dressed in tatters – stood in clusters, while others wandered down the street from the city shelter for derelicts, one of Manhattan's unseen hellholes. But that was all. Most of the 800 people following the coffin were either old friends of Miss Day who lived outside the neighborhood or members of the Catholic Worker community who run St. Joseph's and Maryhouse, the two local shelters for the homeless.

Large numbers of the poor did not come, for a reason as obvious as the open sores on the face of a wino opposite Maryhouse; they were too busy trying to fight death themselves. To mark the passing of someone who loved them – accepted them totally by living here, raising money for them through her newspaper, The Catholic Worker – would, of course, make sense in the rational world of the comfortable, where public tribute to the deceased great and the seemingly great is the proper way of dealing with grief. But here on this street that is full of the homeless and jobless, death was not needed for grief. Hope gets buried every day.

If the turnout of the poor was not strong, there was an almost total absence of Catholic officialdom. This was the genuine affront. Few of the faithful in this century were more committed than Dorothy Day to the church's teachings, both in its social encyclicals – on the distribution of wealth, the evils of the arms race – and its call to private spirituality. She was a daily communicant at mass, rising early to read the Bible and pray the rosary.

Dorothy Day used her faith as a buffer against burnout and despair. Fittingly, it will have to be taken on faith that her life of service made a difference. She issued no progress reports on neighborhood improvement, summoned no task forces on how to achieve greater efficiency on the daily soup line.

Nor did she ever run "follow-up studies" on whether the derelicts of the Bowery renounced their drunken and quarrelsome ways. As her favorite saint, Theresa of Lisieux, taught, results don't matter to the prayerful.

On the subject of results, Dorothy Day had a philosophy of divine patience: "We continue feeding our neighbors and clothing and sheltering them, and the more we do it the more we realize that the most important thing is to love. There are several families with us, destitute to an unbelievable extent, and there, too, is nothing to do but love. What I mean is that there is no chance of rehabilitation – no chance, so far as we see, of changing them, certainly no chance of adjusting them to this abominable world about them, and who wants them adjusted, anyway?"

That was from the June, 1946 issue of The Catholic Worker newspaper, a monthly that has been a voice of pacifism and justice since 1933. The jobless and homeless are so thick in the streets that "Holy Mother City," as Miss Day called it, makes no pretense of even counting them.

It may be just as well. Counters get in the way when there is soup to be made. Even worse, getting too close to the government means a trade-off that Miss Day resisted in words and action. "The state believes in war," she said, "and, as pacifists and philosophical anarchists, we don't"

Because she served the poor for so long and with such tireless intensity, Dorothy Day had a national constituency of remarkable breadth. She was more than merely the conscience of the Left. Whether it was a young millionaire named John F. Kennedy who came to see her (in 1943) or one of the starving, she exuded authenticity.

It was so well-known that she lived among the poor – shared their table, stood in their lines, endured the daily insecurity – that the Catholic Worker became known as the one charity in which contributions truly did reach the poor. It is at St. Joseph's House, 36 E. 1st, New York, 10003.

"It is a strange vocation to love the destitute and dissolute," Miss Day wrote a few years ago. But it is one that keeps attracting the young who come to Catholic Worker as a place to brew the soup and clean the toilets, which is also the work of peacemakers. They are against military wars for sure, but their pacifism resists the violence of the economic wars. "We refuse to fight for a materialistic system that cripples so many of its citizens," the Catholic worker has been saying for half a century.

The only catholic bishop of the church on hand was Terence Cardinal Cooke of New York. As the procession rounded the corner from Maryhouse and went onto the sidewalk leading to the church, the scarlet vestments of the cardinal came into view. The contrast was powerful. In a neighborhood of drab colors, where even the faces of the poor seem to be grayed with depression, the scarlet robes of the cardinal, his scarlet skullcap, had a touch of mock comedy to them; the vestments seemed almost the costume of a clown – a clown who was lost in the saddest of landscapes.

A Catholic Worker priest, a young Dominican who works at Maryhouse and was to celebrate the mass, made the best of the situation. At the head of the procession, he shook hands with Cardinal Cooke. The cardinal took over and prayed aloud, commending the soul of "Dear Dorothy" to the mercy of the Lord. While cameramen of the Associated Press, The Daily News, and the Religious News Service clicked away – getting the coffin in the foreground – the cardinal finished praying in two minutes.

It was just enough time for many in the procession to think beyond the cardinal's brilliantly hued presence at the church door. Some recalled the pacifists from the Catholic Worker who have been standing for the past few months outside Cardinal Cooke's offices uptown and in front of the splendid St. Patrick's Cathedral. They have been leafleting the churchgoers on the immorality of the arms race and pleading with the unseen cardinal to issue a statement in favor of nuclear disarmament. In the most recent issue of The Catholic Worker, one of Dorothy Day's writers said sharply about the vigil at St. Patrick's last August: "We want to remember the victims of the [Hiroshima and Nagasaki] bombings, and to mourn the fact that the hierarchy of our archdiocese is so silent about nuclear disarmament, when statements from the Vatican Council, recent popes, and the U.S. Catholic Bishops Conference have been so clear in their condemnation of the arms race."

Six grandchildren of Miss Day, carrying her coffin, nodded their thanks to the cardinal and proceeded into the church. A moment later, John Shiel went up to Cardinal Cooke. Shiel, a short, half-toothless man who has been repeatedly jailed in peace protests, is something of a lay theologian who can quote every pope back to Boniface I on the subject of war and peace. A friend of Miss Day, he left Washington at 4 a.m. to be here for the mass.

"Hello John," said His Eminence, who knew Shiel from his persistent lobbying for peace at the annual meetings of the hierarchy.

"Hello there, Cardinal," said Sheil. "When are you going to come out against nuclear weapons?"

His Eminence gave no answer, and shortly he was driven off in his limousine to "a previous commitment." The day before, according to a Catholic Worker staff member, Cardinal Cooke's secretary had phoned to request that the mass be held at 10 a.m., because it would then fit into the cardinal's schedule and he could preside. But Miss Day's daughter had already decided on 11 a.m. because that was when the soup kitchen was closed for the morning break between cleaning up after breakfast and getting ready for lunch. The cardinal's presence would be missed, the secretary was told, but with all due respect, feeding the poor came first.

Inside the church, with its unpainted cement-block walls and water-marked ceiling, the breadth of Dorothy Day's friendships was on view. In the pews were Cesar Chavez, Frank Sheed, Michael Harrington, Ed and Kathleen Guinan, Paul Moore, and Father Horace McKenna, the Jesuit who for decades has been serving the poor at his own soup kitchen in Washington.

In the back of the church, after the sermon, the undertaker, a friendly man, tall and properly somber-looking, was asked about the arrangements. "She was a lovely lady," he said. "We're doing this way below cost. The Worker gives us a lot of business, and besides, Miss Day is part of the community."

The undertaker said that the archdiocese was picking up the tab of $380 for opening the grave at the cemetery. If the patron saint of irony were listening in, he or she would call out to the heavenly choir, "Stop the music." During the archdiocese cemetery workers' strike in the mid-1950s, Dorothy Day was personally denounced by Cardinal Spellman for siding with the underpaid gravediggers.

After mass, a young Catholic Worker staff member, who was the candle-bearer at the head of the funeral procession, told the story of the candle – a thick white one, almost three feet tall. "We went around to neighborhood churches. We asked the sacristans for their old candle stubs that would be thrown out anyway. Then we melted them into one large candle."

Class of Nonviolence

Another form of brightness was present – a thought from one of Dorothy Day's books, printed on the bottom of the mass card: "We have all known the long loneliness and we have learned that the only solution is love and that love comes with community."

At about 12:30, some of the crowd drifted back to Maryhouse where lunch was being served. Pea soup was ladled from a 10-gallon kettle. Brown bread was on the table with milk, tea and oranges: enough food for all.

From Washington Post, December 2, 1980

Questions for Lesson Three

1. Dorothy Day, like Mother Teresa, seems to be devoted to healing the symptoms (the victim) of a sick and/or evil society rather than confronting the causes of its illness. Is this a fair assessment; and if so, what would be more fruitful to bring about change?

2. Dorothy Day once said of her church (Catholic Church), that, "She's a whore, but she's my mother." Should we try to reform a corrupt institution by staying within it or is it smarter to abandon it and build a benign alternative? Did Gorbachev's example of reforming the Soviet Union from within argue for this approach of staying "within?"

3. "Where there is no love, put love and you will find love" was Dorothy Day's lifelong theme. Does it play when dealing with unresponsive individuals, the scornful homeless, violent prisoners, those who hate and revile us?

4. What do you think the notion of "turning the other cheek" means within the context of resisting violoence and/or aggression?

5. Would you vote for a pacifist like Dorothy Day to rule America? If so, why; if not, why not?

Readings for Lesson Four

Martin Luther King, Jr.
by Charles De Benedetti

Loving Your Enemies
by Martin Luther King, Jr.

Declaration of Independence from the War in Vietnam
by Martin Luther King, Jr.

Pilgrimage to Nonviolence
by Martin Luther King, Jr.

King and Pacifism: The Other Dimension
by Colman McCarthy

Martin Luther King, Jr.
by Charles De Benedetti

Between 1955 and 1968, a black-led civil rights movement emerged across the United States, and especially in the American South, struggling to end racial segregation and to allow blacks fuller access to the largest promises of the national life. Joining millions of people from all races, creeds, and regions, this movement grew from several deep and tangled historical roots, including: the long black quest for freedom and equality; the egalitarian values inherent in the Declaration of Independence and other fundamental American documents; the strong emphases on social justice of many of America's religious faiths; and, most recently, the labor and liberal reform movements of the 1930s and 1940s. This movement found in Martin Luther King, Jr. a leader capable of transforming millions of inchoate aspirations into an engine of peaceful social change.

The movement's largely peaceful methods and positive results were not preordained. Almost certainly, in view of long-building black frustrations, there would have been a major civil rights movement in the 1950s and 1960s, with or without the Reverend King. Yet, without King's leadership and moral authority, this movement might well have taken a far different course, perhaps even toward a racial bloodbath and severe political repression. Instead, King stepped into history and aggressively deployed the power of Christian nonviolence to move the country away from racial injustice and toward reconciliation. As was noted in a eulogy at his funeral in April 1968, he appeared as "a peaceful warrior who built an army and a movement that is mighty without missiles, able without an atomic arsenal, ready without rockets, real without bullets; an army tutored in living and loving and not in killing." He was that rare phenomenon- "a leader who was willing to die, but not willing to kill." In the process of fighting for civil rights, he helped to shepherd his country through a time of trial and progress in race relations.

Fundamentally, King was an inclusive peacemaker. He sought not only to include as many supporters as possible within the civil rights movement, but also to bring about an eventual reconciliation with their opponents. He saw the circle of support for social justice, which he termed the "beloved community," expanding until it included virtually all Americans. Furthermore, King was an inclusive peacemaker in the sense that he strove to overcome his personal limitations for the sake of greater moral and political effectiveness. The basic outline of King's life before the Montgomery Alabama bus boycott of 1955-56 can be summarized briefly. He was born in Atlanta on January 15, 1929. His parents were Alberta Williams King, the daughter of the pastor of the Ebenezer Baptist Church, and Martin Luther "Daddy" King, the assistant pastor who became pastor upon the death of his father-in-law in 1931. Ebenezer was a thriving church, and Martin grew up in a family with middle class comforts. He attended church faithfully and sang hymns at church meetings at a young age. Growing up in Atlanta, he also experienced white racism firsthand.

A precocious youth, King skipped his senior year in high school and entered the predominantly black Morehouse College in Atlanta at age 15. After graduating from Morehouse with a degree in sociology in spring 1948, he entered the largely white Crozier

Class of Nonviolence

Theological Seminary in suburban Philadelphia. Three years later, as valedictorian of his graduating class, he won a scholarship to attend the graduate school of his choice. That fall King entered Boston University's prestigious School of Theology, which awarded him the Ph.D. degree in 1955. In the meantime, he married Coretta Scott, a student at the Boston Conservatory, and accepted an appointment as minister of the Dexter Avenue Baptist Church in Montgomery, beginning in the summer of 1954.

As a youth, King's most difficult problem involved the choice of a vocation. He wanted to serve others and to make his mark in the world, but he was not sure how he should proceed. While attracted in some ways to the ministry, he did not like the pressure his father "was putting on him to succeed him as pastor at Ebenezer, and he doubted the relevance of his church's fundamentalist religion in modern America. He toyed with the idea of becoming a doctor, and after a bad personal experience with discrimination on a train trip, he considered becoming a lawyer so that he could help in breaking down the legal barriers that trapped blacks in a segregated subcaste.

In sum, during his first 27 years King developed numerous qualities that proved invaluable to him as a peacemaker. He felt a deep concern for the plight of the black masses, especially in his native South. He sustained a strong religious faith combined with a quest for greater spiritual depth and understanding. He maintained a continuing interest in his own intellectual growth and in learning about ways to bring about peaceful social change. He had an ability to communicate with people of diverse racial and educational backgrounds. And, perhaps most significant, he developed a commitment, strengthened in a time of crisis, to continue to work for social justice even if it meant forfeiting his own life.

The decade beginning with the Montgomery bus boycott in fall 1955 and ending with the Voting Rights Act in summer 1965 marked the glory days for King-and for the civil rights movement as a whole. It was during these years that King, the inclusive peacemaker, was most effective. The story of the civil rights movement during these years has been told many times; here the focus is on some key reasons for King's effectiveness, followed by a closer look at the two great events in civil rights in 1963: the springtime Birmingham Alabama campaign and King's "I Have a Dream" speech in Washington, D.C. in August.

One reason for King's effectiveness during these years was his continuing personal and intellectual growth. He broadened himself by visiting West Africa in 1957 and India in 1959. The visit to the "land of my father's fathers" was memorable, and led to what King called a "nonviolent rebirth" and to a continuing interest in Africa's welfare. His trip to India deepened his commitment to Gandhian principles, including an effort upon his return to put less emphasis on material comforts in his own life. In the midst of a hectic schedule, King took time for writing and reflection. In addition to many articles, he published two books about the movement- **Stride Toward Freedom: The Montgomery Story** (1958) and **Why We Can't Wait** (1964)-and a deeply spiritual book of sermons, **Strength to Love** (1964). During these years King was especially interested in learning more about human behavior and the psychological underpinnings of racism and violence. The relatively brief periods of time that King set aside for travel and for personal renewal helped to keep his speeches and writings fresh and cogent, and helped him, at least until the mid-1960s, to avert a clear danger facing prominent peacemakers – exhaustion or burnout.

During 1966, King largely refrained from criticizing the Vietnam War. He was preoccupied with the Chicago campaign, and distracted by growing demands of young black militants for black power. He made some guardedly critical statements regarding U.S. war policy. But it was not until early 1967, after doing careful study of the history of the conflict, that he made the war the theme of several major addresses. In February, he told an audience in Los Angeles that: "the bombs in Vietnam explode at home: they destroy the hopes and possibilities for a decent America." In a sermon at his church in Atlanta, he said that he could "study war no more," and urged blacks opposed to the war to "challenge our young men with the alternative of conscientious objection." "The world now demands a maturity of America that we may not be able to achieve," King continued. "The New Testament says, 'Repent.' It is time for America to repent now." Before a crowd of 3,000 in New York's Riverside Church on April 4, he portrayed the war as a moral tragedy perpetrated by "the greatest purveyor of violence in the world today – my own government." Americans had failed to recognize the Vietnamese opposition to the Vietnam War was still a minority view even among his liberal civil rights allies and supporters. Black leaders, including Roy Wilkins of the NAACP and Whitney Young of the National Urban League, attacked King's position, while normally sympathetic newspapers like the New York Times and the Washington Post blasted the Southern Christian Leadership Conference leader for commenting on matters they considered irrelevant to social justice issues. King, however, believed that his opposition to the war was consistent with his concern about the oppressed and his commitment to nonviolence. He thus decided to stand on principle against a war that was draining so much of the power and potential of black America.

Like Vietnam, the rise of Black Nationalism presented difficult dilemmas for King. He supported many of the ideals of Stokely Carmichael and other black nationalists: pride in black history, emphasis on unity and improvement of living conditions within the black community, and constructive use of black economic and political power. But he did not like the slogan "Black Power" that had corrupted the imagination of many young blacks after Carmichael first used it at a Mississippi rally in 1966. King believed that the slogan had too many negative connotations, and that it would feed the growing white backlash against civil rights. He also believed that it would be impossible for blacks to continue to improve their status in American society without white support. And, even if they could make it on their own, Black Power's emphasis on separatism and its implicit endorsement of violence went against King's commitment to an inclusive Christian community.

King responded in detail to Black Power ideas during winter 1967 in his last full-length book, Where Do We Go From Here: Chaos or Community? He was careful to acknowledge the Black Power arguments that whites had systematically oppressed blacks, and that blacks had made many gains through self-help and racial pride. But he strongly rejected black nationalism's basic premises:

*"In the final analysis the weakness of Black Power is its failure to see that
the black man needs the white man and the white man needs the black man.
However much we may try to romanticize the slogan, there is no separate
black path to power and fulfillment that does not intersect white paths,
and there is no separate white path to power and fulfillment, short of social
disaster, that does not share that power with black aspirations for freedom
and human dignity. We are bound together in a single garment of destiny. The
language, the cultural patterns, the music, the material prosperity, and even
the food of America are an amalgam of black and white."*

King's book epitomized the changes in the black movement during the time since he had completed **Why We Can't Wait** three years earlier. In that book, King had written primarily about the black struggle for equal rights. Now he was writing much more about the systemic problem of economic inequality and the need for massive federal expenditures to "fight poverty, ignorance, and slums." Equally important, in **Why Can't We Wait**, King was speaking for white liberals and for the overwhelming majority of blacks, North and South, with only the relatively small Black Muslim movement in serious opposition. Now he clearly was writing to respond to the growing nationalist movement and to rally the supporters of his nonviolent, integrationist approach. King still possessed a respected voice, but increasingly it was one voice among many.

King's insistence in **Where Do We Go From Here** on large-scale federal programs to end poverty in America provided the focus for the last year of his life. Clearly his vision was now more radical, for he was advocating not only equal rights but also a coalition of the poor to demand economic justice. Earlier, as he was maintaining his coalition of blacks and white liberals (including wealthy white contributors); he had not talked about restructuring the economic system. Now he did so. As he told journalist David Halberstam in spring 1967, "I labored with the idea of reforming the existing institutions of the South, a little change here, a little change there. Now I feel quite differently. I think you've got to have a reconstruction of the entire society, a revolution of values."

This vision, which David Levering Lewis recently called "the promise of nonviolent populism," informed King's planning for the Poor People's Campaign in Washington in 1968. In order to force the government to face up to the continuing problem of poverty in America, King proposed to bring poor black, whites, Puerto Ricans, Indians, and Chicanos to the capital. Initially, plans called for people to come from various parts of the nation and demand the passage of SCLC's $12 billion "Economic Bill of Rights," which included such things as guaranteed jobs for the able bodied, livable incomes for the legitimately unemployed, and a firm federal commitment to open housing and. integrated education. If their efforts failed, thousands more would come and create "major massive dislocations" in the city.

King was unable to carry out what he had called his "last, greatest dream." He was shot down by a white racist assassin on April 4, 1968, in Memphis, Tennessee, where he had gone to lend support to the city's striking garbage workers. Yet, even if he had not been killed, the odds were against the success of the Poor People's Campaign. For one thing, the attitudes of most officials and northerners were extremely hostile. For another, it would have been very difficult to unite poor people of such diverse ethnic and regional backgrounds and to raise the funds required to sustain them in Washington until victory was achieved. But King had not gone with the odds in his other campaigns. Under incessant threat of death, he did not ever have good reason to believe that he would live through them. In faith, he had strived since 1955 to help to bring about the "beloved community." In faith, he would continue to do so until he was "free at last."

On Sunday, February 4, 1968, exactly two months before his death, King delivered a very personal message to the congregation at Ebenezer Baptist Church in Atlanta, where he and his father served as co-pastors. The topic was what he would want said at his own funeral, what he believed his life added up to. Because his words bear so directly on assessing King as peacemaker, they deserve quoting at some length:

> *"Tell them not to mention that I have a Nobel Peace Prize. That isn't important. Tell them not to mention that I have three or four hundred other awards. That's not important. Tell them not to mention where I went to school. I'd like somebody to mention that day that Martin Luther King, Jr. tried to give his life serving others. I'd like for somebody to mention that day that Martin Luther King, Jr. tried to love somebody. I want you to say the day that I tried to be right on the war question. I want you to be able to say that I did try to feed the hungry. I want you to be able to say that day that I did try in my life to clothe those who were naked. I want you to say that I tried to love and serve humanity. Yes, if you want to say that I was a 'drum major, say that I was a drum major for justice. Say that I was a drum major for peace. That I was a drum major for righteousness. And all of the other shallow things will not matter. I won't have any money to leave behind. I won't have the fine and luxurious things of life to leave behind. But I just want to leave a committed life behind. And that's all I want to say."*

The clearest, most powerful theme in this message is King's desire to be remembered as a person who sought to live his Christian faith, to obey God's word as he understood it. Although he appears to have succeeded in this quest, King was far from perfect. He knew the ordinary pressures and temptations of life. He suffered a deep sense of guilt, and periodically knew the agony of depression. He lived through jailings, failures, hatred, and abuse, most of it delivered by his fellow Christians. Yet, as he affirmed in his sermon, he tried to remain faithful to his Christianity and to hope for fuller human community which he believed that it nurtured.

How effective was King as a peacemaker? He surely was correct in his contention that peace within societies is not merely the absence of overt violence (what - he called "negative peace"); instead, peace must involve conscious efforts to build community and bring about greater social justice ("positive peace"). He also was correct to note that means and ends are interrelated, that only nonviolent methods are likely to lead to a more just and peaceful society. Like Gandhi, King's teachings and actions are likely to be studied and discussed as long as there are nonviolent movements for social change.

From Peace Heroes, Indiana University Press, Bloomington, Indiana

Class of Nonviolence

Loving Your Enemies
by Martin Luther King, Jr.

The following sermon was delivered at the Dexter Avenue Baptist Church in Montgomery, Alabama, at Christmas, 1957. Martin Luther King wrote it while in jail for committing nonviolent civil disobedience during the Montgomery bus boycott. Let us be practical and ask the question. How do we love our enemies?

First, we must develop and maintain the capacity to forgive. He who is devoid of the power to forgive is devoid of the power to love. It is impossible even to begin the act of loving one's enemies without the prior acceptance of the necessity, over and over again, of forgiving those who inflict evil and injury upon us. It is also necessary to realize that the forgiving act must always be initiated by the person who has been wronged, the victim of some great hurt, the recipient of some tortuous injustice, the absorber of some terrible act of oppression. The wrongdoer may request forgiveness. He may come to himself, and, like the prodigal son, move up some dusty road, his heart palpitating with the desire for forgiveness. But only the injured neighbor, the loving father back home, can really pour out the warm waters of forgiveness.

Forgiveness does not mean ignoring what has been done or putting a false label on an evil act. It means, rather, that the evil act no longer remains as a barrier to the relationship. Forgiveness is a catalyst creating the atmosphere necessary for a fresh start and a new beginning. It is the lifting of a burden or the canceling of a debt. The words "I will forgive you, but I'll never forget what you've done" never explain the real nature of forgiveness. Certainly one can never forget, if that means erasing it totally from his mind. But when we forgive, we forget in the sense that the evil deed is no longer a mental block impeding a new relationship. Likewise, we can never say, "I will forgive you, but I won't have anything further to do with you." Forgiveness means reconciliation, a coming together again.

Without this, no man can love his enemies. The degree to which we are able to forgive determines the degree to which we are able to love our enemies.

Second, we must recognize that the evil deed of the enemy-neighbor, the thing that hurts, never quite expresses all that he is. An element of goodness may be found even in our worst enemy. Each of us has something of a schizophrenic personality, tragically divided against ourselves. A persistent civil war rages within all of our lives. Something within us causes us to lament with Ovid, the Latin poet, "I see and approve the better things, but follow worse," or to agree with Plato that human personality is like a charioteer having two headstrong horses, each wanting to go in a different direction, or to repeat with the Apostle Paul, "The good that I would I do not: but the evil which I would not, that I do."

This simply means that there is some good in the worst of us and some evil in the best of us. When we discover this, we are less prone to hate our enemies. When we look beneath the surface, beneath the impulsive evil deed, we see within our enemy-neighbor a measure of goodness and know that the viciousness and evilness of his acts are not quite representative of all that he is. We see him in a new light. We recognize that his hate grows out of fear, pride, ignorance, prejudice, and misunderstanding, but in spite of this, we know God's image is ineffably etched in being. Then we love our enemies by realizing that they are not totally bad and that they are not beyond the reach of God's redemptive love.

Third, we must not seek to defeat or humiliate the enemy but to win his friendship and understanding. At times we are able to humiliate our worst enemy. Inevitably, his weak moments come and we are able to thrust in his side the spear of defeat. But this we must not do. Every word and deed must contribute to an understanding with the enemy and release those vast reservoirs of goodwill which have been blocked by impenetrable walls of hate. Let us move now from the practical how to the theoretical why: Why should we love our enemies? The first reason is fairly obvious. Returning hate for hate multiplies hate, adding deeper darkness to a night already devoid of stars. Darkness cannot drive out darkness; only light can do that. Hate cannot drive out hate; only love can do that. Hate multiplies hate, violence multiplies violence, and toughness multiplies toughness in a descending spiral of destruction.

So when Jesus says "Love your enemies," he is setting forth a profound and ultimately inescapable admonition. Have we not come to such an impasse in the modern world that we must love our enemies-or else? The chain reaction of evil—hate begetting hate, wars producing more wars—must be broken, or we shall be plunged into the dark abyss of annihilation. Another reason why we must love our enemies is that hate scars the soul and distorts the personality. Mindful that hate is an evil and dangerous force, we too often think of what it does to the person hated. This is understandable, for hate brings irreparable damage to its victims. We have seen its ugly consequences in the ignominious deaths brought to six million Jews by a hate-obsessed madman named Hitler, in the unspeakable violence inflicted upon Negroes by bloodthirsty mobs, in the dark horrors of war, and in the terrible indignities and injustices perpetrated against millions of God's children by unconscionable oppressors. But there is another side which we must never overlook. Hate is just as injurious to the person who hates. Like an unchecked cancer, hate corrodes the personality and eats away its vital unity. Hate destroys a man's sense of values and his objectivity. It causes him to describe the beautiful as ugly and the ugly as beautiful, and to confuse the true with the false and the false with the true.

A third reason why we should love our enemies is that love is the only force capable of transforming an enemy into a friend. We never get rid of an enemy by meeting hate with hate; we get rid of an enemy by getting rid of enmity. By its very nature, hate destroys and tears down; by its very nature, love creates and builds up. Love transforms with redemptive power.

The relevance of what I have said to the crisis in race relations should be readily apparent. There will be no permanent solution to the, race problem until oppressed men develop the capacity to love their enemies. The darkness of racial injustice will be dispelled only by the light of forgiving love. For more than three centuries American Negroes have been battered by the iron rod of oppression, frustrated by day and bewildered by night by unbearable injustice and burdened with the ugly weight of discrimination. Forced to live with these shameful conditions, we are tempted to become bitter and to retaliate with a corresponding hate. But if this happens, the new order we seek will be little more than a duplicate of the old order. We must in strength and humility meet hate with love.

My friends, we have followed the so-called practical way for too long a time now, and it has led inexorably to deeper confusion and chaos. Time is cluttered with the wreckage of communities which surrendered to hatred and violence. For the salvation of our nation and the salvation of mankind, we must follow another way.

While abhorring segregation, we shall love the segregationist. This is the only way to create the beloved community.

To our most bitter opponents we say: "We shall match your capacity to inflict suffering by our capacity to endure suffering. We shall meet your physical force with soul force. Do to us what you will, and we shall continue to love you. We cannot in all good conscience obey your unjust laws because noncooperation with evil is as much a moral obligation as is cooperation with good. Throw us in jail and we shall still love you. Bomb our homes and threaten our children, and we shall still love you. Send your hooded perpetrators of violence into our community at the midnight hour and beat us and leave us half dead, and we shall still love you. But be ye assured that we will wear you down by our capacity to suffer. One day we shall win freedom but not only for ourselves. We shall so appeal to your heart and conscience that we shall win you in the process and our victory will be a double victory."

Declaration of Independence
from the War in Vietnam
By Martin Luther King, Jr.

An address at Riverside Church
New York City, Tuesday, April 4, 1967

OVER THE PAST TWO YEARS, as I have moved to break the betrayal of my own silences and to speak from the burnings of my own heart, as I have called for radical departures from the destruction of Vietnam, many persons have questioned me about the wisdom of my path. At the heart of their concerns this query has often loomed large and loud: Why are you speaking about the war, Dr. King? Why are you joining the voices of dissent? Peace and civil rights don't mix, they say. Aren't you hurting the cause of your people, they ask. And when I hear them, though I often understand the source of their concern, I am nevertheless greatly saddened, for such questions mean that the inquirers have not really known me, my commitment or my calling. Indeed, their questions suggest that they do not know the world in which they live.

There is at the outset a very obvious and almost facile connection between the war in Vietnam and the struggle I, and others, have been waging in America. A few years ago there was a shining moment in that struggle. It seemed as if there was a real promise of hope for the poor—both black and white—through the Poverty Program. Then came the build-up in Vietnam, and I watched the program broken and eviscerated as if it were some idle political plaything of a society gone mad on war, and I knew that America would never invest the necessary funds or energies in rehabilitation of its poor so long as Vietnam continued to draw men and skills and money like some demonic, destructive suction tube. So I was increasingly compelled to see the war as an enemy of the poor and to attack it as such. Perhaps the more tragic recognition of reality took place when it became clear to me that the war was doing far more than devastating the hopes of the poor at home. It was sending their sons and their brothers and their husbands to fight and to die in extraordinarily high proportions relative to the rest of the population. We were taking the young black men who had been crippled by our society and sending them 8000 miles away to guarantee liberties in Southeast Asia which they had not found in Southwest Georgia and East Harlem. So we have been repeatedly faced with the cruel irony of watching Negro and white boys on TV screens as they kill and die together for a nation that has been unable to seat them together in the same schools. So we watch them in brutal solidarity burning the huts of a poor village, but we realize that they would never live on the same block in Detroit. I could not be silent in the face of such cruel manipulation of the poor. I knew that I could never again raise my voice against the violence of the oppressed in the ghettos without having first spoken clearly to the greatest purveyor of violence in the world today—my own government.

Class of Nonviolence

Somehow this madness must cease. I speak as a child of God and brother to the suffering poor of Vietnam and the poor of America who are paying the double price of smashed hopes at home and death and corruption in Vietnam. I speak as a citizen of the world, for the world as it stands aghast at the path we have taken. I speak as an American to the leaders of my own nation. The great initiative in this war is ours. The initiative to stop must be ours.

This is the message of the great Buddhist leaders of Vietnam. Recently, one of them wrote these words: "Each day the war goes on the hatred increases in the hearts of the Vietnamese and in the hearts of those of humanitarian instinct. The Americans are forcing even their friends into becoming their enemies. It is curious that the Americans, who calculate so carefully on the possibilities of military victory do not realize that in the process they are incurring deep psychological and political defeat. The image of America will never again be the image of revolution, freedom and democracy, but the image of violence and militarism."

In 1957 a sensitive American official overseas said that it seemed to him that our nation was on the wrong side of a world revolution. During the past ten years we have seen emerge a pattern of suppression which now has justified the presence of U.S. military "advisors" in Venezuela. The need to maintain social stability for our investments accounts for the counterrevolutionary action of American forces in Guatemala. It tells why American helicopters are being used against guerrillas in Colombia and why American napalm and Green Beret forces have already been active against rebels in Peru. With such activity in mind, the words of John F. Kennedy come back to haunt us. Five years ago he said, "Those who make peaceful revolution impossible will make violent revolution inevitable."

I am convinced that if we are to get on the right side of the world revolution, we as a nation must undergo a radical revolution of values. When machines and computers, profit and property rights are considered more important than people, the giant triplets of racism, materialism, and militarism are incapable of being conquered. The Western arrogance of feeling that it has everything to teach others and nothing to learn from them is not just. A true revolution of values will lay hands on the world order and say of war: "This way of settling differences is not just." This business of burning human beings with napalm, of filling our nation's homes with orphans and widows, of injecting poisonous drugs of hate into the veins of peoples normally humane, of sending men home from dark and bloody battlefields physically handicapped and psychologically deranged, cannot be reconciled with wisdom, justice, and love. A nation that continues year after year to spend more money on military defense than on programs of social uplift is approaching spiritual death.

There is nothing, except a tragic death wish, to prevent us from re-ordering our priorities, so that the pursuit of peace will take precedence over the pursuit of war. There is nothing to keep us from molding a recalcitrant status quo until we have fashioned it into a brotherhood.

This kind of positive revolution of values is our best defense against communism. War is not the answer. Communism will never be defeated by the use of atomic bombs or nuclear weapons.

We must not engage in a negative anti-communism, but rather in a positive thrust for democracy, realizing that our greatest defense against communism is to take: offensive action in behalf of justice. We must with positive action seek to remove those conditions of poverty, insecurity and injustice which are the fertile soil in which the seed of communism grows and develops.

These are revolutionary times. All over the globe men are revolting against old systems of exploitation and oppression, and out of the wombs of a frail world, new systems of justice and equality are being born. The shirtless and barefoot people of the land are rising up as never before. "The people who sat in darkness have seen a great light." We in the West must support these revolutions. It is a sad fact that, because of comfort, complacency, a morbid fear of communism, and our proneness to adjust to injustice, the Western nations that initiated so much of the revolutionary spirit of the modern world have now become the arch anti-revolutionaries. This has driven many to feel that only Marxism has the revolutionary spirit. Therefore, communism is a judgment against our failure to make democracy real and follow through on the revolutions that we initiated. Our only hope today lies in our ability to recapture the revolutionary spirit and go out into a sometimes hostile world declaring eternal hostility to poverty, racism, and militarism.

Here is the true meaning and value of compassion and nonviolence - when it helps us to see the enemy's point of view, to hear his questions, to know his assessment of ourselves. For from his view we may indeed see the basic weaknesses of our own condition, and if we are mature, we may learn and grow and profit form the wisdom of the brothers who are called the opposition.

Pilgrimage to Nonviolence
By Martin Luther King, Jr.

Often the question has arisen concerning my own intellectual pilgrimage to nonviolence. In order to get at this question it is necessary to go back to my early teens in Atlanta. I had grown up abhorring not only segregation but also the oppressive and barbarous acts that grew out of it. I had passed spots where Negroes had been savagely lynched, and had watched the Ku Klux Klan on its rides at night. I had seen police brutality with my own eyes, and watched Negroes receive the most tragic injustice in the courts. All of these things had done something to my growing personality. I had come perilously close to resenting all white people.

I had also learned that the inseparable twin of racial injustice was economic injustice. Although I came from a home of economic security and relative comfort, I could never get out of my mind the economic insecurity of many of my playmates and the tragic poverty of those living around me. During my late teens I worked two summers, against my father's wishes—he never wanted my brother and me to work around white people because of the oppressive conditions—in a plant that hired both Negroes and whites. Here I saw economic injustice firsthand, and realized that the poor white was exploited just as much as the Negro. Through these early experiences I grew up deeply conscious of the varieties of injustice in our society.

So when I went to Atlanta's Morehouse College as a freshman in 1944 my concern for racial and economic justice was already substantial. During my student days at Morehouse I read Thoreau's Essay on Civil Disobedience for the first time. Fascinated by the idea of refusing to cooperate with an evil system, I was so deeply moved that I reread the work several times. This was my first intellectual contact with the theory of nonviolent resistance.

Not until I entered Crozier Theological Seminary in 1948, however, did I begin a serious intellectual quest for a method to eliminate social evil. Although my major interest was in the fields of theology and philosophy, I spent a great deal of time reading the works of the great social philosophers. I came early to Walter Rauschenbusch's **Christianity and the Social Crisis**, which left an indelible imprint on my thinking by giving me a theological basis for the social concern which had already grown up in me as a result of my early experiences. Of course there were points at which I differed with Rauschenbusch. I felt that he had fallen victim to the nineteenth century "cult of inevitable progress" which led him to a superficial optimism concerning man's nature. Moreover, he came perilously close to identifying the Kingdom of God with a particular social and economic system—a tendency which should never befall the Church. But in spite of these shortcomings Rauschenbusch had done a great service for the Christian Church by insisting that the gospel deals with the whole man, not only his soul but his body; not only his spiritual well-being but his material well-being. It has been my conviction ever since reading Rauschenbusch that any religion which professes to be concerned about the souls of men and is not concerned about the social and economic conditions that scar the soul, is a spiritually moribund religion only waiting for the day to be buried. It well has been said: "A religion that ends with the individual, ends."

After reading Rauschenbusch, I turned to a serious study of the social and ethical theories of the great philosophers, from Plato and Aristotle down to Rousseau, Hobbes, Bentham, Mill and Locke. All of these masters stimulated my thinking—such as it was—and, while finding things to question in each of them, I nevertheless learned a great deal from their study.

The Challenge of Marxism

During the Christmas holidays of 1949 I decided to spend my spare time reading Karl Marx to try to understand the appeal of communism for many people. For the first time I carefully scrutinized **Das Kapital** and **The Communist Manifesto**. I also read some interpretive works on the thinking of Marx and Lenin. In reading such Communist writings I drew certain conclusions that have remained with me to this day.

First, I rejected their materialistic interpretation of history. Communism, avowedly secularistic and materialistic, has no place for God. This I could never accept, for as a Christian I believe that there is a creative personal power in this universe who is the ground and essence of all reality—a power that cannot be explained in materialistic terms. History is ultimately guided by spirit, not matter.

Second, I strongly disagreed with Communism's ethical relativism. Since for the Communist there is no divine government, no absolute moral order, there are no fixed, immutable principles; consequently almost anything—force, violence, murder, lying—is a justifiable means to the "millennial" end. This type of relativism was abhorrent to me. Constructive ends can never give absolute moral justification to destructive means, because in the final analysis the end is preexistent in the mean.

Third, I opposed communism's political totalitarianism. In communism the individual ends up in subjection to the state. True, the Marxist would argue that the state is an "interim" reality which is to be eliminated when the classless society emerges; but the state is the end while it lasts, and man only a means to that end. And if any man's so-called rights or liberties stand in the way of that end, they are simply swept aside. His liberties of expression, his freedom to vote, his freedom to listen to what news he likes or to choose his books are all restricted. Man becomes hardly more, in communism, than a depersonalized cog in the turning wheel of the state.

This deprecation of individual freedom was objectionable to me. I am convinced now, as I was then, that man is an end because he is a child of God. Man is not made for the state; the state is made for man. To deprive man of freedom is to relegate him to the status of a thing, rather than elevate him to the status of a person. Man must never be treated as a means to the end of the state, but always as an end within himself.

Yet, in spite of the fact that my response to communism was and is negative, and I considered it basically evil, there were points at which I found it challenging. The late Archbishop of Canterbury, William Temple, referred to Communism as a Christian heresy.

By this he meant that communism had laid hold of certain truths which are essential parts of the Christian view of things, but that it had bound up with them concepts and practices which no Christian could ever accept or profess. Communism challenged the late Archbishop and it should challenge every Christian—as it challenged me—to a growing concern about social justice. With all of its false assumptions and evil methods, communism grew as a protest against the hardships of the underprivileged. Communism in theory emphasized a classless society, and a concern for social justice, though the world knows from sad experience that in practice it created new classes and a new lexicon of injustice. The Christian ought always to be challenged by any protest against unfair treatment of the poor, for Christianity is itself such a protest, nowhere expressed more eloquently than in Jesus' words: "The Spirit of the Lord is upon me, because he hath anointed me to preach the gospel to the poor; he hath sent me to heal the brokenhearted, to preach deliverance to the captives, and recovering of sight to the blind, to set at liberty them that are bruised, to preach the acceptable year of the Lord."

I also sought systematic answers to Marx's critique of modern bourgeois culture. He presented Capitalism as essentially a struggle between the owners of the productive resources and the workers, whom Marx regarded as the real producers. Marx interpreted economic forces as the dialectical process by which society moved from feudalism through capitalism to socialism, with the primary mechanism of this historical movement being the struggle between economic classes whose interests were irreconcilable. Obviously this theory left out of account the numerous and significant complexities—political, economic moral, religious and psychological—which played a vital role in shaping the constellation of institutions and ideas known today as Western civilization. Moreover, it was dated in the sense that the capitalism Marx wrote about bore only a partial resemblance to the capitalism we know in this country today.

Toward a New Social Synthesis

But in spite of the shortcomings of his analysis, Marx had raised some basic questions. I was deeply concerned from my early teen days about the gulf between superfluous wealth and abject poverty, and my reading of Marx made me ever more conscious of this gulf. Although modern American capitalism had greatly reduced the gap through social reforms, there was still need for a better distribution of wealth. Moreover, Marx had revealed the danger of the profit motive as the sole basis of an economic system; capitalism is always in danger of inspiring men to be more concerned about making a living than making a life. We are prone to judge success by the index of our salaries or the size of our automobiles, rather than by the quality of our service and relationship to humanity—thus capitalism can lead to a practical materialism that is as pernicious as the materialism taught by communism.

In short, I read Marx as I read all of the influential historical thinkers—from a dialectical point of view, combining a partial "yes" and a partial "no." In so far as Marx posited a metaphysical materialism, an ethical relativism, and a strangulating totalitarianism, I responded with an unambiguous "no"; but in so far as he pointed to weaknesses of traditional capitalism, contributed to the growth of a definite self-consciousness in the masses, and challenged the social conscience of the Christian churches, I responded with a definite "yes."

My reading of Marx also convinced me that truth is found neither in Marxism nor in traditional Capitalism. Each represents a partial truth. Historically Capitalism failed to see the truth in collective enterprise, and Marxism failed to see the truth in individual enterprise. Nineteenth century Capitalism failed to see that life is social and Marxism failed and still fails to see that life is individual and personal. The Kingdom of God is neither the thesis of individual enterprise nor the antithesis of collective enterprise, but a synthesis which reconciles the truths of both.

Muste, Nietzsche and Gandhi

During my stay at Crozier, I was also exposed for the first time to the pacifist position in a lecture by A. J. Muste. I was deeply moved by Mr. Muste's talk, but far from convinced of the practicability of his position. Like most of the students of Crozier, I felt that while war could never be a positive or absolute good, it could serve as a negative good in the sense of preventing the spread and growth of an evil force. War, horrible as it is, might be preferable to surrender to a totalitarian system—Nazi, Fascist, or Communist.

During this period I had about despaired of the power of love in solving social problems. Perhaps my faith in love was temporarily shaken by the philosophy of Nietzsche. I had been reading parts of **The Genealogy of Morals** and the whole of **The Will to Power**. Nietzsche's glorification of power—in his theory all life expressed the will to power—was an outgrowth of his contempt for ordinary morals. He attacked the whole of the Hebraic-Christian morality—with its virtues of piety and humility, its otherworldliness and its attitude toward suffering—as the glorification of weakness, as making virtues out of necessity and impotence. He looked to the development of a superman who would surpass man as man surpassed the ape.

Then one Sunday afternoon I traveled to Philadelphia to hear a sermon by Dr. Mordecai Johnson, president of Howard University. He was there to preach for the Fellowship House of Philadelphia. Dr. Johnson had just returned from a trip to India, and, to my great interest, he spoke of the life and teachings of Mahatma Gandhi. His message was so profound and electrifying that I left the meeting and bought a half dozen books on Gandhi's life and works.

Like most people, I had heard of Gandhi, but I had never studied him seriously. As I read I became deeply fascinated by his campaigns of nonviolent resistance. I was particularly moved by the Salt March to the Sea and his numerous fasts. The whole concept of "Satyagraha" (Satya is truth which equals love, and agraha is force; "Satyagraha," therefore, means truth-force or loveforce) was profoundly significant to me. As I delved deeper into the philosophy of Gandhi my skepticism concerning the power of love gradually diminished, and I came to see for the first rime its potency in the area of social reform. Prior to reading Gandhi, I had about concluded that the ethics of Jesus were only effective in individual

Class of Nonviolence

relationship. The "turn the other cheek" philosophy and the "love your enemies" philosophy were only valid, I felt, when individuals were in conflict with other individuals; when racial groups and nations were in conflict a more realistic approach seemed necessary. But after reading Gandhi, I saw how utterly mistaken I was.

Gandhi was probably the first person in history to lift the love ethic of Jesus above mere interaction between individuals to a powerful and effective social force on a large scale. Love, for Gandhi, was a potent instrument for social and collective transformation. It was in this Gandhian emphasis on love and nonviolence that I discovered the method for social reform that I had been seeking for so many months. The intellectual and moral satisfaction that I failed to gain from the utilitarianism of Bentham and Mill, the revolutionary methods of Marx and Lenin, the social-contracts theory of Hobbes, the "back to nature" optimism of Rousseau, the superman philosophy of Nietzsche, I found in the nonviolent resistance philosophy of Gandhi. I came to feel that this was the only morally and practically sound method open to oppressed people in their struggle for freedom.

An Encounter With Niebuhr

But my intellectual odyssey to nonviolence did not end here. During my last year in theological school, I began to read the works of Reinhold Niebuhr. The prophetic and realistic elements in Niebuhr's passionate style and profound thought were appealing to me, and I became so enamored of his social ethics that I almost fell into the trap of accepting uncritically everything he wrote.

About this time I read Niebuhr's critique of the pacifist position. Niebuhr had himself once been a member of the pacifist ranks. For several years, he had been national chairman of the Fellowship of Reconciliation. His break with pacifism came in the early thirties, and the first full statement of his criticism of pacifism was in Moral Man and Immoral Society. Here he argued that there was no intrinsic moral difference between violent and nonviolent resistance. The social consequences of the two methods were different, he contended, but the differences were in degree rather than kind. Later Niebuhr began emphasizing the irresponsibility of relying on nonviolent resistance when there was no ground for believing that it would be successful in preventing the spread of totalitarian tyranny. It could only be successful, he argued, if the groups against whom the resistance was taking place had some degree of moral conscience, as was the case in Gandhi's struggle against the British. Niebuhr's ultimate rejection of pacifism was based primarily on the doctrine of man. He argued that pacifism failed to do justice to the reformation doctrine of justification by faith, substituting for it a sectarian perfectionism which believes "that divine grace actually lifts man out of the sinful contradictions of history and establishes him above the sins of the world."

At first, Niebuhr's critique of pacifism left me in a state of confusion. As I continued to read, however, I came to see more and more the shortcomings of his position. For instance, many of his statements revealed that he interpreted pacifism as a sort of passive nonresistance to evil expressing naive trust in the power of love. But this was a serious distortion. My study of Gandhi convinced me that true pacifism is not nonresistance to evil, but nonviolent resistance to evil. Between the two positions, there is a world of difference. Gandhi resisted evil with as much vigor and power as the violent resister, but he resisted with love instead of hate. True pacifism is not unrealistic submission to evil power, as Niebuhr contends. It is rather a courageous confrontation of evil by the power of love, in the faith that it is better to be the recipient of violence than the inflicter of it, since the latter only multiplied the existence of violence and bitterness in the universe, while the former may develop a sense of shame in the opponent, and thereby bring about a transformation and change of heart.

The next stage of my intellectual pilgrimage to nonviolence came during my doctoral studies at Boston University. Here I had the opportunity to talk to many exponents of nonviolence, both students and visitors to the campus. Boston University School of Theology under the influence of Dean Walter Muelder and Professor Allan Knight Chalmers, had a deep sympathy for pacifism. Both Dean Muelder and Dr. Chalmers had a passion for social justice that stemmed, not from a superficial optimism, but from a deep faith in the possibilities of human beings when they allowed themselves to become co-workers with God. It was at Boston University that I came to see that Niebuhr had overemphasized the corruption of human nature. His pessimism concerning human nature was not balanced by an optimism concerning divine nature. He was so involved in diagnosing man's sickness of sin that he overlooked the cure of grace.

I studied philosophy and theology at Boston University under Edgar S. Brightman and L. Harold DeWolf. Both men greatly stimulated my thinking. It was mainly under these teachers that I studied personalistic philosophy—the theory that the clue to the meaning of ultimate reality is found in personality. This personal idealism remains today my basic philosophical position. Personalism's insistence that only personality—finite and infinite—is ultimately real strengthened me in two convictions: it gave me metaphysical and philosophical grounding for the idea of a personal God, and it gave me a metaphysical basis for the dignity and worth of all human personality.

Just before Dr. Brightman's death, I began studying the philosophy of Hegel with him. Although the course was mainly a study of Hegel's monumental work, **Phenomenology of Mind**, I spent my spare time reading his **Philosophy of History** and **Philosophy of Right**. There were points in Hegel's philosophy that I strongly disagreed with. For instance, his absolute idealism was rationally unsound to me because it tended to swallow up the many in the one. But there were other aspects of his thinking that I found stimulating. His contention that "truth is the whole" led me to a philosophical method of rational coherence. His analysis of the dialectical process, in spite of its shortcomings, helped me to see that growth comes through struggle.

In 1954 I ended my formal training with all of these relative divergent intellectual forces converging into a positive social philosophy. One of the main tenets of this philosophy was the conviction that nonviolent resistance was one of the most potent weapons available to oppressed people in their quest for social justice. At this time, however, I had merely an

Class of Nonviolence

intellectual understanding and appreciation of the position, with no firm determination to organize it in a socially effective situation.

When I went to Montgomery as a pastor, I had not the slightest idea that I would later become involved in a crisis in which nonviolent resistance would be applicable. I neither started the protest nor suggested it. I simply responded to the call of the people for a spokesman. When the protest began, my mind, consciously or unconsciously, was driven back to the Sermon on the Mount, with its sublime teachings on love, and the Gandhian method of nonviolent resistance. As the days unfolded, I came to see the power of nonviolence more and more. Living through the actual experience of the protest, nonviolence became more than a method to which I gave intellectual assent; it became a commitment to a way of life. Many of the things that I had not cleared up intellectually concerning nonviolence were now solved in the sphere of practical action.

The philosophy of nonviolence

Since the philosophy of nonviolence played such a positive role in the Montgomery movement, it may be wise to turn to a brief discussion of some basic aspects of this philosophy.

First, it must be emphasized that nonviolent resistance is not a method for cowards; it does resist. If one used this method because he is afraid, he is not truly nonviolent. That is why Gandhi often said that if cowardice is the only alternative to violence, it is better to fight. He made this statement conscious of the fact that there is always another alternative: no individual or group need ever submit to any wrong, nor need they use violence to right the wrong; there is the way of nonviolent resistance. This is ultimately the way for the strong man. It is not a method of stagnant passivity. The phrase "passive resistance" often gives the false impression that this is a sort of "do-nothing method" in which the resister quietly and passively accepts evil. But nothing is further from the truth. For while the nonviolent resister is passive in the sense that he is not physically aggressive toward his opponent, his mind and emotions are always active, constantly seeking to persuade his opponents that he is wrong. The method is passive physically, but strongly active spiritually. It is not passive resistance to evil, it is active nonviolent resistance to evil.

A second basic fact that characterizes nonviolence is that is does not seek to defeat or humiliate the opponent, but to win his friendship and understanding. The nonviolent resister may often express his protest through noncooperation or boycotts, but he realizes that these are not ends in themselves; they are merely means to awaken a sense of moral shame in the opponent. The end is redemption and reconciliation. The aftermath of nonviolence is the creation of the beloved community, while the aftermath of violence is tragic bitterness.

A third characteristic of this method is that the attack is directed against forces of evil rather than against persons who happen to be doing the evil. It is evil that the nonviolent resister seeks to defeat, not the person victimized by the evil. If he is opposing racial injustice, the nonviolent resister has the vision to see that the basic tension is not between races. As I like to say to the people in Montgomery: "The tension in the city is not between white people and Negro people. The tension is, at bottom, between justice and injustice, between the forces of light and the forces of darkness. And if there is a victory, it will be a victory not merely for 50,000 Negroes, but a victory for justice and the forces of light. We are out there to defeat injustice and not white persons who may be unjust."

A fourth point that characterizes nonviolent resistance is a willingness to accept suffering without retaliation, to accept blows from the opponent without striking back. "Rivers of blood may have to flow before we gain our freedom, but it must be our blood," Gandhi said to his countrymen. The nonviolent resister is willing to accept violence if necessary, but never to inflict it. He does not seek to dodge jail. If going to jail is necessary, he enters it "as a bridegroom enters the bride's chamber."

One may well ask: "What is the nonviolent resister's justification for this ordeal to which he invites men, for this mass political application of the ancient doctrine of turning the other cheek?" The answer is found in the realization that unearned suffering is redemptive. Suffering, the nonviolent resister realizes, has tremendous educational and transforming possibilities. "Things of fundamental importance to people are not secured by reason alone, but have to be purchased with their suffering," said Gandhi. He continued: "Suffering is infinitely more powerful than the law of the jungle for converting the opponent and opening his ears which are otherwise shut to the voice of reason."

A fifth point concerning nonviolent resistance is that it avoids not only external physical violence but also internal violence of spirit. The nonviolent resister not only refuses to shoot his opponent but he also refuses to hate him. At the center of nonviolence stands the principle of love. The nonviolent resister would contend that in the struggle for human dignity, the oppressed people of the world must not succumb to the temptation of becoming bitter or indulging in hate campaigns. To retaliate in kind would do nothing but intensify the existence of hate in the universe. Along the way of life, someone must have sense enough and morality enough to cut off the chain of hate. This can only be done by projecting the ethic of love to the center of our lives.

In speaking of love at this point, we are not referring to some sentimental or affectionate emotion. It would be nonsense to urge men to love their oppressors in an affectionate sense. Love in this connection means understanding, redemptive good will. Here the Greek language comes to our aid. There are three words for love in the Greek New Testament. First, there is eros. In Platonic philosophy eros meant the yearning of the soul for the realm of the divine. It has come now to mean a sort of aesthetic or romantic love. Second, there is philia which means intimate affection between personal friends. Philia denotes a sort of reciprocal love; the person loves because he is loved. When we speak of loving those who oppose us, we refer to neither eros nor philia; we speak of love which is expressed in the Greek word agape. Agape means understanding, redeeming good will for all men. It is an overflowing love which is purely spontaneous, unmotivated, groundless, and creative. It is not set in motion by any quality or function of its object. It is the love of God operating in the human heart.

Agape is disinterested love. It is a love in which the individual seeks not his own good, but the good of his neighbor (1 Cor. 10-24). 'Agape does not begin by discriminating between worthy and unworthy people, or any qualities people possess. It begins by loving others for their sakes. It is an entirely "neighbor-regarding concern for others," which discovers the neighbor in every man it meets. Therefore, agape makes no distinction between friend and enemy; it is directed toward both. If one loves an individual merely on account of his friendliness, he loves him for the sake of benefits to be gained from the friendship, rather than for the friend's sake. Consequently, the best way to assure oneself that love is disinterested is to have love for the enemy-neighbor from whom you can expect no good in return, but only hostility and persecution.

Another basic point about agape is that it springs from the need of the other person - his need for belonging to the best of the human family. The Samaritan who helped the Jew in the Jericho Road was "good" because he responded to the human need that he was presented with. God's love is eternal and fails not, because man needs his love. St. Paul assures us that the loving act of redemption was done "while we were yet sinners," that is, at the point of our greatest need for love. Since the white man's personality is greatly distorted by segregation, and his soul is greatly scarred, he needs the love of the Negro. The Negro must love the white man, because the white man needs his love to remove his tensions, insecurities and fears.

Agape is not a weak, passive love. It is love in action. Agape is love seeking to preserve and create community. It is insistence on community even when one seeks to break it. Agape is a willingness to sacrifice in the interest of mutuality. Agape is a willingness to go to any length to restore community. It doesn't stop at the first mile, but goes the second mile to restore community. The cross is the eternal expression of the length to which God will go in order to restore broken community. The resurrection is a symbol of God's triumph over all the forces that that seek to block community. The Holy Spirit is the continuing community creating reality that moves through history. He who works against community is working against the whole of creation. Therefore, if I respond to hate with a reciprocal hate I do nothing but intensify the cleavage in broken community. I can only close the gap in broken community by meeting hate with love. If I meet hate with hate, I become depersonalized, because creation is so designed that my personality can only be fulfilled in the context of community. Booker T. Washington was right: "Let no man pull you so low that he makes you hate him." When he pulls you that low he brings you to the point of working against community; he drags you to the point of defying creation, and thereby becoming depersonalized.

In the final analysis, agape means recognition of the fact that all life is interrelated. All humanity is involved in a single process, and all men are brothers. To the degree that I harm my brother, no matter what he is doing to me, to that extent I am harming myself. For example, white men often refuse federal aid to education in order to avoid giving the Negro his rights; but because all men are brothers they cannot deny Negro children without harming their own. They end, all efforts to the contrary, by hurting themselves. Why is this?

Because men are brothers. If you harm me, you harm yourself.

Love, agape, is the only cement that can hold this broken community together. When I am commanded to love, I am commanded to restore community, to resist injustice, to meet the needs of my brothers.

A sixth basic fact about nonviolent resistance is that it is based on the conviction that the universe is on the side of justice. Consequently, the believer in nonviolence has deep faith in the future. This faith is another reason why the nonviolent resister can accept suffering without retaliation. For he knows that in his struggle for justice he has cosmic companionship. It is true that there are devout believers in nonviolence who find it difficult to believe in a personal God. But even these persons believe in the existence of some creative force that works for universal wholeness. Whether we call it an unconscious process, an impersonal Brahman, or a Personal Being of matchless power and infinite love, there is a creative force in this universe that works to bring the disconnected aspects of reality into a harmonious whole.

excerpted from "Stride Toward Freedom", 1958

Class of Nonviolence

King and Pacifism: The Other Dimension
by Colman McCarthy

Why the uproar over the remarks of Jesse Helms on Martin Luther King, Jr.? The North Carolina senator, in raising questions about King's character and his links with Communists, was temperate compared with what we have heard before. J. Edgar Hoover said that King was "the most notorious liar in the country." In 1965, Sheriff Jim Clark, the keeper at the time of Alabama's attack dogs and water hoses, said that "an agitator" like King "is the lowest form of humanity."

During the Senate debate on whether to honor King with a national holiday, Helms, in his twisted way, actually helped the cause. His speeches assured publicity. Without the oversized mouth of Helms, the issue might have passed unnoticed.

King's reputation was damaged more by the supporters of the holiday legislation than by its opponents. He was praised as only a civil rights leader. Sen. Edward Kennedy said that "King worked tirelessly to remove the stain of discrimination from our nation."

King was much, much more than that. At the core - of both his thinking and of his commitment as a Christian clergyman was pacifism, as practiced through the techniques of organized nonviolent confrontation. His constituency was not limited to blacks. Liberals like Kennedy do a disservice to King. In limiting their praise of him to civil rights they sanitize the record.

It was King the pacifist who said in April 1967 that "the greatest purveyor of violence in the world today (is) my own government." That Statement was not quoted on the Senate floor. Nor was his Statement that we are "a society gone mad with war. If America's soul becomes totally poisoned, part of the autopsy must read 'Vietnam.' It can never be saved so long as it destroys the deepest hopes of men the world over."

At some moment, the city of Washington will need a statue of King to go along with his national holiday. Several of King's thoughts are suitable to be chiseled into stone, with a number of sites around town being appropriate for the statue.

In front of the Pentagon, why not a bronzed King saluting the flag with these words underneath: "War is not the answer. Communism will never be defeated by the use of atomic bombs or nuclear weapons."

Or perhaps the King statue should be placed between the Treasury and the Department of Commerce, with this thought: "Capitalism may lead to a practical materialism that is as pernicious as the theoretical materialism taught by communism." Maybe Congress will want the King presence on the lawn before the Capitol. If so, King's quote—uttered in early 1968 when the House and Senate were cutting social programs and increasing military spending—is fit: "The Congress is sick."

For a fourth possible site, there is the new memorial for the 59,000 Americans who died in Vietnam. Put in stone King's memorable words about the troops being sent to Southeast Asia: "Before long they must know that their government has sent them into a struggle among Vietnamese, and the more sophisticated surely realize that we are on the side of the wealthy and the secure while we create a hell for the poor."

'These aren't the soothing nosegays found in quotation books under "Patriotism" where the comments of George Washington, our only other leader to be honored with a national holiday, can be found by schoolchildren. By categorizing King as only a civil rights leader, the Senate of 1983 has pulled off what King himself would not allow his detractors to get away with in the 1960s. After his tactics of nonviolence led to the passage of the 1961 civil rights law, voices of respectability told King to stick to race and leave antiwar dissent to others.

It was the new way of telling blacks to stay in their place. King replied that racism and militarism are diseases spread by the same germ: the contempt of the powerful for the weak. With the world armed with nukes, he said, "It will be worthless to talk about integration if there is no world to integrate."

If the Senate liberals avoided the real King, Ronald Reagan will certainly do so when he signs the bill for the holiday. 'That leaves it up to the followers of King. To accept him as anything less than a revolutionary pacifist will mean that we are getting just another irrelevant plastic hem.

From Washington Post October 30,1983

Class of Nonviolence

Questions for Lesson Four

1. Why was "forgiveness" and "inclusive peacemaking" the crucial underpinning of Martin Luther King's approach to confronting a racist society?

2. Define and give an example of institutional racism. How might you be contributing to such an entity unknowingly?

3. Do you believe affirmative action programs are justified? If so, why?

4. Have you tried to become personally acquainted with and appreciative of people from ethnic and racial backgrounds different from your own? How did it change you?

5. King assumed the basic oneness of humanity as a means of overcoming racism. How have you advanced this notion in your life?

Readings for Lesson Five

Feminism, Peace and Power
by Mary Roodkowsky

Rape is all too Thinkable for Quite the Normal Sort of Man
by Neal King and Martha McCaughey

To the Women of India
by Mohandas Gandhi

Narrowing the Battlefield
by Carol Ascher

Patriarchy: A State of War
by Barbara Hope

An American Shero of 1941
by Colman McCarthy

Feminism, Peace, and Power
By Mary Roodkowsky

"Who then will do it? The men are all fighting, and some women, too."
Betty Williams, Nobel Peace laureate, when asked why women created the People's Peace Movement in Ireland.

Fighting, vanquishing, attacking, and counterattacking are so-called masculine skills shed of the metaphors of business, sports, and social competition which usually clothe them. War creates heroes, supermen, known by their performance: true men, on whose chests medals and stripes glitter and ribbons flap. Strong men, whose very survival proves brains and brawn. Men in charge of their own lives, and with the power and authority to direct and mold the lives of others.

Victory in war derives from comparative advantage—no stronger or wiser for the battle, perhaps poorer than before—to conqueror is defined by his superior position, his lower losses. The loot consists mainly of positional goods, those which can be held only at the expense of others. Use and control over the opponent's natural resources and social status—the ability to determine if and how others will share in those resources.

Because it seems that conflict's only rationale is acquisition of goods or power from another, only those who are enfranchised, or who might hope to be, need involve themselves. No wonder, then, that women neither profit from nor join in wars. The round tables where strategic decisions are made never include women—in fact, women rarely approach them save with memos or coffee for the real decision makers.

While men wage war, women keep house and also the economy. Their perpetual care of the hearth and of the children maintains a social structure and ensures a home where soldiers may return. Women labor in factories and offices, in seats left vacant by men called to the front.

Women also take on new burdens in wartime. They sacrifice butter to churn out guns in factories, they expand their roles as society's washers, nurses, and caretakers, to include the extra destruction created by war. Women make and roll bandages, and then use them to bind wounds they never inflicted. At the war's close they comfort combat-tattered psyches, of both sides. Their wartime jobs—and the newly acquired earning power it brought—are pre-empted by those to whom they really belong, the boys back from the front. Thus, wars that are fought for goods and position benefit women little. In fact, rather than acquiring goods or position in war, women often are the goods, the spoils, acquired by war. Rape has been standard operating procedure during armed conflict, from the Trojan War to the Vietnam War. In her book Against Our Will, Susan Brownmiller suggests that soldiers' abuse of women ranks along with looting, burning, and bombing as a means of subduing the enemy. Later, the women become a part of the victor's booty:

"The body of a raped woman becomes a ceremonial battlefield, a parade ground for the victor's trooping of the colors. The act that is played out upon her is a message passed between men—vivid proof of victory for one and loss and defeat for the other."

Class of Nonviolence

Some of glory's light does shine on women, but indirectly and through their relationships to men, as in so many other areas of life. Army nurses who have bravely cared for wounded men may receive medals, and exceptional female military personnel may also be rewarded for their contributions. But the "glory" comes mostly through their men—the fathers, husbands, sons—"given" to the effort. All women in wartime must sacrifice those men's presence, as well as their contributions to home and family. Later, the ultimate honor consists in welcoming back the womb's fruit like the Spartan woman who will only greet her son with his shield, victorious, or on it, dead. Today's reward consists of a body in a bag, and a yearly appearance in the Memorial Day parade. While triumphant men split the spoils and bask in power, women replace their life's love and the result of their caring work with a Gold Star banner fluttering in the wind. Only one-half of the men in a battle can win, one side must lose; however, no woman, on either side of the battle line, can ever claim victory or its prerogatives.

Women Propose Peace

Given their suffering—in themselves, in the destruction of what is most important to them, in the violation of their bodies—and given that women receive little compensation for what they give, it is not surprising that many peace movements and movements for nonviolent change throughout history have been led by women. A history of such involvement might include the imagery of Euripides' Lysistrata, or the way the Pilate's unnamed wife tried to save Christ; it could also tell of Angelina Grimke's impassioned pleas that women work for an end to slavery, without bloodshed; it might discuss Mrs. Rosa Parks' refusal to move to the rear of a bus in Montgomery, Alabama, sparking the civil rights movement; it might document the women's strike for peace during the Vietnam War years, and describe Betty Williams and Mairead Corrigan and the other women in the Irish People's Peace Movement. It might discuss how the woman's suffrage movement of the 19th and 20th centuries in America diligently overturned law and social order, without violence. Given the deep state of powerlessness of most women and the extra effort it takes for women to work in the organized realms of government, law, and broad scale organization, this record is even more remarkable.

Winning Over Others

Nonviolence not only opposes war; it also upholds a way of living where conflict creates rather than destroys. Feminism, too, goes beyond its rejection of arms and battle, to suggest and to practice nondestructive patters of conflict resolution. It is perhaps rooted in women's socialization, or perhaps due to women's economic and political powerlessness, or perhaps because of the common female roles. But whatever its source, feminist understandings of conflict can help to clarify and expand nonviolent theory.

One major aspect of Gandhi's nonviolence embodied a stance of non-injury, or ahimsa, to the enemy. Destruction of the opponent merely perpetuates the injustice one tries to overcome. Instead, the goal is to win the opponent over to one's own side. Gandhi wrote:

"We must try patiently to convert our opponents. If we wish to evolve the spirit of democracy out of slavery, we must be scrupulously exact in our dealings with opponents. We must concede to our opponents the freedom we claim for ourselves and for which we are fighting."

Ahimsa has been very much a part of women's attitudes, even with respect to the most emotional, basic issues of feminism. For instance, at the national convention sponsored by the State Department, the most volatile issues included abortion rights, the Equal Rights Amendment, and freedom for sexual preference (lesbian rights). All three passed, but not without debate, debate which adhere in various ways to nonviolent principles of respect for the opponent, and of winning over those with whom one disagrees.

Because of socialization from girlhood on, reinforced by the expectations of womanhood, a woman perceives her fate as intimately tied to that of others in a variety of ways—her choices are not always hers alone. A woman has far less decision-making power in the social structures that govern her, whether she lives in the United States, Ireland, Egypt, or India. Likewise, on an individual level, her husband, children, and other family steer her life's course. What happens to these people and to the dominant social structures affect her with a more conclusive impact than they do a man with more autonomy. Economically, for example, when a woman depends on a man for her sustenance, the political or social factors which increase or decrease his status will likely do the same for her—either directly, when he gets a raise, or indirectly, when a slow economy pushes the "least important" elements out of the work force, as after a war or when labor is costly. He may have alternative choices in his job, and hers depend upon his. Women's relationship to men, for better and usually for worse, is a derivative one. For women as a group this has led to a greater cognizance of the interrelatedness of all humans, with each other and with the earth. Women's relationships to other women likewise recognize such interrelatedness, but on a far more egalitarian basis. Contrary to stereotypes of calculating, competitive women, documentation of women in developing nations and histories of women in Western civilization demonstrate norms of cooperation, caring, and nurture among women.

For example, female midwives through the Middle Ages often expertly delivered children at minimal cost. When two male doctors introduced the forceps, many midwives scorned them—for their expense, and for the fact that they foresaw an era when less compassionate, more technological childbirth would become the norm. Women in many developing nations sustain informal exchanges of goods and services among themselves, swapping household foods and childcare on a cooperative, nonprofit basis. In contemporary society, wherever neighborhoods still exist and women's communities live despite pressures of urbanization, such bartering still occurs, despite the counterpressures of consumerism.

An adherent of nonviolence cannot injure another, because their fates intertwine. How, then, can women make a policy of winning their need and more by destroying or subjugating the adversary, when so much of their own well-being so clearly depends on the welfare of the adversary?

Not only are women's fates combined with those of their community, but women's roles in society are constructed with a notion of responsibility to others and to the physical world—such accountability intrinsically leads to nonviolence.

Women bear the brunt of their own actions more directly than do men. Men's work is supported by others—by those lower on the social ladder, by secretaries, and subordinates in the workplace, by women at home. A woman's work, however, receives no such subsidy. She takes final responsibility for the children's and the men's lifestyles and daily physical and material needs, as well as for her own, since there is no one further down the ladder to whom she can shunt the blame or the chores. Cooking dinner, washing laundry, feeding the baby, are all tasks created by the needs of many but only met by the work of one woman. Such "women's work" is not the whole of the females' responsibilities. The world over, women perform not only such womanly chores, but other "male" work as well. In Africa, 80 percent of the farmers are women; in the United States, 48 percent of women work or need work outside the home. Dual workloads complicate women's accountability and burden. A woman doctor in a remote Himalayan mountain area comments that women in her district "work three times as hard as men," for they must do all the things men do, and then care for the family.

Without someone down the line to blame, the unpleasant, ugly fallout of violent action might deter more women from participating in it. The desecration of the earth in strip-mining, for example, is encouraged and financed not by those displaced by or living near the site, but by corporations in cities. Nuclear power irresponsibly manufactures energy, allowing others—future generations—to grapple with the radioactive waste it creates. No one thoroughly socialized in female responsibilities could ever dream such a system. Nonviolent action asserts the value and necessity of acting in support of the truth (the Satyagraha of Gandhi), that doing for self means also doing for others. The U.S. peace group, Mobilization for Survival, made four demands in 1977, the first three were all injunctions against violence: zero nuclear weapons, ban nuclear power, and stop the arms race; the fourth demand was the advocacy for the justice central to nonviolent action: fund human needs.

The psychology of women supports this policy of non-injury. A woman judges her own worth, and others judge her, in terms of how well she serves others. Rather that basing her worth on the domination of others or on comparative strength, the normative criteria have been sacrifice and service.

Such advocacy is in many ways the raison d'etre of the traditional female role. Psychoanalyst Jean Baker Miller states:

> "In our culture serving others is for losers, it is low-level stuff. Yet serving others is a basic principle around which women's lives are organized; it is far from such for men. In fact, there are psychoanalytic data to suggest that men's lives are psychologically organized against such a principle, that there is a potent dynamic at work forcing men away from such a goal."

When conflict produces an either/or, have/have-not situation, a woman is apt to opt for the subordinate role. The ideal of serving is so firmly implanted in the consciousness, in letting the other win—tennis, and argument, or a job—that not to do so is unfeminine, and therefore attacks the core of the woman's worth. Women's spirituality is beautifully described by the French mystic, Simone Weil, who states that love is merely attention to the other's needs.

However, in doing such service, we can make another kind of connection between feminism on the one hand, and nonviolence on the other. This ideal of living-for-others not only has avoided overt violence aimed at others by women, its reverse side is the exploitation of that service by men, to hurt women and women's extreme internalization of that ideal and negation of their own needs.

Because nonviolence promotes action for justice, nothing can be less passive than its "truth-force." For their own sake women need to emphasize this active side far more than the avoidance of violence to others. Many ethics, nonviolent codes included, speak largely to the male psyche, to its aggressive, competitive, against-others nature. Applying ethical principles of self-denial and service to the already self-sacrificing woman can sometimes overwhelm her into increased living-for-others to the point where any living-for-self seems invalid. Jean Baker Miller writes that the unilateral assignation of women to a service role is the source of overwhelming problems for men and women alike, denying to the former (men), their justly due community responsibility, to the latter (women), a necessary and realistic understanding of self-worth.

Gandhi sometimes glorified suffering for the cause of truth. But he, and other non-violent activists, also stressed the need for noncooperation with the forces of evil. Angelina Grimke urged her Christian sisters to throw away their submissive behavior in order to work to end slavery. Peace activist Dorothy Day illegally asserted herself against nuclear armaments and for the United Farm Workers' union struggle. Women can apply this principle of noncooperation to their oppression, and to those who hurt them. Nonviolence never assents to the demands of the oppressors, even though it may cause anger or resentment. It strips the oppressors of authority to which they are not entitled, at the same time ascertaining that all enjoy what they rightfully own.

Feminist and nonviolent activist Barbara Deming connects feminism with nonviolent cooperation in application of ahimsa to both the other and the self:
"We act out respect for ourselves by refusing to cooperate with those who oppress or exploit us. And as their power never resides in their single selves, always depends upon the cooperation of others—by refusing that cooperation...refusing our labor, our wits, our money, or blood upon their battlefields, our deference, we take their power away from them."

Our actions bear upon ourselves as well as on others. Injuring others means injuring ourselves—our capacity to love, to care, to create, and to learn. And this dynamic works in reverse: to respect ourselves will mean to respect others, to expect them to respect, learn, and create in return. Feminism has set in motion a process by which women—in caring, nonviolent ways—are learning to respect themselves, value their own work, and to evoke, expect, and demand that respect from others. In this way, another dichotomy—that between oppressor and oppressed, powerful and powerless—dissolves.

For women, such noncooperation with the degradation of sexism and the self-hatred it brings is non-violent to others and to self. Doubtless, non-cooperation with sexist structures—refusal to make coffee, criticism of policies made by men with high-ego involvement in their work, insisting on equal wages; or going to school—will be threatening to men, who will then accuse women of being angry and even violent. Affirmative action in the U.S.A., for example, is really such noncooperation with the male WASP workworld. Yet, if women are not to continue to judge themselves with violence, noncooperation is essential.

Using Power Creatively

At their cores, both feminism and nonviolence perceive power differently from male-centered ideology and are alien to the reality principle that directs our world and which encourages violent struggles for position. Power, as the dominant ideology understands it, cannot coexist with love or caring—it is an imposition over others, rather than a force to help us compose, or create, together.

Those who know that only one side can be victorious in war can well understand the corollary of this truism: that any concept of a loving or interdependent ethic must mean a relinquishing of social and positional goods and therefore, powerlessness. Power so conceptualized cannot be used for the general good of the society—only for the aggrandizement of an individual or state—hence, a state of war. Feminist philosopher Mary Daly suggests that this split degrades humanity: "Power split off from love makes an obscenity out of what we call love, forcing us unwillingly to destroy ourselves and each other.

Feminists and advocates of nonviolence live by the contrary force, the power of love, which compels us to ahimsa. Learning to use our human energies as a loving force in the process of empowerment—a process which enables us to act critically and creatively to end injustice, not accept it. Empowerment comes both from the community—in the consciousness-raising group or the affinity group—and from the individual's new reconceptualizing of his/her own loving capabilities.

For poet and feminist Adrienne Rich, motherhood dissolves many dichotomies between power and powerlessness. While a mother has ultimate power over, responsibility for, and control over her baby since the baby depends on the mother for all sustenance and warmth, the baby also controls the mother—her psyche and her body, as in the flow of milk from her breasts. Rich writes of the sense of confused power and powerlessness, of being taken over in the one hand and of touching new physical and psychic potentialities in the other, a heightened sensibility which can be exhilarating, bewildering, and exhausting. For Rich, motherhood dramatizes the interactions of "exclusive" opposites, impresses upon us, for example, that "love and anger can exist concurrently."

The women's health care movement generally, and feminist attitudes toward both specifically, understand the concurrence of power and powerlessness and use it as a principle of developing nonviolent attitudes toward the body. The women's health care movement seeks to change the physical alienation affecting women, replacing a variety of attitudes that deny the body's goodness and fear of its function. Rather than labeling menstruation "the curse," women are learning to accept and celebrate their cyclical rhythms. Instead of birth control pills which, although "sure," chemically dominate and sometimes injure the body, women are turning to methods that are perhaps more limited but far safer.

The movement toward home births and toward "childbirth without violence" integrates many principles of nonviolence in the relationships involved in childbirth. Modern technological obstetrics sterilizes, shaves, and generally obfuscates the nature of childbirth, dehumanizing the most profound of human experiences. Mothers become passive observers, while their bodies become objects. Babies likewise are objectified, not considered to be people affected by their environment. The goal of such obstetrics is, of course, total control through the domination of the doctor. The entire birth experience is subject to manipulation, not only its labor and its pain, but also its passion, creativity, and satisfaction. Home births have developed an alternative to this, where midwife, mother, child, father, and others all participate and cooperate with natural forces. The benefits of such non-injury to mother and child alike include physically healthy birth without drugs, less birth trauma for the baby, early development of emotional ties between mother, father, and baby. Beyond these, new attitudes toward birth signify the development of supportive and less destructive attitudes toward our bodies, and to the natural environment generally.

Feminism and Nonviolence as Creativity

New thinking by women shedding old oppressive roles, yet retaining the real joys of womanness, can become one of the most creative political forces society has ever known. Women, like all oppressed groups, have had to know well, and bargain with, the structures which hurt them. Feminism has helped to evoke new social understandings based on women's experience and sisterhood. Many of these are implicitly grounded in nonviolence. Sisterhood implies democracy, for the needs and points of view are all-important in community. Women's responsibility provides a rationale for self-reliance and an end to exploitation.

Perhaps, as men take on new roles which encourage human values, nonviolence will seem more realistic to them too. Those who care for children and who understand their value as derived from caring will be less willing to kill. Environmental accountability will be encouraged when men take more responsibility for their day-to-day actions, and deal more closely with the consequences. Competition may lose some of its importance to those with other priorities.

Life is not a zero-sum game, where some must win at the others' expense. Violence and sexism in their many forms destroy our bonds with each other and our standing on the earth. They are ideologies which deny the ways in which we need each other and our natural order, and attempt to do what cannot be done—discard human needs and emotions and the natural workings of the earth.

Rape is All Too Thinkable
for Quite the Normal Sort of Man
By Neal King and Martha McCaughey

Men have trouble discussing rape. Some men rape, say some men, imagining that members of a subspecies abuse women in this culture. But let's be honest and tell it like it is: Normal men rape.

We are not being metaphorical or loose with our terms: we mean this the way it sounds. The vast majority of men who rape are quite ordinary.

If this sounds absurd, let's review some facts.

Rape is the bodily penetration of an unconsenting person. Men need to be reminded what this means. It is not listening when your partner says "no;" it's getting your date drunk to get sex from her; it's taking advantage of an unconscious women at a party; it's using your economic or political power to intimidate a coworker into sex. These forms of rape are far more common than the stereotypical scene of a stranger jumping out from the bushes and attacking a woman.

Nearly half of all American women have had at least one man try, successfully or not, to rape them. And many women have been attacked a number of times. The men who did this must be normal; there are not enough "abnormal" men in this society to accomplish abuse on that scale.

When a rape is grotesquely violent, or when its perpetrated on the wife of another man or on a very young girl, many men get upset to the point of proclaiming their desire to kill the rapist. But people have grown so accustomed to the sexual coercion of women that most rapes go unnoticed, especially by the men who commit them.

Most rapists are not strangers or even strange; they are their victims' friends, acquaintances, co-workers, neighbors, dates, lovers, husbands, brothers, fathers. They are the everyday, run-of-the-mill normal men in the lives of normal women.

Male readers may be getting defensive at this point, thinking, "I'm not one of them!" and they might not be. But the fact is, most men do not know what rape is. To these men, forcing a woman who is not willing is part of the game, perfectly normal, and, for many, especially satisfying. These men may acknowledge that using physical force is rape, but prevailing over a woman through trickery, blackmail, or other means is simply sex. This implies that men don't want to know - that rape may be part of their normal sexual encounters. Normal men rape because they engage in normal sex - normal sex often being coercive and abusive to women.

Though these women feel injured and demeaned in such encounters, they are not surprised to feel that they have been raped. Men don't define the experience as rape, and men are oblivious to the pain they've inflicted. Many a man who forces his date to have sex will call her up the next day and ask her out again. Normal men can be that out of touch with women's feelings.

So often women hear men refer to rape as if it were some kind of compliment, "You're so attractive that I have to have you," or "She's too ugly to get raped," or, "You look so good, I can't control myself." The notion that rape can be normal is evident in the inevitable questions about what a woman was wearing at the time: "Dressed like that, what did she expect?"

If men respected women as peers, they would see the fixation on women's body parts as a fetish, the fascination with adolescent women as pedophilia, and the desire for female passivity as necrophilia. They would also see the sexual coercion of women for what it is — rape.

In this culture, sadly, a man can be normal in believing that sex is what women are for. But that is not what women are for.

If sex is not consensual, it is rape, and men must start learning the difference by looking at it from women's perspectives.

The man who can truthfully say that he has never forced or tricked a women into sex may dismiss all of this - "It's not my concern." It is. All men must work to create a culture where sexual aggression is unthinkable for normal men. Men have to examine their own relationships with women and talk to other men about rape. The man who says that rape is a women's issue is part of the problem. The wall of silence that men have put up against this "normal" violence must come down. Normal men rape, and normal men, together, have the responsibility to stop it.

From Los Angeles Times, August 13, 1989

Class of Nonviolence

To the Women of India
By Mohandas Gandhi

The impatience of some sisters to join the good fight is to me a healthy sign. It has led to the discovery that however attractive the campaign against the salt tax may be, for them to confine themselves to it would be to change a pound for a penny. They will be lost in the crowd, there will be in it no suffering for which they are thirsting.

In this nonviolent warfare, their contribution should be much greater than men's. To call women the weaker sex is a libel; it is man's injustice to woman. If by strength is meant brute strength, then indeed is woman less brute than man. If by strength, is meant moral power, then woman is immeasurably man's superior. Has she not greater intuition, is she not more self-sacrificing, has she not greater powers of endurance, has she not greater courage? Without her man could not be. If nonviolence is the law of our being, the future is with women.

I have nursed this thought now for years. When the women of the Ashram insisted on being taken along with men something within me told me that they were destined to do greater work in this struggle than merely breaking salt laws.

I feel that I have now found that work. The picketing of liquor shops and foreign cloth shops by men, though it succeeded beyond expectations up to a point for a time in 1921, failed because violence crept in. If a real impression is to be created, picketing must be resumed. If it remains peaceful to the end, it will be the quickest way of educating the people concerned. It must never be a matter of coercion but conversion, moral suasion. Who can make a more effective appeal to the heart than woman?

From: Gandhi's Autobiography

Narrowing the Battlefield
By Carol Ascher

The attitude of nonviolence stems from a reverence and respect for life. It is the commandment: "Thou shalt not kill," understood in its widest meaning: physical and psychic harm, short of death, are included in the assumption that in this bountiful world there can be sufficient space, time, and resources for each of us to get what we need without violently taking from others. There is an appealing optimism in this attitude, and I believe also the truth. Its complications arise, of course, when there are vast differences in the power to procure or command resources, and when violence is declared the order of the day. At times like this, when editorial writers congratulate their readers for getting over the "Vietnam Syndrome," as if a reluctance to kill people and destroy another country were a disease, nonviolence can seem like a sweet pipedream.

The irony of the nonviolent attitude, of course, is that it only has a living meaning in exactly those moments when an individual or group has the power to kill or destroy, or when a person's or group's safety is threatened.

When we talk about women and men in relation to nonviolence, I think we are talking about an urgent and ultimate good for both. But because of real differences in strength and power created by both nature and society, the nonviolent attitude has had a quite different meaning for women than for men. Most obviously, for men in our society, nonviolence means relinquishing physical and mechanical powers to which they usually have had easy access, and probably even learned to believe they have a right; it means deciding not to go to war, to carry weapons, or to hit their wives. For women, on the other hand, a nonviolent world immediately conjures images of walking in safety and ease on the street, feeling unafraid to argue heatedly with a lover, not worrying about the loss of husbands and sons in war. If women must give up anything to accept a nonviolent world, it seems to me, it is their age-old standards for judging "manliness" in men. At the risk of bifurcating the world too sharply, I suspect that when you ask a man to picture a gun he most often imagines himself holding it; while to a woman, the gun in the picture is pointed at her or at someone she loves.

The problem for women who want to take a nonviolent stance in this still extremely violent world is, in fact, rather like the problem for men who decide to become pacifists while on the battlefield. They must invent tactics, strategies, and states of mind which take them out of real-world and internalized victimization. Insofar as it is possible to get off the battlefield, they must do so. But men can shoot their guns into the air, volunteer to drive an ambulance, or go AWOL. Women in their homes and in the cities of today have a more difficult time discovering the demarcations of the battlefield. What are the equivalents for women of shooting a gun into the air? I myself am not always sure.

It will come as a surprise that for thousands of years, without being pacifists, women have largely taken a defensive position towards violence. Whether they believed violence was right or wrong, they knew that they could get killed; and having children under their wing, they stayed out of the line of fire. In primitive societies, women cultivate the soil while the men hunt or make war. There is no value system which judges the men's activities as pejorative; on the contrary, they are most often accorded a higher status exactly because of their closeness to death. It is the connection between men's higher status and their activities as hunters and warriors that made Simone de Beauvoir write in The Second Sex that, "If blood were but a nourishing fluid, it would be valued no higher than milk. For it is not in giving life but in risking life that man is raised above the animal; that is why superiority has been accorded in humanity not to the sex that brings forth but to that which kills." Although I think we are deeply embedded in nature exactly because of both our violence and the oppression of women which our consciousness could enable us to overcome, I believe that the two phenomena are linked.

In our urbanized industrial society, beyond the very real dangers which women rationally try to avoid, an elaborate culture has developed through which women indicate their inferiority to men at the same time as showing their "sensitivity" to violence. The hands over the eyes during the murder scene at the movies, squeamish shrieks in the face of bugs that must be removed or killed, an avoidance of certain kinds of articles on the front page of the newspaper or stories on the evening news - these are the images that rush to my mind. But again, these sensitivities do not reflect more than the dullest adherence to the commandment against killing; and I doubt that the connection is more than rarely even made. Instead, all this acting out is largely ritualized drama, a kind of pageant play affirming men's important role as gun bearers, bug squashers, and decision-makers on those front page issues of destruction and violence. The women will wash and clean up and bear whatever life and death bring them.

Of course, the men have their reciprocal role: they not only risk their lives to "defend" the homeland (experiencing "life" and friendship at its peak while out alone with their buddies), but with due chivalry they protect their women from knowing the grisly and glorious truths about the violent atrocities they may have committed away from home.

A wave of American feminism arose out of the ashes of the anti-draft and anti-war movements of the 1960s. Women, gathering political skills at the same time as a new understanding of their second place in the violent world of men, began to strike out on their own. During the 1970s, as a result of the women's movement, a change occurred in this country in women's relationship to violence. In large part, women lessened their fear of it, but they themselves at times also became more involved in it. Early on there was the anger that men had controlled the streets too long with their threats of mugging and rape, and the cry that women had to reclaim the right to walk about freely at night. I recall vigilante squads of women who, for a time, tried to ensure other women's safety in the dark hours. One friend of mine joined a women's group which organized regular rifle practice so that women could become at ease with the control side of a gun. I myself took karate lessons - a chance to learn the limits of my own physical power and to lose my feminine fear of violence, I thought - until after three months its militaristic elements repelled me too much to continue. For the first time, too, there were publicized cases of women who defended themselves against rape with guns and knives. Joanne Little became a legend when, herself already a prisoner, she killed a guard who had tried to rape her, using his own weapon. Women have become sensitive to the cultural violence against them, and some began to picket in front of theaters which showed images of sexual violence against women. I attended uncomfortable meetings where women admitted to being battered wives and asked other women for help. And there was the drive by women to join the military, and the resulting machinations for and against the Equal Rights Amendment and the revival of the draft.

On the other side, although it sometimes seems less publicized, has been an active feminist-pacifist movement. Feminists with a nonviolent perspective have been at the core of anti-nuclear organizing, and their sensitivity to the preciousness of life has made them turn up at the forefront of a variety of ecological issues from Love Canal to uranium mining on Native American territories. The idea of nonviolence has been extended from the relationship between people to the ties between human beings and our delicate earth. A significant number of feminists-pacifists have also chosen to live in rural areas, in women's communities, without men. They have said, in effect, it is too hard to live one's private life ethically and comfortably on the battlefield.

Strangely, there is one area of battle and conflict that women carry with them even unto the furthest rural reaches. Within feminist-pacifists circles, the issue of abortion has been upsetting and unresolved. Most feminists without a nonviolence perspective, perhaps wisely, argue in public for women's right to control their own bodies, including their reproductive systems, and reserve their sadness and moral concern about the fate of a fetus for quiet discussions, behind closed doors. But feminist-pacifists have made a commitment to sanctify life, and so some feel they cannot simply argue the expedience of first winning a right for women that they may then pronounce unethical to use. There have been angry and hurtful interchanges among these women, but more recently also open discussion, including an enormously interesting transcribed discussion among several feminist-pacifists in the August 1, 1980 issue of WIN, the War Resisters League magazine.

I believe a nonviolent approach to the universe is more urgent than ever before. But I also believe that both the "violent" as well as the nonviolent aspects of the women's movement over the past decade have been largely to the good. Both sides, each in its way, have worked to narrow the gap and so have an effect on the violent world of men. I suspect that there are fewer women now than 10 years ago who worship men's capacity for violence from afar, while denigrating their own life-giving activities - however much noise Phyllis Schafly, Maribel Morgan, and the men who finance them may be making. Also, psychologically, many women may need to move from seeing themselves as passive victims of violence through a phase of anger and violence before they can become nonviolent activists. From this perspective, even women entering the military may have some good results. The problem is: do we have time, given our capacity for destruction, for women to get this experience, and can it be gotten without creating its own added waves of violence? I said before that I hold to the connection between the sharp bifurcation of genders, with

Class of Nonviolence

its concomitant oppression of women, and the violence and destruction we experience throughout the world. In her book The Mermaid and the Minotaur, one of the great theoretical contributions of this wave of the women's movement, Dorothy Dinnerstein has elaborately argued how female-dominated child-rearing guarantees "male insistence upon, and female compliance with, a double-standard of sexual behavior," including male aggression and violence and "certain forms of antagonism - rampant in men, and largely shared by women as well - against women." Turning away from their mothers, who they must not be like, men also run from their own softness and nurturance, their "fleshy mortality," the memory of infancy when they experienced both boundless and helpless passion. With their infantile longing neither satisfied nor transcended, war and conquest are the "amoral greed of infancy turned loose on the world; and the death and destruction which they create is the fear of both which they must deny in themselves. Arguing the urgency for men to share in child-rearing with women, Dinnerstein writes, "They cannot be our brothers until we stop being their mothers: until, that is, we stop carrying the main responsibility - and taking the main blame - for their early introduction to the human condition." Of course, as she adds, what also stops true solidarity among women is that women share men's anti-female feelings.

If Dinnerstein is right, as I believe she is, then a nonviolent world must be worked toward at home, in a differently structured family, as well as on the street and in the recruitment center. The battlefield that must be narrowed includes those widely differing roles deemed appropriate for men and women. This is an enormously difficult task: when one talks to people about murder, most will have to concede that it is wrong; but there still are many who see nothing amiss with one-half the world, women, taking full responsibility for bringing to adulthood each new generation of human beings. Yet the enormity of the task is matched by the risks on the other side, as men continue to develop technology that can not only wipe out an entire hemisphere of our planet but also make life impossible for countless future generations.

From Confrontation, Winter, 1991, Long Island University Library Journal.

Patriarchy: A State of War
By Barbara Hope

Why weren't we prepared for this — the imminence of nuclear holocaust. The final silencing of life. The brutal extinction of the planet. Surely there have been substantial clues throughout history. Male supremacy. Wars. Witch-burning. Male religious myths. Institutionalized greed. The enslavement of half the human race. Centuries of violence.

Why weren't we prepared for this? We have lived with violence for so long. We have lived under the rule of the fathers so long. Violence and patriarchy: mirror images. An ethic of destruction as normative. Diminished love for life, a numbing to real events as the final consequence. We are not even prepared.

Mary Daly, in Gyn/Ecology: The Metaethics of Radical Feminism, writes, "The rulers of the patriarchy - males with power - wage an unceasing war against life itself. Since female energy is essentially biophilic, the female spirit/body is the primary target in the perpetual war of aggression against life. Women must understand that the female self is the enemy under fire from the patriarchy." She further writes that "clearly the primary and essential object of aggression is not the opposing military force. The members of the opposing team play the same war games and share the same values. The secret bond that binds the warriors together is the violation of women, acted out physically and constantly replayed on the level of language and shared fantasies."

We needn't look far for evidence to support her theory. Recall the U.S. Army basic training jingle: "This is my rifle (slaps rifle). This is my gun (slaps crotch). One is for killing, the other for fun." The language of war is the language of genocide. Misogynist obscenities are used to train fighters and intensify feelings of violence. War provides men with a context to act out their hatred of women without the veneer of chivalry or civilization. War is rape.

In the male world of war, toughness is the most highly-prized virtue. Some even speak of the "hairy chest syndrome." The man who recommends violence does not endanger his reputation for wisdom, but a man who suggests negotiation becomes known as soft, as willing to settle for less. To be repelled by mass murder is to be irresponsible. It is to refuse the phallic celebration. It is to be feminine, to be a dove. It means walking out of the club of bureaucratic machismo. To be a specialist in the new violence is to be on the frontier. It is no accident that patriarchy related history as the history of war; that is precisely their history. In remembering their battles, the fathers recall the deep experience of their own violent proclivities and relive the ecstatic euphoria of those ultimate moments of male bonding.

The history of war speaks volumes about national will in a patriarchal culture. Wars are nothing short of organized killing presided over by men deemed as the best. The fact is - they are. They have absorbed, in the most complete way, the violent character of their own ethos. These are the men who design missiles and technologies as extensions of themselves. These men are ready to annihilate whole societies. These are the men honored as heroes with steel minds, resolute wills, insatiable drives for excellence, capable of planning demonic

Class of Nonviolence

acts in a detached non-emotional way. These are the dead men, the hollow men, capable of nothing but violence.

It is significant that, after the accident at Three Mile Island, women were more concerned about the danger than men; women felt they were being lied to about the real-life effects of nuclear technology. Women were resistant to the repeated declaration of the male decision makers that everything was under control, that there was nothing to be alarmed about, that nuclear engineers could solve any difficulties. Women felt the lies. Women know and feel the lies that maintain nuclear technology because we have been lied to. We are the victims of patriarchal lies. We know the deceit that grounds patriarchal colonization of women. We know, feel and intuit the deep truth that falsehoods, deceptions and lies form the very character of male rule. Women are the first victims of the patriarchal state of war.

Violence to our bodies: A women is raped every three minutes. A woman is battered every eighteen seconds. Women are physically threatened by a frightening social climate structured in male might. Women are depicted in pornography as objects to be beaten, whipped, chained and conquered. The myth prevails that women like it.

Violence to our hearts: The positing of male comradeship as the model of human relationships. The systematic separation of women from one another. The degradation of women's culture. The erasure of women's history. The sanctifying of the heterosexual norm with its rigid understanding of the giving and receiving of affection.

Violence to our spirit: The dismemberment of the goddess and the enthronement of the male god. The ripping of women away from a life in tune with natural patterns of rhythm and flow in the universe. The ongoing patriarchal work of rendering women unconscious to ourselves.

Violence to our work: The exploitation and devaluation of women's labor. The regulation of women to supportive, maintenance roles. The deliberate structure of women's economic dependence. Violence to women. Under the patriarchy, women are the enemy. This is a war across time and space, the real history of the ages.

In this extreme situation, confronted by the patriarchy in its multiple institutional forms, what can women do? We can name the enemy: patriarchy. We can break from deadly possession by the fathers. We can move from docility, passivity and silence to liberation, courage and speech. We can name ourselves, cherish ourselves, courageously take up our lives. We can refuse to sell our bodies and we can refuse to sell our minds. We can claim freedom from false loyalties. We can band with other women and ignite the roaring fire of female friendship.

This much we have learned from our living: life begets life. Life for women, life for the earth, the very survival of the planet is found only outside the patriarchy. Beyond their sad and shallow definitions. Beyond their dead and static knowledge. Beyond their amnesia. Beyond their impotence. Beyond their wars. Wars which unmask the fear, insecurity and powerlessness that form the very base of patriarchal rule.

To end the state of war, to halt the momentum toward death, passion for life must flourish. Women are the bearers of life-loving energy. Ours is the task of deepening that passion for life and separating from all that threatens life, all that diminishes life. Becoming who we are as women. Telling/living the truth of our lives. Shifting the weight of the world.

Will such measures put an end to war? What we already know is that centuries of other means have failed. In the name of peace, war is raged, weapons developed, lives lost. Testimonies are announced. Treaties signed. Declarations stated. Pronouncements issued. And the battle still goes on. The patriarchy remains intact. Women are not free. Nothing changes. This time the revolution must go all the way. In the words of the poet:

> This is what we are watching: watching the
> Spider rebuild – patiently, the say,
> But we recognize in her
> Impatience - our own –
> The passion to make and make again
> Where such unmakings reigns
> The refusal to be a victim
> We have lived with violence so long.
> *Adrienne Rich,*
> *Natural Resources*

Peacework: Twenty years of Nonviolent Social Change, edited by Pat Farren, American Friends Service Committee, 1991

Class of Nonviolence

An American Hero of 1941
By Colman McCarthy

Washington — For those feeling glutted with Pearl Harbor tales and left cold by them — I'm freezing—the worthier anniversary is on Dec. 8. On that day in 1941, Rep. Jeannette Rankin, brave and defiantly sensible, stood alone in Congress to vote against America's entry into World War II.

The Montana Republican, 61 at the time and a lifelong pacifist, went to the House floor believing that "you can no more win a war than win an earthquake." The vote was 338-1.

Miss Rankin was hissed. Colleagues asked her to reconsider and make the vote unanimous. After declining, she left the House floor and avoided assault from power zealots by hiding in a phone booth.

Miss Rankin would later explain her vote: "There can be no compromise with war, it cannot be reformed or controlled; cannot be disciplined into decency or codified into common sense, for war is the slaughter of human beings, temporarily regarded as enemies, on as large a scale as possible."

Were Jeanette Rankin a member of Congress in modern times, she would have joined the minority who opposed American militarism in Grenada, Libya, Panama, and Iraq, as she did in 1969 when leading a peace march in Washington to protest the Vietnam War.

She would be vocal, too, about current preparations for America's next war against whoever dares cross it. Miss Rankin's stand in 1941 had the strength of consistency. On April 6, 1917, she had voted against U.S. involvement in World War I, saying, "We cannot settle disputes by eliminating human beings."

That was the first vote of the first woman in Congress. For defying the military ethic, A New York Times editorialist saw Miss Rankin as "almost final proof of feminine incapacity for straight reasoning."

A majority of Montanans apparently agreed. They gave her only one term in 1917 and only one after that 1941 vote. Both times, Miss Rankin found the rejections as bothersome as pebbles in her shoe. She marched ahead, combining her pacifism with the feminism she had championed in her first term when introducing suffrage legislation that would give federal voting rights to women in the 19th amendment.

Between the two wars, Miss Rankin fortified her ideals by a life of study and service. She moved to Georgia, living near Athens in Thoreau-like simplicity in a cabin with no phone, electricity, or running water but plenty of books.

She founded the Georgia Peace Society and taught "peace habits" to local children. For her toil, she received a high honor from the Atlanta post of the American Legion: The old boys called her a Communist.

Neither Jeanette Rankin nor her politics has wafted off into obscurity. On May 1, 1985, 500 Montanans, historians, politicians, and a few pacifists gathered in the rotunda of the Capitol for the unveiling of a bronze likeness of Miss Rankin.

In a speech, Rep. Pat Williams, the Montana Democrat who represents the congresswoman's old district, offered a memorable line: Miss Rankin "realized and brought us to understand the meaning of the power and influence of an individual in this democracy carrying out her conscience."

The following year, some Rankinites in Missoula, the congresswoman's hometown, organized to form the Jeanette Rankin Peace Resource Center. In five years, it has become nationally known for carrying on the kind of educational, social justice, and conflict resolution programs that Miss Rankin believed in. At a ceremony last April, the center reminded the citizens of Missoula County what it cost them to live in militaristic America: $344,284 a day — the Pentagon's share of the local federal tax haul.

The event prompted the chairman of the economics department at the University of Montana to state the most obvious political reality of our day: Military spending is the "crushing burden that has substantially decreased our ability to take care of our basic needs." Pure Rankin, pure truth.

Internationally, knowledge of this American hero grows. The Japanese have been reading the 1989 book A Single Dissenting Voice: The Life of Jeanette Rankin. Its author, Yunosuke Ohkura of the Tokyo Broadcasting Co., was in Washington in May 1973 and read the obituary of Miss Rankin who died at 93. He was astonished to read of her stand in 1941.

"We are a nation of unity," Yonosuke Ohkura, now a professor at Tokyo University, told Montanan magazine last year. "I've never heard of a single dissenting vote in Japanese life. But in the United States, even after this powerful attack, there was a person against the war. I was amazed."

Professor Ohkura's book, soon to be translated into English, will join two other biographies of Miss Rankin. More are needed—as are more of her kind in Congress when war hysteria next arises.

From Washington Post, December 6, 1991

Questions for Lesson Five

1. Given the chance, are women just as prone to violence as men? Is it beyond men's capacity to establish a peaceful world? Are women's views of peace different from men; after all, don't women expect men to "protect" them at all costs?

2. If a woman is in a man's apartment after a date, a night of partying at 3 a.m., should she be surprised if "date rape" occurs?

3. In what sense is sexism a justice related issue?

4. Men's liberation must accompany women's liberation. Explain.

5. Sexual stereotypes are created and sustained by society. Why do you think this is true and why do people go along with it?

Readings for Lesson Six

The Technique of Nonviolent Action
by Gene Sharp

The Politics of Nonviolent Action
by Gene Sharp

The Methods of Nonviolent Protest and Persuasion
by Gene Sharp

Albert Einstein on Pacifism

Letter to Ernesto Cardenal: Guns Don't Work
by Daniel Berrigan

Building Confidence at Prairie Creek
by Colman McCarthy

The Technique of Nonviolent Action
by Gene Sharp

A ruler's power is ultimately dependent on support from the people he would rule. His moral authority, economic resources, transport system, government bureaucracy, army, and police—to name but a few immediate sources of his power—rest finally upon the cooperation and assistance of other people. If there is general conformity, the ruler is powerful.

But people do not always do what their rulers would like them to do. The factory manager recognizes this when he finds his workers leaving their jobs and machines, so that the production line ceases operation; or when he finds the workers persisting in doing something on the job which he has forbidden them to do. In many areas of social and political life comparable situations are commonplace. A man who has been a ruler and thought his power sure may discover that his subjects no longer believe he has any moral right to give them orders, that his laws are disobeyed, that the country's economy is paralyzed, that his soldiers and police are lax in carrying out repression or openly mutiny, and even that his bureaucracy no longer takes orders. When this happens, the man who has been ruler becomes simply another man, and his political power dissolves, just as the factory manager's power does when the workers no longer cooperate and obey. The equipment of his army may remain intact, his soldiers uninjured and very much alive, his cities unscathed, the factories and transport systems in full operational capacity, and the government buildings and offices unchanged. Yet because the human assistance which had created and supported his political power has been withdrawn, the former ruler finds that his political power has disintegrated.

Nonviolent Action

The technique of nonviolent action, which is based on this approach to the control of political power and the waging of political struggles, has been the subject of many misconceptions: for the sake of clarity the two terms are defined in this section.

The term technique is used here to describe the overall means of conducting an action or struggle. One can therefore speak of the technique of guerrilla warfare, of conventional warfare, and of parliamentary democracy.

The term nonviolent action refers to those methods of protest, noncooperation, and intervention in which the actionists, without employing physical violence, refuse to do certain things which they are expected, or required, to do; or do certain things which they are not expected, or are forbidden, to do. In a particular case there can of course be a combination of acts of omission and acts of commission.

Nonviolent action is a generic term: it includes the large class of phenomena variously called nonviolent resistance, satyagraha, passive resistance, positive action, and nonviolent direct action. While it is not violent, it is action, and not inaction; passivity, submission, and cowardice must be surmounted if it is to be used. It is a means of conducting conflicts and waging struggles, and is not to be equated with (though it may be accompanied by) purely verbal dissent or solely psychological influence. It is not pacifism, and in fact has in the vast majority of cases been applied by nonpacifists. The motives for the adoption of nonviolent action may be religious or ethical or they may be based on considerations of expediency. Nonviolent action is not an escapist approach to the problem of violence, for it can be applied in struggles against opponents relying on violent sanctions. The fact that in a conflict one side is nonviolent does not imply that the other side will also refrain from violence. Certain forms of nonviolent action may be regarded as efforts to persuade by action, while others are more coercive.

Methods of Nonviolent Action

There is a very wide range of methods, or forms, of nonviolent action, and at least 197 have been identified. They fall into three classes - nonviolent protest and persuasion, noncooperation, and nonviolent intervention.

Generally speaking, the methods of nonviolent protest are symbolic in their effect and produce an awareness of the existence of dissent. Under tyrannical regimes, however, where opposition is stifled, their impact can in some circumstances be very great. Methods of nonviolent protest include marches, pilgrimages, picketing, vigils, "haunting" officials, public meetings, issuing and distributing protest literature, renouncing honors, protest emigration, and humorous pranks.

The methods of nonviolent noncooperation, if sufficient numbers take part, are likely to present the opponent with difficulties in maintaining the normal efficiency and operation of the system; and in extreme cases the system itself may be threatened. Methods of nonviolent noncooperation include various types of social noncooperation (such as social boycotts); economic boycotts (such as consumers' boycott, traders' boycott, rent refusal, and international trade embargo); strikes (such as the general strike, strike by resignation, industry strike, go-slow, and economic shutdown); and political noncooperation (such as boycott of government employment, boycott of elections, administrative noncooperation, civil disobedience, and mutiny).

The methods of nonviolent intervention have some features in common with the first two classes, but also challenge the opponent more directly; and, assuming that fearlessness and discipline are maintained, relatively small numbers may have a disproportionately large impact. Methods of nonviolent intervention include sit-ins, fasts, reverse strikes, nonviolent obstructions, nonviolent invasion, and parallel government.

The exact way in which methods from each of the three classes are combined varies considerably from one situation to another. Generally speaking, the risks to the actionists on the one hand, and to the system against which they take action on the other, are least in the case of nonviolent protest, and greatest in the case of nonviolent intervention. The methods of noncooperation tend to require the largest numbers, but not to demand a large degree of special training from all participants. The methods of nonviolent intervention are generally effective if the participants possess a high degree of internal discipline and are willing to accept severe repression; the tactics must also be selected and carried out with particular care and intelligence.

Several important factors need to be considered in the selection of the methods to be used in a given situation. These factors include the type of issue involved, the nature of the opponent, his aims and strength, the type of counteraction he is likely to use the depth of feeling both among the general population and among the likely actionists, the degree of repression the actionists are likely to be able to take, the general strategy of the overall campaign, and the amount of past experience and specific training the population and the actionists have had. Just as in military battle weapons are carefully selected, taking into account such factors as their range and effect, so also in nonviolent struggle the choice of specific methods is very important.

Mechanisms of Change

In nonviolent struggles there are, broadly speaking, three mechanisms by which change is brought about. Usually there is a combination of the three. They are conversion, accommodation, and nonviolent coercion.

George Lakey has described the conversion mechanism thus: "By conversion we mean that the opponent, as the result of the actions of the nonviolent person or group, comes around to a new point of view which embraces the ends of the nonviolent actor." This conversion can be influenced by reason or argument, but in nonviolent action it is also likely to be influenced by emotional and moral factors, which can in turn be stimulated by the suffering of the nonviolent actionists, who seek to achieve their goals without inflicting injury on other people.

Attempts at conversion, however, are not always successful, and may not even be made. Accommodation as a mechanism of nonviolent action falls in an intermediary position between conversion and nonviolent coercion, and elements of both of the other mechanisms are generally involved. In accommodation, the opponent, although not converted, decides to grant the demands of the nonviolent actionists In a situation where he still has a choice of action. The social situation within which he must operate has been altered enough by nonviolent action to compel a change in his own response to the conflict; perhaps because he has begun to doubt the rightness of his position, perhaps because he does not think the matter worth the trouble caused by the struggle, and perhaps because he anticipates coerced defeat and wishes to accede gracefully or with minimum or losses.

Nonviolent coercion may take place in any of three circumstances. Defiance may become too widespread and massive for the ruler to be able to control it by repression; the social and political system may become paralyzed; or the extent of defiance or disobedience among the ruler's own soldiers and other agents may undermine his capacity to apply repression. Nonviolent coercion becomes possible when those applying nonviolent action succeed in withholding, directly or indirectly, the necessary sources of the ruler's political power. His power then disintegrates, and he is no longer able to control the situation, even though he still wishes to do so.

Just as in war danger from enemy fire does not always force front line soldiers to panic and flee, so in nonviolent action repression does not necessarily produce submission. True, repression may be effective, but it may fail to halt defiance, and in this case the opponent will be in difficulties. Repression against a nonviolent group which persists in face of it and maintains nonviolent discipline may have the following effects: it may alienate the general population from the opponent's regime, making them more likely to join the resistance; it may alienate the opponent's usual supporters and agents, and their initial uneasiness may grow into internal opposition and at times into noncooperation and disobedience; and it may rally general public opinion (domestic or international) to the support of the nonviolent actionists; though the effectiveness of this last factor varies greatly from one situation to another, it may produce various types of supporting actions. If repression thus produces larger numbers of nonviolent actionists, thereby increasing the defiance, and if it leads to internal dissent among the opponent's supporters, thereby reducing his capacity to deal with the defiance, it will clearly have rebounded against the opponent.

Naturally, with so many variables (including the nature of the contending groups, the issues involved, the context of the struggle, the means of repression. and the methods of nonviolent action used), in no two instances will nonviolent action "work" in exactly the same way. However, it is possible to indicate in very general terms the ways in which it does achieve results. It is, of course, sometimes defeated: no technique of action can guarantee its user short-term victory in every instance of its use. It is important to recognize, however, that failure in nonviolent action may be caused, not by an inherent weakness of the technique, but by weakness in the movement employing it, or in the strategy and tactics used.

Strategy is just as important in nonviolent action as it is in military action. While military strategic concepts and principles cannot be automatically carried over into the field of nonviolent struggle, since the dynamics and mechanisms of military and nonviolent action differ greatly, the basic importance of strategy and tactics is in no way diminished. The attempt to cope with strategic and tactical problems associated with civilian defense (national defense by prepared nonviolent resistance) therefore needs to be based on thorough consideration of the dynamics and mechanisms of nonviolent struggle; and on consideration of the general principles of strategy and tactics appropriate to the technique—both those peculiar to it and those which may be carried over from the strategy of military and other types of conflict.

Development of the Technique

Nonviolent action has a long history but because historians have often been more concerned with other matters, much information has undoubtedly been lost. Even today, this field is largely ignored, and there is no good history of the practice and development of the technique. But it clearly began early. For example, in 494 B.C. the plebeians of Rome, rather than murder the Consuls, withdrew from the city to the Sacred Mount where they remained for some days, thereby refusing to make their usual contribution to the life of the city, until an agreement was reached pledging significant improvements in their life and status.

A very significant pre-Gandhian expansion of the technique took place in the 19th and early 20th centuries. The technique received impetus from three groups during this period: first from trade unionists and other social radicals who sought a means of struggle—largely strikes, general strikes, and boycotts—against what they regarded as an unjust social system, and for an improvement in the condition of working men; second, from nationalists who found the technique useful in resisting a foreign enemy such as the Hungarian resistance against Austria between 1850 and 1867, and the Chinese boycotts of Japanese goods in the early 20th century; and third, on the level of ideas and personal example, from individuals, such as Leo Tolstoy in Russia and Henry David Thoreau in the U.S.A., who wanted to show how a better society might be created.

With Gandhi's experiments in the use of nonviolent action to control rulers, alter policies, and undermine political systems, the character of the technique was broadened and refinements were made in its practice. Many modifications were introduced: greater attention was given to strategy and tactics; the armory of methods was expanded; and a link was consciously forged between mass political action and the ethical principle of nonviolence. Gandhi, with his political colleagues and fellow Indians, demonstrated in a variety of conflicts in South Africa and India that nonviolent struggle could be politically effective on a large scale. He termed his refinement of the technique "satyagraha," meaning roughly insistence and reliance upon the force of truth. "In politics, its use is based upon the immutable maxim, that government of the people is possible only so long as they consent either consciously or unconsciously to be governed."

From: The Politics of Nonviolent Action

The Politics of Nonviolent Action
By Gene Sharp

India – 1930-1931

For the 1930 campaign Gandhi formulated a program of political demands and a concrete plan for nonviolent rebellion, including civil disobedience. Pleas to the Viceroy produced no concessions.

Focusing initially on the Salt Act (which imposed a heavy tax and a government monopoly), Gandhi set out with disciples on a 26-day march to the sea to commit civil disobedience by making salt. This was the signal for mass nonviolent revolt throughout the country. As the movement progressed, there were mass meetings, huge parades, seditious speeches, a boycott of foreign cloth, and picketing of liquor shops and opium dens. Students left government schools. The national flag was hoisted. There were social boycotts of government employees, short strikes (hartals), and resignations by government employees and members of the Legislative Assembly and Councils. Government departments were boycotted, as were foreign insurance firms and the postal and telegraph services. Many refused to pay taxes. Some renounced titles. There were nonviolent raids and seizures of government-held salt, and so on.

The government arrested Gandhi early in the campaign. About 100,000 Indians (including 17,000 women) were imprisoned or held in detention camps. There were beatings, injuries, censorship, shootings, confiscation, intimidation, fines, banning of meetings and organizations, and other measures. Some persons were shot dead. During the year the normal functioning of government was severely affected, and great suffering was experienced by the resisters. A truce was finally agreed on, under terms settled by direct negotiations between Gandhi and the Viceroy.

Although the concessions were made to the nationalists, the actual terms favored the government more than the nationalists. In Gandhi's view it was more important, however, that the strength thus generated in the Indians meant that independence could not long be denied, and that by having to participate in direct negotiations with the nonviolent rebels, the government had recognized India as an equal with whose representatives she had to negotiate. This was as upsetting to Winston Churchill as it was reassuring to Gandhi.

Jawaharlal Nehru, who was later to become Prime Minister of independent India, was no believer in an ethic of nonviolence or Gandhi's philosophy or religious explanations. However, like many other prominent and unknown Indians, he became a supporter of Gandhi's "grand strategy" for obtaining a British evacuation from India, and he spent years in prison in that struggle. Nehru wrote in his autobiography:

"We had accepted that method, the Congress had made that method its own, because of a belief in its effectiveness. Gandhiji had placed it before the country not only as the right method but also as the most effective one for our purpose."

In spite of its negative name it was a dynamic method, the very opposite of a meek, submission to a tyrant's will. It was not a coward's refuge from action, but a brave man's defiance of evil and national subjection.

Struggle Against Nazis

Independent of the continuing Gandhian campaigns, significant nonviolent struggles under exceedingly difficult circumstances also emerged in Nazi-occupied Europe. Almost without exception these operated in the context of world war and always against a ruthless enemy. Sometimes the nonviolent forms of resistance were closely related to parallel violent resistance; occasionally they took place independently. Often the nonviolent elements in the resistance struggles were highly important, sometimes even overshadowing the violent elements in the resistance.

Nonviolent resistance in small or large instances took place in a number of countries but was especially important in the Netherlands, Norway, and probably to a lesser degree, Denmark. In no case does there appear to have been much if anything in the way of special knowledge of the technique, and certainly no advanced preparations or training. The cases generally emerged as spontaneous or improvised efforts to "do something" in a difficult situation. Exceptions were certain strikes in the Netherlands which the London-based government –in-exile requested in order to help Allied landings on the continent.

Norway, 1942

The Norwegian teacher's resistance is but one of these resistance campaigns. During the Nazi occupation, the Norwegian Fascist "minister-President," Vidkun Quisling, set out to establish the Corporative State on Mussolini's model, selecting teachers as the first "corporation." For this he created a new teacher's organization with compulsory membership and appointed as its leader the head of the Hird, the Norwegian S.A. (storm troopers.) A compulsory Fascist youth movement was also set up.

The underground called on the teachers to resist. Between 8,000 and 10,000 of the country's 12,000 teachers wrote letters to Quisling's Church and Education Department. All signed their names and addresses to the wording prescribed by the underground for the letter. Each teacher said he (or she) could neither assist in promoting fascist education of the children nor accept membership in the new teacher's organization.

The government threatened them with dismissal and closed all schools for a month. Teachers held classes in private homes. Despite censorship, news of the resistance spread. Tens of thousands of letters of protest from parents poured into the government office.

After the teachers defied the threats, about 1,000 male teachers were arrested and sent to concentration camps. Children gathered and sang at railroad stations as teachers were shipped through in cattle cars. In the camps, the Gestapo imposed an atmosphere of terror intended to induce capitulation. On starvation rations, the teachers were put through "torture gymnastics" in deep snow. When only a few gave in, "treatment" continued.

Class of Nonviolence

The schools reopened, but the teachers still at liberty told their pupils they repudiated membership in the new organization and spoke of a duty to conscience. Rumors were spread that if these teachers did not give in, some or all of those arrested would be killed. After difficult inner wrestling, the teachers who had not been arrested almost without exception stood firm.

Then, on cattle car trains and overcrowded steamers, the arrested teachers were shipped to a camp near Kirkenes, in the far north. Although Quisling's Church and Education Department stated that all was settled and that the activities of the new organization would cease, the teachers were kept at Kirkenes in miserable conditions, doing dangerous work.

However, their suffering strengthened morale on the home front and posed problems for Quisling's regime. As Quisling once raged at the teachers in a school near Oslo: "You teachers have destroyed everything for me!" Fearful of alienating Norwegians still further, Quisling finally ordered the teachers' release. Eight months after the arrests, the last teachers returned home to triumphal receptions.

Quisling's new organization for teachers never came into being, and the schools were never used for fascist propaganda. After Quisling encountered further difficulties in imposing the Corprorative State, Hitler ordered him to abandon the plan entirely.

Berlin, 1943

It is widely believed that once the "Final Solution," the annihilation of Europe's Jews, was under way, no nonviolent action to save German Jews occurred and that none could have been effective. This belief is challenged by an act of nonviolent defiance by the non-Jewish wives of arrested Berlin Jews. This limited act of resistance occurred in the midst of the war, in the capital of the Third Reich, toward the end of the inhuman effort to make Germany free of Jews – all highly unfavorable conditions for successful opposition. The defiance not only took place, but was completely successful, even in 1943. The following account is by Heinz Ullstein, one of the men who had been arrested; his wife was one of the women who acted:

"The Gestapo was preparing for large-scale action. Columns of covered trucks were drawn up at the gates of factories and stood in front of private houses. All day long they rolled through the streets, escorted by armed SS men – heavy vehicles under whose covers could be discerned the outlines of closely packed humanity. On this day, every Jew living in Germany was arrested and for the time being lodged in mass camps. It was the beginning of the end.

"People lowered their eyes, some with indifference, others perhaps with a fleeting horror and shame. The day wore on, there was a war to be won, provinces were conquered. "History was made," we were on intimate terms with the millennium. And the public eye missed the flickering of a tiny torch which might have kindled the fire of general resistance to despotism. From the vast collecting centers to which the Jews of Berlin had been taken, the Gestapo sorted out those with 'Aryan kin' and concentrated them in a separate prison in the

Rosenstrasse. No one knew what was to happen to them.

"At this point the wives stepped in. Already by the early hours of the next day they had discovered the whereabouts of their husbands and as by common consent, as if they had been summoned, a crowd of them appeared at the gate of the improvised detention center. In vain the security police tried to turn away the demonstrators, some 6,000 of them, and to disperse them. Again and again they massed together, advanced, called for their husbands, who despite strict instructions to the contrary, showed themselves at the windows, and demanded their release.

"For a few hours the routine of a working day interrupted the demonstration, but in the afternoon the square was again crammed with people, and the demanding, accusing cries of the women rose above the noise of the traffic like passionate avowals of a love strengthened by the bitterness of life.

"Gestapo headquarters was situated in the Burgstrasse, not far from the square where the demonstration was taking place. A few salvoes from a machine gun could have wiped the women off the square, but the SS did not fire, not this time. Scared by an incident which had no equal in the history of the Third Reich, headquarters consented to negotiate. They spoke soothingly, gave assurances, and finally released the prisoners."

Latin American Civilian Insurrection

Latin America is more famous for its political violence than for nonviolent action. This may be an unbalanced view. There have apparently been a large number of instances in Latin America of general strikes and several cases of nonviolent civilian insurrections. For example, within a few weeks in 1944 two Central American dictators, in El Salvador and Guatemala, fell before massive civil resistance. These cases are especially important because of the rapidity with which the nonviolent action destroyed these entrenched military dictatorships. Attention here is focused on the Guatemala case.

Guatemala, 1944

With the help of the secret police, General Jorge Ubico had ruled Guatemala since 1932. Ubico was extolled in some U.S. magazines as a "road-and-school dictator" the men who had faced his political police knew better. Time Magazine called him an admirer of Hitler's 1934 blood purge, and quoted Ubico: "I am like Hitler, I execute first and give trial afterwards."

During World War II many U.S. troops were in Guatemala, which had joined the Allies. The Americans there promoted ideas of democracy for which, they said, the war was being fought. These appealed especially to Guatemalan students and young professional men. Other changes were undermining Ubico's position. Seizure of German-owned coffee fincas (plantations) in 1942 removed some of his supporters. Domestic issues were causing unrest, both among workers and within the business community. The dictator of nearby El Salvador, Martinez, had fallen a few weeks previously in the face of widespread nonviolent resistance. That proved to be a dangerous and contagious example. Action began in Guatemala, mildly — at first.

In late May 1944, 45 lawyers asked the removal of the judge who tried most political opponents of the regime brought before a civil court. Ubico asked for specific charges against the judge. Surprisingly, one newspaper was allowed to publish them.

On the day prior to the annual parade of teachers and schoolchildren in tribute to the dictator, 200 teachers petitioned Ubico for a wage increase. Those who drafted the petition were arrested and charged with conspiracy against the social institution of the supreme government. The teachers replied with a boycott of the parade; they were fired.

On June 20 a manifesto announced the formation of the Social Democrat party and called for opposition parties, social justice, lifting of the terror, and hemispheric solidarity. Students petitioned for university autonomy, rehiring of two discharged teachers, and release of two imprisoned law students. Unless the demands were granted within 24 hours, they threatened a student strike.

Ubico declared a state of emergency. He called the opposition "Nazi-Fascist." Fearful, many student leaders sought asylum in the Mexican Embassy. However, young lawyers and professional men refused to submit to intimidation, and supported the students. On June 23rd the schoolteachers went on strike.

Ubico had once said that if 300 respected Guatemalans were to ask him to resign, he would do so. On June 24th two men delivered the Memorial de los 311 to Ubico's office. The 311 prominent signers risked their lives. The document explained the reasons for unrest, asked effective constitutional guarantees, and suspension of martial law. The same day, students marched past the U.S. Embassy and emphasized reliance on nonviolent means. Officials seemed surprised at the form of this demonstration. A peaceful meeting that evening demanded Ubico's resignation. Later that night, however, police beat and arrested hundreds at a neighborhood religious and social celebration. Some blamed "drunken bandits, previously coached by the police"; others pointed to clashes between persons shouting anti-Ubico slogans and the dictator's strong-arm men.

The next day the foreign minister summoned to the National Palace the two men who had delivered the Memorial de los 311 – Carbonell and Serrano. The ex-head of the secret police joined in the meeting. Simultaneously, a demonstration took place before the National palace; against it the government massed platoons of soldiers, cavalry, tanks, armored cars, machine guns, and police armed with guns and tear gas bombs. Carbonell and Serrano were asked to "calm the people." Although all meetings had been banned, the men were permitted to meet with other "leaders" of the movement to seek a solution to the crisis.

That afternoon women dressed in deep mourning prayed for an end to the night's brutalities at the Church of San Francisco in the center of Guatemala City. Afterward they formed an impressive silent procession; the cavalry charged and fired into the crowd. An unknown number were wounded and one, Maria Chincelli Recinos, a teacher, was killed. She became the first martyr: "The mask had been torn form the Napoleonic pose, revealing Ubico and his regime standing rudely on a basis of inhumanity and terror."

Guatemala City responded with a silent paralysis. The opposition broke off talks with the government. Workers struck. Businessmen shut stores and offices. It was an economic shutdown. Everything closed. The streets were deserted.

After attempts at a new parley failed, at Ubico's request the diplomatic corps arranged a meeting that afternoon between the opposition and the government. The delegates told Ubico to his face that during his rule "Guatemala has known nothing but oppression." Ubico insisted: "As long as I am president, I will never permit a free press, nor free association, because the people of Guatemala are not ready for a democracy and need a strong hand." The possibility of Ubico's resigning and the question of succession were discussed. The delegates were to sample public opinion.

The opposition later reported to Ubico by letter the unanimous desire of the people that he resign. They again demanded the lifting of martial law, freedom of the press and association, and an end to attacks on the people. Petitions and messages from important people poured into the palace; they also asked Ubico to resign. The silent economic shutdown of Guatemala City continued. The dictator's power was dissolving.

On July 1st Ubico withdrew in favor of a triumvirate of generals. Immediate and unaccustomed political ferment followed. Labor and political organizations mushroomed, and exiles returned. General Ponce, one of the triumvirates, tried to install himself in Ubico's place. In October he faced another general strike and a student strike and was ousted by a coup d'etat. Difficult times were still ahead.

"Energetic and cruel, Jorge Ubico could have put down an armed attack. He could have imposed his will on any group of disgruntled, military or civilian, and stood them up against a wall. But he was helpless against civil acts of repudiation, to which he responded with violence, until these slowly pushed him into the dead-end street where all dictatorships ultimately arrive: kill everybody who is not with you or get out."

The movement that brought Waterloo to Guatemala's Napoleon was, fittingly, a peaceful, civilian action; the discipline, serenity and resignation with which it was conducted made it a model of passive resistance.

Extensive use of nonviolence has occurred despite the absence of attention to the development of the technique itself. Its practice has been partly spontaneous, partly intuitive, partly vaguely patterned after some known case. It has usually been practiced under highly unfavorable conditions and with a lack of experienced participants or even experienced leaders. Almost always there were no advance preparations or training; little or no planning or prior consideration of strategy and tactics and of the range of methods. The people using it have usually had little real understanding of the nature of the technique which they sought to wield and were largely ignorant of its history. There were no studies of strategy and tactics for them to consult, or handbooks on how to organize the "troops," conduct the struggle, and maintain discipline. Under such conditions it is not surprising that there have been defeats or only partial victories, or that violence has sometimes erupted – which, as we shall see, helps to bring defeat. With such handicaps, it is amazing that the practice of the technique has been as widespread, successful, and orderly as it has.

Some men and women are now trying to learn more of the nature of this technique and to explore its potentialities. Some people are now asking how nonviolent action can be refined and applied in place of violence to meet complex and difficult problems. These intellectual efforts are a potentially significant new factor in the history of this technique. It remains to be seen what consequences this factor may have for the future development of nonviolent action.

Czechoslovakia, 1968

The Soviet leaders expected that the massive invasion of Czechoslovakia by more than half a million Warsaw Treaty Organization troops would overwhelm the much smaller Czechoslovak army within days, leaving the country in confusion and defeat. The invasion would also make possible a coup d'etat to replace the reform-minded Dubcek regime with a conservative pro-Moscow one. With this in mind, the Soviet K.G.B. (state police) kidnapped the Communist Party's First Secretary, Alexander Dubcek; the Prime Minister, Oldrich Cernik; the National Assembly President, Josef Smrkovsky; and the National Front Chairman, Frantisek Kriegel. The Soviet officials held under house arrest the President of the Republic, Ludvik Svoboda, who was a popular soldier-statesman in both Czechoslovakia and the Soviet Union. They hoped that he would give the mantle of legitimacy to the new conservative regime. The kidnapped leaders might have been killed once the coup had been successful, as happened in Hungary in 1957.

But the country was not demoralized as a result of military defeat, for it was a different type of resistance which was waged. Nor did a puppet regime quickly replace the kidnapped leaders. The Czechoslovak officials sent emergency orders to all the armed forces to remain in their barracks. The Soviet leaders had expected that the situation would be so effectively under control within three days that the invading troops could then be withdrawn. This did not happen, and as a result there were serious logistical and morale problems among the invading troops. Owing to resistance at several strategic points a collaborationist government was prevented, at least for about eight months – until April, 1969 when the Husak regime came in.

Resistance began in early hours of the invasion. Employees of the government news agency (C/T.K.) refused orders to issue a release stating that certain Czechoslovak party and government officials had requested the invasion. Also, President Svoboda courageously refused to sign the document presented to him by the conservative clique. Finally, it was possible through the clandestine radio network to convene several official bodies, and these opposed the invasion.

The Extraordinary 14th Party Congress, the National Assembly, and what was left of the government ministers all issued statements by the Party Presidium before the arrival of the K.G.B. – that the invasion had begun without the knowledge of party governmental leadership; there had been no "request." Some of the bodies selected interim leaders who carried out certain emergency functions. The National Assembly went on to "demand the release from detention of our constitutional representatives — in order that they can carry out their constitutional functions entrusted to them by the Sovereign people of the country," and to "demand immediate withdrawal of the armies of the five states."

The clandestine radio network during the first week both created many forms of resistance and shaped others: it convened the Extraordinary 14th Party Congress, called one-hour general strikes, requested the rail workers to slow the transport of Russian tracking and jamming equipment, and discouraged collaboration within the C.S.S.R. State Police. There is no record of any collaboration among the uniformed Public Police; indeed, many of them worked actively with the resistance. The radio argued the futility of acts of violence and the wisdom of nonviolent resistance. It instructed students in the streets to clear out of potentially explosive situations and cautioned against rumors. The radio was the main means through which a politically mature and effective resistance was shaped. Colin Chapman has observed that "each form of resistance, however effective it might have been alone, served to strengthen the other manifestations," and through the radio different levels of resistance and different parts of the country were kept in steady communication. With many government agencies put out of operation by Russian occupation of their offices, the radio also took on certain emergency functions (such as obtaining manpower to bring in potato and hops harvest) and provided vital information. This ranged from assuring mothers that their children in summer camp were safe to reporting meager news of the Moscow negotiations.

Militarily totally successful, the Russians now faced a strong political struggle. In face of unified civilian resistance, the absence of a collaborationist government, and the increasing demoralization of their troops, the Soviet leaders agreed on Friday, the 23rd that President Svoboda would fly to Moscow for negotiations. Svoboda refused to negotiate until Dubcek, Cernik, and Smrkovsky joined the discussions. In four days a compromise was worked out. This left most of the leaders in their positions but called for the party to exercise more fully in its "leading role," and left the Russian troops in the country. The compromise seems also to have included the sacrifice of certain reform-minded leaders and reforms.

That first week the entire people had in a thousand ways courageously and cleverly fought an exhilarating battle for their freedom. The compromise, called the Moscow Protocol, created severely mixed feelings among the people. Observers abroad saw this as an unexpected success for the nation and its leaders; an occupied country is not supposed to have bargaining power. But most Czechs and Slovaks saw it as a defeat and for a week would not accept it. The leaders were apparently doubtful of the disciplined capacity of the populace for sustained resistance in the face of severe repression.

Despite the absence of prior planning or explicit training for civilian resistance, the Dubcek regime managed to remain in power until April 1969, about eight months longer than would have been possible with military resistance. The Russians subsequently gained important objectives, including the establishment of a conservative regime. The final outcome of the struggle and occupation remains undetermined at this writing. Nevertheless, this highly significant case requires careful research and analysis of its methods, problems, successes, and failures.

The Methods of
Nonviolent Protest and Persuasion
by Gene Sharp

Nonviolent protest and persuasion is a class which includes a large number of methods which are mainly symbolic acts of peaceful opposition or of attempted persuasion, extending beyond verbal expressions but stopping short of noncooperation or nonviolent intervention. Among these methods are parades, vigils, picketing, posters, teach-ins, mourning, and protest meetings.

Their use may simply show that the actionists are against something; for example, picketing may express opposition to a law which restricts dissemination of birth control information. The methods of this class may also be applied for something; for example, group lobbying may support a clean-air bill pending in the legislature or overseas aid. Nonviolent protest and persuasion also may express deep personal feelings or moral condemnation on a social or political issue; for example, a vigil on Hiroshima Day may express penance for the American atomic bombing of that Japanese city. The "something" with which the nonviolent protestors may be concerned may be a particular deed, a law, a policy, a general condition, or a whole regime or system.

The act may be intended primarily to influence the opponent—by arousing attention and publicity for the issue and thereby, it is hoped, support, which may convince him to accept the change; or by warning him of the depth or extent of feeling on the issue which is likely to lead to more severe action if a change is not made. Or the act may be intended primarily to communicate with the public, onlookers, or third parties, directly or through publicity, in order to arouse, attention and support for the desired change. Or the act may by intended primarily to influence the grievance group—the persons directly affected by the issue—to induce them to do something themselves, such as participate in a strike or an economic boycott.

What, then, are the specific methods of nonviolent action which may be classified as nonviolent protest and persuasion? This is a sampling.

Sit-ins

In a sit-in the interventionists occupy certain facilities by sitting on available chairs, stools, and occasionally on the floor for a limited or unlimited period, either in a single act or in a series of acts, with the objective of disrupting the normal pattern of activities. The purpose may be to establish a new pattern, such as opening particular facilities to previously excluded persons, or to make a protest which may not be directly connected with the facilities occupied. This method has often been used in the civil rights movement in the United States.

Student Strikes

Students and pupils of all types of schools, from elementary schools to universities, may as a means of protest or resistance temporarily refuse to attend classes. Or they may refuse to cooperate in a related way—by boycotting only some, not all, lectures, for example; or students may attend classes but refuse to pay attention, as was done at the University of Madrid in 1965 as part of the campaign for an independent student union. Possible variations are legion. It is more usual, however, for all classes to be boycotted. (Student strikes are also called school boycotts or class boycotts.)

The student strike has long been widely used in China, Latin America, and to a lesser degree Africa; in 1970, following the United States' invasion of Cambodia, it became a prominent part of university life in the United States. The student strike is not a modern invention, as the Chinese examples show. Student strikes in China have sometimes taken the form of refusal to take the examinations, sometimes in protest against the lack of impartiality by the examiners.

Sit-downs

The sit-down is an act of noncooperation in which the participants actually sit down on the street, road, ground, or floor and refuse to leave voluntarily, for either a limited or an indefinite period of time. The sit-down may be a spontaneous act, or a reaction decided on in advance, as a response to orders for a march or other demonstration to disperse. Or it may be combined with civil disobedience to some regulatory law as a serious type of symbolic resistance. The sit-down may also be used to halt ordinary traffic or tanks, or to prevent workers or officials from carrying out their work. In these cases it becomes a method of nonviolent intervention (either nonviolent interjection or nonviolent obstruction, which are described in the next chapter). In recent years the sit-down appears to have been more widely used than previously.

Toward the end of April 1960, during the Algerian War, over 500 demonstrators protested the internment of 6,000 North Africans in France, without trial or hearing, by marching to the Centre de Tri de Vincennes (one of the French reception centers for Arabs) and sitting down in front of it. New waves of demonstrators came when the first persons were arrested and driven away in vehicles.

Turning One's Back

Silent disapproval may be emphasized by turning one's back (whether standing or sitting) to the person or persons who are or represent the opponent. For example, when in his proclamation of a day of fasting and prayer in 1771, Governor Hutchinson of Massachusetts Bay had included a call for thanks for the "Continuance of our Privileges," the radicals took this as an open insult because of the implication of support for British policies. The proclamation was to be read in the churches, but, Philip Davidson writes, "Dr. Pemberton alone of the Boston pastors read the proclamation—and he did so simply because the Governor was a member of his congregation—and he did so with evident embarrassment, for many of the members turned their backs or left the building."

After the dramatic days of the June 16th-17th East German Rising, on June 18th, 1953, East Berlin strikers returned to their factories but refused to work. "They squatted in front of their lathes and benches and turned their backs on Party officials."

Vigils

A vigil is an appeal normally addressed not to one or a few persons, but to many people. Like picketing, a vigil consists of people remaining at a particular place as a means of expressing a point of view. It differs from picketing, however, in that it is frequently maintained over a longer period of time, sometimes around the clock, and is associated with a more solemn attitude, often of a pleading or religious character. It often involves late hours and loss of sleep.

"Haunting" Officials

As a means of reminding officials of the "immorality" of their behavior in repressing a nonviolent resistance movement and of the determination and fearlessness of the population, volunteers may sometimes follow and "haunt" officials everywhere they go, thus constantly reminding them of the population's determination. For example, as Joan Bondurant has reported, during the 1928 Bardoli campaign in India: "Volunteers followed officials everywhere, camping on roads outside official bungalows. When arrested, they were replaced by others until authorities tired of the process."

Protest Disrobings

One of the rarer old—but newly reactivated— forms of nonviolent protest is the public removal of clothes as a means of expressing one's religious disapproval or political protest. During the Quaker "invasion" of the intolerant Massachusetts Bay Colony in the seventeenth century, Lydia Wardel entered Newbury Church naked as a protest. Members of the Sons of Freedom sect of the Doukhobors in British Columbia, Canada, have been credited with "uncounted nude parades" and in some cases individual women have disrobed in front of their own burning homes, to which they set fire as a protest against alleged government interference or prosecution of their husbands for resistance activities, including demolitions. When Prime Minister John Diefenbaker was attending a political rally at Trail, British Columbia, on May 28, 1962, Doukhobor women whose husbands were awaiting trial for terrorist acts interrupted the meeting, tearfully protesting "unfair treatment" of their group, and took off their clothing as part of their protest.

One of several cases of protest disrobing in the United States in recent years by young people in the antiwar and social protest movements took place at Grinnell College, in Grinnell, Iowa, on February 5, 1969. The Students staged a "nude-in" during a speech by a representative of Playboy magazine, in protest of the magazine's "sensationalism of sex."

From: The Politics of Nonviolent Action

Albert Einstein on Pacifism

The United States has reached a point where she feels compelled to fortify islands, produce more atomic bombs, and hamper free scientific exchange; the army, demands huge budgets to stimulate research and guide it into specific channels; and youth is being indoctrinated with the spirit of nationalism. All this is done in preparation for the day when the specter may come to life. Unfortunately, these very policies are the most effective way of actually bringing the specter into being.

Developments have taken the same course everywhere. But our responsibility is particularly great, for circumstances have temporarily placed the United States in so powerful a position that our influence on current affairs is of very great significance. In the face of so heavy a responsibility, the temptation to abuse one's power is great and potentially very dangerous.

You cannot simultaneously prevent and prepare for war. The very prevention of war requires more faith, courage and resolution than are needed to prepare for war. We must all do our share, that we may be equal to the task of peace.

Two months later, on March 8th, 1955, Einstein discussed the Arab question in a letter to his Indian friend:

Of course, I regret the constant state of tension existing between Israel and the Arab states. Such tension could hardly have been avoided. in view of the nationalistic attitude of both sides, which has only been intensified by the war and its implications. Worst of all has been the policy of the new administration in the United States [the Eisenhower administration] which, due to its own imperialist and militaristic interests, seeks to win the sympathy of the Arab nations by sacrificing Israel. As a consequence the very existence of Israel has become seriously imperiled by the armament efforts of her enemies. This man Dulles is a real misfortune! While pretending to serve the cause of peace, he in fact threatens everybody, hoping thereby to achieve his imperialist aims without becoming involved in a "big" war. Such a policy is not only morally objectionable but will prove dangerous to the United States in the long run. How few people realize this! In a surprisingly brief time, they have come to accept this shortsighted militaristic point of view.

I must confess that the foreign policy of the United States since the end of hostilities often irresistibly reminds me of the foreign policy of Germany under Kaiser Wilhelm II. I know that others have independently recognized this painful analogy.

It is characteristic of the military mentally to consider material factors, such as atomic bombs, strategic bases, arms of every description, raw material resources, and the like as important while, at the same time, regarding man himself, his thoughts, and aspirations as quite inferior. In its theoretical approach the military mentality bears some resemblance to Marxism. In both, man is minimized as being merely "capacity" or "manpower." Under the impact of this kind of thinking, the goals which normally determine human aspirations simply disappear. To fill the gap, the military mentality makes the possession of "naked power" a goal in itself. This surely is one of the strangest delusions to which man can fall victim.

Class of Nonviolence

Today, the existence of the military mentality is more dangerous than ever; for the weapons which are available to aggressor nations have become much more powerful than weapons of defense. This fact will inevitably produce the kind of thinking which leads to preventive wars. Because of the general insecurity resulting from these developments, the civil rights of citizens are being sacrificed to the alleged cause of national interest. Political witch hunting and government interference in many forms, such as official control over teaching, research, and the press, appear inevitable and, consequently, do not encounter the kind of popular resistance that ought otherwise serve to protect the population. All traditional values are changing and anything which does not clearly serve the utopian goal of militarism is considered inferior.

In our own days the struggle is primarily waged for freedom of political conviction and discussion as well as for freedom of research and teaching. The fear of communism has led to policies that expose our country to ridicule by the rest of civilized mankind. How long shall we tolerate power-hungry politicians who try to generate a fear of communism in order to gain political advantage? Sometimes it seems that the people of today have lost their sense of humor to such a degree that the French saying "Ridicule kills," has lost its validity.

To A.J. Muste of the Fellowship of Reconciliation, Einstein wrote on April 11th. 1951:

I agree wholeheartedly in all essential points with the opinions expressed in the article "The Paranoia Race." I wish to mention, however, that I do not consider it reasonable to compare a disease in the medical sense with the hatred and fear toward Russia which have been installed in the American people since the death of Roosevelt. It is, of course, incontestable that the arming of individual countries can lead only to war and destruction, not to security. Under present conditions, those countries which have a minimum of armament are most secure. The only reasonable policy the United States could pursue is to declare unconditionally that security in the world depends upon the establishment of a world government which would be open to all nations and would have the duty and power to solve all international conflicts and put an end to colonial oppression.

A Hungarian survivor of the Dachau concentration camp, who had emigrated to Australia, asked in referring to the atomic bomb whether Einstein had discarded the old and noble traditions of his profession and had put his conscience and his faith in human ideals in cold storage; was Einstein working for the benefit of the people or had he plotted a revolt against their lives? Einstein took these insinuations seriously and replied on October 1st, 1952: "You are mistaken in regarding me as a kind of chieftain of those scientists who abuse science for military purposes. I have never worked in the field of applied science, let alone for the military."

I condemn the military mentality of our time just as you do. Indeed, I have been a pacifist all my life and regard Gandhi as the only truly great political figure of our age.

My name is linked to the atomic bomb in two different ways. Almost 50 years ago I discovered the equivalence of mass and energy, a relationship which served as the guiding principle in the work leading to the release of atomic energy. Secondly, I signed a letter to President Roosevelt stressing the need for work in the field of the atomic bomb. I felt this was necessary because of the dreadful danger that the Nazi regime might be the first to come into possession of the atomic bomb.

Thus, your letter, as you will no doubt realize, was based on incorrect assumptions.

On February 16th, 1931, the Yale Daily News published Einstein's answers to a long series of questions relating to the field of science. Only one of the questions touched upon politics. In his reply, Einstein once again emphasized the view that science in itself could have no direct influence in building the international organization that was necessary if world chaos were to be avoided; man's determination alone could solve that problem.

On February 16th, 1931, Einstein addressed several hundred students at the California Institute of Technology:

I could sing a hymn of praise about the progress made in the field of applied science; and, no doubt, you yourselves will promote further progress during your lifetime. I could speak in such terms since this is the century of applied science, and America is its fatherland. But I do not want to use such language. Why does applied science, which is so magnificent, saves work, and makes life easier, bring us so little happiness? The simple answer is that we have not yet learned to make proper use of it.

In times of war, applied science has given men the means to poison and mutilate one another. In times of peace, science has made our lives hurried and uncertain. Instead of liberating us from much of the monotonous work that has to be done, it has enslaved men to machines; men who work long, wearisome hours mostly without joy in their labor and with the continual fear of losing their pitiful income.

You may feel that this old man before you is singing an ugly song. I do it, however, for the purpose of making some suggestions to you. If you want your life's work to be useful to mankind, it is not enough that you understand applied science as such. Concern for man himself must always constitute the chief objective of all technological effort, concern for the big, unsolved problems of how to organize human work and the distribution of commodities in such a manner as to assure that the results of our scientific thinking may be a blessing to mankind, and not a curse.

Never forget this when you are pondering over your diagrams and equations!

There is enough money, enough work, and enough food, provided we organize our resources according to our necessities rather than be slaves to rigid economic theories or traditions. Above all, we must not permit our minds and our activities to be diverted from constructive work by preparations for another war. I agree with the great American Benjamin Franklin, who said that there never was a good war or a bad peace.

I am not only a pacifist but a militant pacifist. I am willing to fight for peace. Nothing will end war unless the peoples themselves refuse to go to war.

Every great cause is first championed by an aggressive minority. Is it not better for a man to die for a cause in which he believes, such as peace, than to suffer for a cause in which he does not believe, such as war? Every war merely enlarges the chain of vicious circles which impedes the progress of mankind. A handful of conscientious objectors can dramatize the protest against war.

The masses are never militaristic until their minds are poisoned by propaganda. I agree with you that we must teach them to resist propaganda. We must begin to inoculate our children against militarism by educating them in the spirit of pacifism. The trouble with Europe is that her people have been educated on a wrong psychology. Our schoolbooks glorify war and conceal its horrors then indoctrinate children with hatred. I would teach peace rather than war, love rather than hate.

The textbooks should be rewritten. Instead of perpetuating ancient rancors and prejudices, we should infuse a new spirit into our educational system. Education should begin in the cradle. Mothers throughout the world have the responsibility of sowing the seeds of peace into the souls of their children.

It may not be possible in one generation to eradicate the combative instinct. It is not even desirable to eradicate it entirely. Men should continue to fight, but they should fight for things worthwhile, not for imaginary geographical lines, racial prejudices, and private greed draped in the colors of patriotism. Their arms should be weapons of the spirit, not shrapnel and tanks.

Think of what a world we could build if the power unleashed in war were applied to constructive tasks! One tenth of the energy that the various belligerents spent in the World War, a fraction of the money they exploded in hand grenades and poison gas, would suffice to raise the standard of living in every country and avert the economic catastrophe of worldwide unemployment.

We must be prepared to make the same heroic sacrifices for the cause of peace that we make ungrudgingly for the cause of war. There is no task that is more important or closer to my heart.

Nothing that I can do or say will change the structure of the universe. But maybe, by raising my voice, I can help the greatest of all causes—goodwill among men and peace on earth.

A climactic point in Einstein's career as a militant pacifist came on December 14th, 1930, when he spoke at a meeting in New York's Ritz Carlton Hotel, under the auspices of the New History Society. The speech was delivered extemporaneously, and when the interpreter originally designated proved unequal to the task. Mrs. Rosika Schwimmer volunteered to translate Einstein's remarks into English:

When those who are bound together by pacifist ideals hold a meeting they are usually consorting only with their own kind. They are like sheep huddled together while wolves wait outside. I believe that pacifist speakers face this difficulty: they ordinarily reach only their own group, people who are pacifists any how and hardly need to be convinced. The sheep's voice does not reach beyond this circle and is, therefore ineffectual. That is the real weakness of the pacifist movement.

Genuine pacifists, those whose heads are not in the clouds but who think in realistic terms, must fearlessly endeavor to act in a manner which is of practical value to the cause rather than remain content merely to espouse the ideals of pacifism. Deeds, not words, are needed; mere words get pacifists nowhere. They must initiate action and begin with what can be achieved now.

As to what our next step should be, I should like you to realize that under the present military system every man is compelled to commit the crime of killing for his country. The aim of all pacifists must be to convince others of the immorality of war and rid the world of the shameful slavery of military service. I wish to suggest two ways to achieve that aim.

The first has already been put into practice: uncompromising war resistance and refusal to do military service under any circumstances. In countries where conscription exists, the true pacifist must refuse military duty. Already, a considerable number of pacifists in many countries have refused and are refusing, at great personal sacrifice, to serve a military term in peacetime. By doing so, it becomes manifest that they will not fight in the event of war.

In countries where compulsory service does not exist, true pacifists must publicly declare in time of peace that they will not take up arms under any circumstances. This, too, is an effective method of war resistance. I earnestly urge you to try to convince people all over the world of the justice of this position. The timid may say, "What is the use? We shall be sent to prison." To them I would reply: Even if only two percent of those assigned to perform military service should announce their refusal to fight, as well as urge means other than war of settling international disputes, governments would be powerless, they would not dare send such a large number of people to jail.

A second line of action for war resisters, which I suggest, is a policy which would not involve personal involvement with the law. That is, to try to establish through international legislation the right to refuse military service in peacetime. Those who are unwilling to accept such a position might prefer to advocate legislation which would permit them, in place of military service, to do some strenuous or even dangerous work, in the interest of their own country or of mankind as a whole. They would thereby prove that their war resistance is unselfish and merely a logical consequence of the belief that international differences can be sealed in ways other than fighting; it would further prove that their opposition to war could not be attributed to cowardice or the desire for personal comfort or unwillingness to accept work of a dangerous nature; we shall have advanced far on the road to a more peaceful world.

I further suggest that pacifists of all countries start raising funds to support those who would want to refuse military service but who cannot actually do so for lack of financial means. I, therefore, advocate the establishment of an international organization and an international pacifist fund to support the active war resisters of our day.

In conclusion, may I say that the serious pacifists who want to accomplish peace must have the courage to initiate and to carry on these aims; only then will the world be obliged to take notice. Pacifists will then be heard by people who are not already pacifists; and once they are listened to, their message is bound to be effective. If they are too restrained, their voices will continue to reach only those in their own circle. They will remain sheep, pacifist sheep.

I am very glad that you have given me this opportunity to make a few remarks about the problem of pacifism. The developments of the last few years have once more indicated that we are hardly justified in assuming that the struggle against armaments and the spirit of militarism can be safely left in the hands of governments. Even the creation of pacifist organizationss with large memberships will not bring us much closer to our goal.

I am convinced that the only way to be effective is through the revolutionary method of refusing military service. We need organizations in different countries to give material and moral support to all those who have the courage to resist war. This is the only way to make pacifism a vital issue and to inaugurate a vigorous campaign that will attract men of strong character. It is a fight not sanctioned by law, but one which must be fought if people are to have the right to resist the demands of governments that they perform criminal actions."

Many who consider themselves good pacifists will not want to participate in such a radical form of pacifism; they will claim that patriotism prevents them from adopting such a policy. But, in an emergency, such people cannot be counted on anyhow, as we learned so well during the World War.

On May 28th 1940, the Columbia Broadcasting System originated a special broadcast on atomic energy. The broadcast, called "'Operation Crossroads," emanated from the Coolidge Auditorium of the Library of Congress in Washington, D.C.:

Newscaster Robert Trout:

There are many people who—while they hope and pray that war can be averted—{are} pessimistic about the chance of avoiding war. They say it's just "human nature, " and that while mankind may possibly, change some old habits of thinking in a million years, there's certainly no chance of changing them in the next five. What about that "you can't change human nature" argument, Dr. Albert Einstein?

Einstein (speaking from Princeton):

When you speak of "human nature," what do you mean?

Trout (from Washington):

Why, I suppose the hates and fears and prejudices that make for wars.

Einstein:

Then I would say that it is precisely because we cannot change human nature in a million years that we must do what we have to do very quickly, in order to prevent the terrible destruction of an atomic war. This "human nature" which likes wars is like a river. It is impossible in geological time to change the nature of the river. But when it continually overflows its banks and destroys our lives and homes, do we sit down and say, "It is too bad. We can't change the river. We can do nothing about it. "

Trout:

No, Dr. Einstein. We get together and build a dam which will keep the river in check.

Einstein:

Exactly. And what do we use to build the dam?

Trout:

We use reason, I suppose, our ability to think.

Einstein:

That is correct. And this ability to think is also a part of human nature. It is intelligence, which is the ability to learn from experience, to plan ahead. It includes the capacity to give up immediate, temporary benefits far permanent ones. This part of human nature recognizes that a man's security and happiness depend on a well-functioning society; that a well-functioning society depends on the existence and observance of laws; and that men must submit to these laws in order to have peace. It is this reasoning faculty which is responsible for all of man's progress in art, science, agriculture, industry, and government.

Trout:

And you believe, Dr. Einstein, that this thinking man can solve our great problem for us?

Einstein:

I believe nothing else can. Just as we use our reason to build a dam to hold a river in check, we must now build institutions to restrain the fears and suspicions and greed which move peoples and their rulers. Such institutions, as have been described by Mr. Stassen and Mr. Douglas, must be based on law and justice. They must have authority over atomic bombs and other weapons, and they must have the power to enforce this authority. To do this is difficult, yes; but we must remember that if the animal part of human nature is our foe, the thinking part is our friend. We do not have to wait a million years to use our ability to reason. It does not depend on time. We are using it every day of our lives.

On March 21st, 1952, Einstein responded to a troubled pacifist who, like others, asked for clarification of apparent inconsistencies in Einstein's various statements on pacifism and suggested that he make a public pronouncement about his actual pacifist position. Einstein wrote:

"I am indeed a pacifist, but not a pacifist at any price. My views are virtually identical with those of Gandhi. But I would, individually and collectively resist violently any attempt to kill me or to take away from me, or my people, the basic means of subsistence.
I was, therefore, of the conviction that it was justified and necessary to fight Hitler. For his was such an extreme attempt to destroy people.

"Furthermore, I am of the conviction that realization of the goal of pacifism is possible only through supranational organization. To stand unconditionally for this cause is, in my opinion, the criterion of true pacifism."

Letters urging him to clarify his change of views followed him to England and even America. Professor C.C. Heringa of the University of Amsterdam was another pacifist who could not believe the published reports. On September 11, 1933, Einstein wrote him from Cromer, England:

"I assure you that my present attitude toward military service was arrived at with the greatest reluctance and after a difficult inner struggle. The root of all evil lies in the fact that there is no powerful international police force, nor is there a really effective international court of arbitration whose judgments could be enforced. All the same, antimilitarists were justified in refusing military service as long as the majority of the nations of Europe were intent upon peace. This no longer holds true. I am convinced that developments in Germany tend toward belligerent acts similar to those in France after the Revolution. Should this trend meet with success, you may be sure that the last remnants of personal freedom on the continent of Europe will be destroyed.

"While it is quite true that the deterioration of conditions in Germany is partially attributable to the policies of neighboring countries, there seems little purpose at this juncture in blaming them for these policies. The plain fact is that the gospel of force and repression, currently prevailing in Germany, poses grave threats to the continent of Europe and the independence of its inhabitants. This threat cannot be combated by moral means; it can be met only by organized might. To prevent the greater evil, it is necessary that the lesser evil—the hated military—be accepted for the time being. Should German armed might prevail, life will not be worth living anywhere in Europe.

"I believe, nonetheless, that even now it is not too late to avert war by preventing German rearmament through diplomatic pressure. But such pressure will require absolute military superiority on the part of Germany's neighbors. To destroy such superiority or to prevent its achievement is tantamount to betraying the cause of European freedom.

"You cannot compare French militarism to German militarism. The French people, even those at the top, have remained preponderantly pacifist in outlook and are maintaining an army merely for the defense of their country. This is even more true of the Belgian people.

"To summarize: In the present circumstances, realistic pacifists should no longer advocate the destruction of military power; rather, they should strive for its internationalization. Only when such internationalization has been achieved will it be possible to work toward the reduction of military power to the dimensions of an international police force. We do not cause the danger to disappear by merely closing our eyes to it."

Letter to Ernesto Cardenal:
Guns Don't Work
by Daniel Berrigan

Editor's note: Ernesto Cardenal had helped establish a Christian community on Solentiname Island in Nicaragua. Some members joined the armed resistance to Samosa, and Cardenal issued a declaration of his support for them and the Sandinista Front.

Dear Brother Ernesto Cardenal,

Your account of events in your community of Solentiname has been widely distributed in the United States, especially by the religious press. One translation appended a word: "It is important for us in this country to be able to listen and not to judge this."

Indeed. But at least we can talk together. Please consider what follows, then, as a continuing reflection on matters you have had the courage to open up, and indeed, to act on.

May I also summon a memory or two, as you do so poignantly in you statement? You visited my brother Philip and myself in jail in February of 1977, when we were locked up after a demonstration at the Pentagon. I hope you could read in our faces all your visit meant; a visit from a fellow priest, a poet, a good communitarian, a struggling friend, whose fame was great but whose human warmth was his best gift. Thank you once more for coming to us.

Then there was our first meeting a few years previous, when you brought the art of Solentiname to New York for an exhibition. I had the joy of greeting you, this poet, the intense quiet Latino, known in the southern countries for his sandals and flowing hair and beard, his kinky myopic eyes; known here for his poetry, his courage.

The shadow of Thomas Merton's death lay heavy on us. I think we were seeking consolation in one another's eyes. And we found it.

I am not going to start with the customary disclaimers about your statement. Such are not only superfluous, they verge on the insulting. What Latino. What Yankee doesn't know by now the deadly mutual interests which in Washington prop up the Nicaraguan military government of the Somozas? And who would regard you—an exile, a priest who must now anoint your forehead with the ashes of your dream—regard your convictions, your choices, with anything but the utmost respect? All this is implicit in friendship itself.
I would like to do you a better courtesy, that of taking you seriously: your words, and the actions which by now, I presume, you have taken.

Let me say too that the questions you raise are among the most crucial that Christians can spell out today. Indeed, in your own country, your life raises them. But you thrust them also at us, and rightly so. They are far more than a matter of domestic importance.

There is, first of all, no parallel in America to the violence you describe—whether of the Somozas or the Sandinistas.

What indeed are a few guns, or even a few hundred guns, in the hands of guerrillas in comparison with the doomsday cache of nuclear horrors lurking in our mountains and bunkers? What reasonable comparison can be made between the sorties of your Frente Sandinista, and the lunar devastation of Vietnam, Laos, Cambodia? On your part, a few deaths, much love, exalted goals. On the part of America—but words fail me.

These things I grant with all my heart. What then nags at me, when I ponder your words? I have some inkling of what you face, what your companions face, the students and workers and peasants of your country. I know that the Somozas, given the leash, could swallow all of you tomorrow. I know that on the same day, the U.S. military could swallow the Somozas who had swallowed you—the mouse within the dog within the python—and hardly feel sated. On the world scale where the stakes are piled high—oil, uranium, laisse-faire larcenies, predatory markets, ripoffs, and stand- offs; in a world where the superpowers warily circle one another like urban thugs, nuclear firebombs in hand; in such a world, you or your followers, or even your persecutors, count for very little.

You and the Frente, and the Somozas, could disappear tomorrow. Only a minor breeze would stir the papers on the desk of some sub-secretary of the State Department. A lie or two at a presidential conference would be your obituary, the Nicaraguan folder transferred to a dead file. The empire, in sum, can take your life, and take your death, and take your theology, and the destruction of your community, and your resistance, all in stride.

I say this in no spirit of cynicism. Merely to suggest that in a way I find both strange and exhilarating, your situation lies quite near the realities of the gospel. It ought not, after all, depress us beyond measure, if the empire finds you and me expendable. That is quite normal and constant in the history of such entities. What is of import finally is whether we are able to salvage something in the open season on humans.

I do not mean salvage our lives; I mean our humanity. Our service to one another, of compassion—our very sanity.

I hope I am inching toward the contents of your letter. You discuss quite freely and approvingly the violence of a violated people, yourselves. You align yourself with that violence, regretfully but firmly, irrevocably.

I am sobered and saddened by this. I think of the consequences of your choice, within Nicaragua and far beyond. I sense how the web of violence spins another thread, draws you in, and so many others for whom your example is primary, who do not think for themselves, judging that a priest and poet will lead them in the true way.

I think how fatally easy it is, in a world demented and enchanted with the myth of shortcuts and definitive solutions, when nonviolence appears increasingly naive, old hat, freakish—how easy it is to cross over, to seize the gun. How easy to conclude: the deck is stacked, first: card to last, in favor of the Big Sharks; the outcome of the game, of life itself, is settled before the cards are dealt. Why then isn't taking a few lives (of dubious value at best, torturers, lackeys, police) preferable to the taking of many lives of great value, students, the poor, the victimized and defenseless, the conscientious, those easily identifiable as gospel brothers and sisters? There is, after all, a long tradition of legitimate self-defense.

It may be true, as you say, that "Gandhi would agree with us." Or it may not be true. It may be true, as you imply, that Merton would agree with you. It may be true that Christ would agree with you. I do not believe he would, but I am willing to concede your argument, for the sake of argument.

You may be correct in reporting that "those young Christians fought without hate—and especially without hate for the guards they shortly killed (though this must be cold comfort to the dead). Your vision may one day be verified of a Nicaragua free of "campesino guards killing other campesinos." The utopia you ache for may one day be realized in Nicaragua: "an abundance of schools, child care centers, hospitals, and clinics for everyone-and most importantly, love between everyone." This may all be true: the guns may bring on the kingdom.

But I do not believe it.

One religious paper here published your words under the following headline: "When they take up arms for love of the kingdom of God." How sublime, I thought, how ironic. We have had "just" wars of the Right, a long history of blood, the blood of colonials and natives and slaves and workers and peasants. But we are through with all that. Now we are enlightened. We are to have "just" wars of the Left!

So the young men of Solentiname resolved to take up arms. They did it for one reason: "on account of their love for the kingdom of God." Now here we certainly speak within a tradition! In every crusade that ever marched across Christendom, murder—the most secular of undertakings, the most worldly, the one that enlists and rewards us along with the other enlistees of Caesar—this undertaking is invariably baptized in religious ideology: the kingdom of God.

The power of such language we know too well. Religious battle cries induct hearts and minds as no secular slogans can. Religious ideology raises its flag in every nation, even as it denies the final authority of every nation. It offers to transcendent longings a task that is simple and forthright: kill. It offers a slogan that is as immediately tactile and hot as a fired gun: kill for the kingdom. And perhaps most important of all, it offers a way out: out of anger, out of frustration, out of poverty, out of political stagnation, out of the harsh and dreadful necessity of love. God wills it! The kingdom requires it!

Blood and iron, nukes and rifles. The leftists kill the rightists, the rightists kill the leftists, both, given time and occasion, kill the children, the aged, the ill, the suspects. Given time and occasion, both torture prisoners. Always, you understand inadvertently, regretfully. Both sides, moreover, have excellent intentions, and call on God to witness them. And some god or other does witness them, if we can take the word of whatever bewitched church.

And of course nothing changes. Nothing changes in Beirut, in Belfast, or in Galilee, as I have seen. Except that the living die. And that old, revered distinction between combatant and noncombatant, which was supposed to protect the innocent and helpless, goes down the nearest drain, along with the indistinguishable blood of any and all.

Alas, I have never seen anyone morally improved by killing; neither the one who aimed the bullet, nor the one who received it in his or her flesh.

Class of Nonviolence

Of course we have choices, of course we must decide. When all is said, we find that the gospel makes sense, that it strikes against our motives and actions or it does not. Can that word make sense at all today, can it be something more than utopian or extravagant? The gospel is after all a document out of a simpler age, a different culture. It may even be our duty to construct for ourselves another ethic, based on our own impasse or insights or ego. And go from there, with whatever assurance we can muster, amid the encircling gloom.

Or on the other hand, we can bow our heads before a few truths, crude, exigent, obscure as they are. The outcome of obedience we cannot know, the outcome of disobedience we can deceive ourselves about, indefinitely and sweetly. Thou shalt not kill. Love one another as I have loved you. If your enemy strikes you on the right cheek, turn to him the other. Practically everyone in the world, citizens and believers alike, consign such words to the images on church walls, or the embroideries in front parlors.

We really are stuck. Christians are stuck with this Christ, the impossible, unteachable, irreformable loser. Revolutionaries must correct him, act him aright. That absurd form, shivering under the crosswinds of power, must be made acceptable, relevant. So a gun is painted into his empty hands. Now he is human! Now he is like us.

Does it all have a familiar ring? In the old empires, the ragged rabbi must be cleaned up, invested in Byzantine robes of state, raised in glittering splendor to the dome of heaven. Correction! Correction! we cry to those ignorant gospel scribes, Matthew and the rest. He was not like that, he was not helpless, he was not gentle, he was under no one's heel, no one pushed him around! He would have taken up a gun if one had been at hand, he would have taken up arms, "solely for one reason; on account of his love for the kingdom of God." Did he not have fantasies like ours, in hours out of the public glare, when he too itched for the quick solution, his eyes narrowed like gun sights?

How tricky it all gets! We look around at our culture: an uneasy mix of gunmen, gun makers, gun hucksters, gun researchers, gun runners, guards with guns, property owners with guns. A culture in which the guns put out contracts on the people, the guns own the people, the guns buy and sell the people, the guns practice targets on the people, the guns kill the people. The guns are our second nature, and the first nature is all but obliterated; it is gunned down.

And who will raise it up, that corpse with the neat hole in its temple, ourselves? It is impossible, it is against nature.

Christ asks the literally impossible. And then, our radical helplessness confessed, he confers what was impossible.

Dear brother Ernesto, when I was underground in 1970 with J. Edgar Hoover's hounds on my tail, I had long hours to think of these things. At that time I wrote: "The death of a single human is too heavy a price to pay for the vindication of any principle, however sacred." I should add that at the time, many among the anti-war Left were playing around with bombings, in disarray and despair.

I am grateful that I wrote those words. I find no reason eight years later to amend or deny them. Indeed, in this bloody century, religion has little to offer, little that is not contaminated or broken or in bad faith. But one thing we have: our refusal to take up bombs or guns, aimed at the flesh of brothers and sisters, whom we persist in defining as such, refusing the enmities pushed at us by war-making state or war-blessing church.

This is a long loneliness, and a thankless one. One says "no" when every ache of the heart would say "yes." We, too, long for a community on the land, heartening liturgies, our own turf, the arts, a place where sane ecology can heal us. And the big boot comes down. It destroys everything we have built. And we recoil. Perhaps in shock, perhaps in a change of heart, we begin to savor on our tongues a language that is current all around us: phrases like "legitimate violence," "limited retaliation," "killing for love of the kingdom." And the phrases makes sense—we have crossed over. We are now an army, like the pope's army, or Luther's, or the crusaders, or the Muslims. We have disappeared into this world, into bloody, secular history. We cannot adroitly handle both gospel and gun; so we drop the gospel, as impediment in any case.

And our weapons?

They are contaminated in what they do, and condemned in what they cannot do. There is blood on them, as on our hands. And like our hands, they cannot heal injustice or succor the homeless.

How can they signal the advent of the kingdom of God? How can we, who hold them? We announce only another bloody victory for the emperor of necessity, whose name in the Bible is Death.

Shall we have dominion?

Brother, I think of you so often. And pray with you. And hope against hope.

From: To Dwell in Peace

Building Confidence at Prairie Creek
by Colman McCarthy

Castle Rod, Minn.- Boxes of soapwort, lavender, and daffodil bulbs sit near the front door of the Prairie Creek Community School. In a day or two, the 103 kindergarten through fifth-grade children will be planting the flowers in front of the one-story schoolhouse that rests on five acres of rural grassland 50 miles south of Minneapolis.

The planting is bringing together students and teachers in another cooperative effort of learning-by-doing that is earning the Prairie Creek Community School a national reputation for innovative and effective education.

This is my second visit here, the first being last spring to observe the students' self-run conflict-resolution program. Few schools have one and fewer still in early grades. What Prairie Creek children learn in their conflict-resolution sessions are the same skills they acquire in planting flowers: how to use shovels.

Linda Crawford, the school's director, explains: ''Our purpose is not to do away with all quarrels among the children. I have no illusions that we will ever accomplish that, and I certainly don't want to accomplish it through repression. Our job seems to be to continue to provide them creative way to get out of the holes they dig for themselves. The best present I know to give a kid is a good shovel.''

The luster at Prairie Creek has a second shine, one that is winning attention as more and more national reports are issued on the problems of American education and commissions are appointed to find solutions. One of those solutions is here. It goes back to 1982, when a group of local parents, many of them faculty members at Carleton and Saint Olaf colleges in nearby Northfield, decided their children deserved more than conventional, standardized education. They founded and funded their own school.

At Prairie Creek, neither the intelligence nor creativity of the young is insulted with tests, grades, report cards, or do-it-or-else homework assignments. Schools that rely on those artificialities are teaching inmates not learners. At Prairie Creek, it's been different. Respect for children's variances in intellectual and spiritual development, plus the availability of a small abandoned public school building back off a dirt road amid some cornfields, moved the families to experiment with learning. Twenty children came and two teachers taught them. The inflow has been heavy since.

This isn't another elite private school where monied parents think they can buy the best in education and then turn their minds elsewhere, like making more money. The wealth at Prairie Creek is in the richness of the parents' involvement in the school. The other morning, a father of a kindergartener was volunteering in the library, sorting and cataloging books. He is a professor and coach at Saint Olaf. Other parents come into the school regularly. Some are here to teach and some to putter around, but all of them, obviously, come because they love their children and because, too, the tuition of $3,200 is an investment they wish to protect.

In my two visits to Prairie Creek, nothing struck me more than the students' affection for Linda Crawford. Children are uninhibited in speaking with her, perhaps because they have sensed she is not another adult control freak. Her philosophy of power-sharing was visible, the other morning at the student council meeting when 12 students—5-year-olds to 10-yearolds—gathered in a room next to her office to decide how the school's sports equipment should be loaned out at recess. It was a decision she could have made herself in 10 seconds, but she let the children devise a strategy. They learned a lesson or two about organizing as well as understanding that the equipment is theirs to care for and not someone else's problem.

Crawford said after the meeting: "All educators want to think they know how to teach every child who walks in. But every person is ultimately mysterious, and if the awareness of that mystery doesn't accompany all that you're doing pedagogically, then there's a thinness to it. It's just a veneer."

Parents of Prairie Creek students have told me that their children leave the school at the end of fifth grade with stirred minds grounded in self-confidence. They believe they can do anything, because for the past six years they have. Most go on to the public middle school and high school in Northfield, where conventional methods— tests, grades, and the rest—prevail. The Prairie Creek kids, however startled they may be to confront another style of education, survive and most flourish.

On leaving Prairie Creek, they take their shovels with them.

From Washington Post, October 19. 1991

Questions for Lesson Six

1. The principle of a "just war" is merely the clever dodge of a government bent on violence. Explain.

2. Many believe that Britain could have been removed from America nonviolently. Explain.

3. If "guns don't work" as Daniel Berrigan asserts, why do humans keep resorting to them to resolve conflict?

4. Explain why pacifism is an active and not a passive approach to conflict resolution.

5. Research and report on a creative demonstration of nonviolent conflict resolution

Readings for Lesson Seven

On the Duty of Civil Disobedience
by Henry David Thoreau

The Judge and the Bomb
by Miles Lord

Patriotism or Peace
by Leo Tolstoy

What Would You Do If?
by Joan Baez

Pray for Peace but Pay for War
by Maurice F. McCrackin

A Vigil for Life While We Celebrate Death
by Colman McCarthy

On the Duty of Civil Disobedience
Henry David Thoreau

I heartily accept the motto, "That government is best which governs least"; and I should like to see it acted up to more rapidly and systematically. Carried out, it finally amounts to this, which also I believe — "That government is best which governs not at all"; and when men are prepared for it, that will be the kind of government which they will have. Government is at best but an expedient; but most governments are usually, and all governments are sometimes, inexpedient. The objections which have been brought against a standing army, and they are many and weighty, and deserve to prevail, may also at last be brought against a standing government. The standing army is only an arm of the standing government. The government itself, which is only the mode which the people have chosen to execute their will, is equally liable to be abused and perverted before the people can act through it. Witness the present Mexican war, the work of comparatively a few individuals using the standing government as their tool; for in the outset, the people would not have consented to this measure.

Unjust laws exist: shall we be content to obey them, or shall we endeavor to amend them, and obey them until we have succeeded, or shall we transgress them at once? Men, generally, under such a government as this, think that they ought to wait until they have persuaded the majority to alter them. They think that, if they should resist, the remedy would be worse than the evil. But it is the fault of the government itself that the remedy is worse than the evil. It makes it worse. Why is it not more apt to anticipate and provide for reform? Why does it not cherish its wise minority? Why does it cry and resist before it is hurt? Why does it not encourage its citizens to put out its faults, and do better than it would have them? Why does it always crucify Christ and excommunicate Copernicus and Luther, and pronounce Washington and Franklin rebels?

If the injustice is part of the necessary friction of the machine of government, let it go, let it go: perchance it will wear smooth — certainly the machine will wear out. If the injustice has a spring, or a pulley, or a rope, or a crank, exclusively for itself, then perhaps you may consider whether the remedy will not be worse than the evil; but if it is of such a nature that it requires you to be the agent of injustice to another, then I say, break the law. Let your life be a counter-friction to stop the machine. What I have to do is to see, at any rate, that I do not lend myself to the wrong which I condemn.

As for adopting the ways of the State has provided for remedying the evil, I know not of such ways. They take too much time, and a man's life will be gone. I have other affairs to attend to. I came into this world, not chiefly to make this a good place to live in, but to live in it, be it good or bad. A man has not everything to do, but something; and because he cannot do everything, it is not necessary that he should be petitioning the Governor or the Legislature any more than it is theirs to petition me; and if they should not hear my petition, what should I do then? But in this case the State has provided no way: its very Constitution is the evil. This may seem to be harsh and stubborn and unconcilliatory; but it is to treat with the utmost kindness and consideration the only spirit that can appreciate or deserves it. So is all change for the better, like birth and death, which convulse the body.

I do not hesitate to say, that those who call themselves Abolitionists should at once effectually withdraw their support, both in person and property, from the government of Massachusetts, and not wait till they constitute a majority of one, before they suffer the right to prevail through them. I think that it is enough if they have God on their side, without waiting for that other one. Moreover, any man more right than his neighbors constitutes a majority of one already.

I meet this American government, or its representative, the State government, directly, and face to face, once a year — no more — in the person of its tax-gatherer; this is the only mode in which a man situated as I am necessarily meets it; and it then says distinctly, recognize me; and the simplest, the most effectual, and, in the present posture of affairs, the indispensablest mode of treating with it on this head, of expressing your little satisfaction with and love for it, is to deny it then. My civil neighbor, the tax-gatherer, is the very man I have to deal with — for it is, after all, with men and not with parchment that I quarrel — and he has voluntarily chosen to be an agent of the government. How shall he ever know well that he is and does as an officer of the government, or as a man, until he is obliged to consider whether he will treat me, his neighbor, for whom he has respect, as a neighbor and well-disposed man, or as a maniac and disturber of the peace, and see if he can get over this obstruction to his neighborliness without a ruder and more impetuous thought or speech corresponding with his action. I know this well, that if one thousand, if one hundred, if ten men whom I could name — if ten honest men only — ay, if one honest man, in this State of Massachusetts, ceasing to hold slaves, were actually to withdraw from this co-partnership, and be locked up in the county jail therefore, it would be the abolition of slavery in America. For it matters not how small the beginning may seem to be: what is once well done is done forever. But we love better to talk about it: that we say is our mission. Reform keeps many scores of newspapers in its service, but not one man. If my esteemed neighbor, the State's ambassador, who will devote his days to the settlement of the question of human rights in the Council Chamber, instead of being threatened with the prisons of Carolina, were to sit down the prisoner of Massachusetts, that State which is so anxious to foist the sin of slavery upon her sister — though at present she can discover only an act of inhospitality to be the ground of a quarrel with her — the Legislature would not wholly waive the subject of the following winter.

Under a government which imprisons unjustly, the true place for a just man is also a prison. The proper place today, the only place which Massachusetts has provided for her freer and less despondent spirits, is in her prisons, to be put out and locked out of the State by her own act, as they have already put themselves out by their principles. It is there that the fugitive slave, and the Mexican prisoner on parole, and the Indian come to plead the wrongs of his race should find them; on that separate but more free and honorable ground, where the State places those who are not with her, but against her — the only house in a slave

State in which a free man can abide with honor. If any think that their influence would be lost there, and their voices no longer afflict the ear of the State, that they would not be as an enemy within its walls, they do not know by how much truth is stronger than error, nor how much more eloquently and effectively he can combat injustice who has experienced a little in his own person. Cast your whole vote, not a strip of paper merely, but your whole influence. A minority is powerless while it conforms to the majority; it is not even a minority then; but it is irresistible when it clogs by its whole weight. If the alternative is to keep all just men in prison, or give up war and slavery, the State will not hesitate which to choose. If a thousand men were not to pay their tax bills this year, that would not be a violent and bloody measure, as it would be to pay them, and enable the State to commit violence and shed innocent blood. This is, in fact, the definition of a peaceable revolution, if any such is possible. If the tax-gatherer, or any other public officer, asks me, as one has done, "But what shall I do?" my answer is, "If you really wish to do anything, resign your office." When the subject has refused allegiance, and the officer has resigned from office, then the revolution is accomplished. But even suppose blood shed when the conscience is wounded? Through this wound a man's real manhood and immortality flow out, and he bleeds to an everlasting death. I see this blood flowing now.

The only obligation which I have a right to assume is to do at any time what I think right. It is truly enough said that a corporation has no conscience; but a corporation on conscientious men is a corporation with a conscience. Law never made men a whit more just; and, by means of their respect for it, even the well-disposed are daily made the agents of injustice. A common and natural result of an undue respect for the law is, that you may see a file of soldiers, colonel, captain, corporal, privates, powder-monkeys, and all, marching in admirable order over hill and dale to the wars, against their wills, ay, against their common sense and consciences, which makes it very steep marching indeed, and produces a palpitation of the heart. They have no doubt that it is a damnable business in which they are concerned; they are all peaceably inclined. Now, what are they? Men at all? or small movable forts and magazines, at the service of some unscrupulous man in power? Visit the Navy Yard, and behold a marine, such a man as an American government can make, or such as it can make a man with its black arts — a mere shadow and reminiscence of humanity, a man laid out alive and standing, and already, as one may say, buried under arms with funeral accompaniment, though it may be,

> "Not a drum was heard, not a funeral note,
>   As his corse to the rampart we hurried;
>   Not a soldier discharged his farewell shot
>   O'er the grave where out hero was buried."

The mass of men serve the state thus, not as men mainly, but as machines, with their bodies. They are the standing army, and the militia, jailers, constables, posse comitatus[1], etc. In most cases there is no free exercise whatever of the judgment or of the moral sense; but they put themselves on a level with wood and earth and stones; and wooden men can perhaps be manufactured that will serve the purpose as well. Such command no more

Class of Nonviolence

respect than men of straw or a lump of dirt. They have the same sort of worth only as horses and dogs. Yet such as these even are commonly esteemed good citizens. Others — as most legislators, politicians, lawyers, ministers, and office-holders — serve the state chiefly with their heads; and, as the rarely make any moral distinctions; they are as likely to serve the devil.

----

[1]Posse Comitatus (Latin: "power or force of the county"), ancient English institution consisting of the shire's force of able-bodied private citizens summoned to assist in maintaining public order.

The Judge & the Bomb
by Judge Miles Lord

The following is a statement by U.S. District Judge Miles Lord at his sentencing of two persons convicted of destroying war-related computer equipment at a Sperry plant in Minnesota.

It is the allegation of these young people that they committed the acts here complained of as a desperate plea to the American people and its government to stop the military madness which they sincerely believe will destroy us all, friend and enemy alike.

As I ponder over the punishment to be meted out to these two people who were attempting to unbuild weapons of mass destruction, we must ask ourselves: Can it be that those of us who build weapons to kill are engaged in a more sanctified endeavor than to see who would by their acts attempt to counsel moderation and mediation as an alternative method of settling international disputes? Why are we so fascinated by a power so great that we cannot comprehend its magnitude? What is so sacred about a bomb, so romantic about a missile? Why do we condemn and hang individual killers while extolling the virtues of warmongers? What is that fatal fascination which attracts us to the thought of mass destruction of our brethren in another country? How can we even entertain the thought that all people on one side of an imaginary line must die and, if we be so ungodly cynical as to countenance that thought, have we given thought to the fact that in executing that decree we will also die?

Who draws these lines and who has so decreed?

How many people in this democracy have seriously contemplated the futility of committing national suicide in order to punish our adversaries? Have we so little faith in our system of free enterprise, our capitalism, and the fundamental concepts that are taught us in our constitutions and in our several bibles that we must, in order to protect ourselves from the spread of foreign ideologies, be prepared to die at our own hands? Such thinking indicates a great deal of lack of faith in our democracy, our body politic, our people, and our institutions.

There are those in high places that believe Armageddon is soon to be upon us, that Christ will soon come to earth and take us all back with him to heaven. It would appear that much of our national effort is being is devoted to helping with the process. It may even be a celebration of sorts. When the bombs go off, Christ won't have to come to earth—we will all, believers and nonbelievers alike, meet him halfway.

The anomaly of this situation is that I am here called upon to punish two individuals who were charged with having caused damage to the property of a corporation in the amount of $33,000. It is this self-same corporation which only a few months ago was before me accused of having wrongfully embezzled from the U.S. government the sum of $3.6 million. The employees of this company succeeded in boosting the corporate profits by wrongfully and feloniously juggling the books. Since these individuals were all employees of the corporation, it appears that it did not occur to anyone in the office of the Attorney General of the United States that the actions of these men constituted a criminal conspiracy for which they might be punished. The government demanded only that Sperry pay back a mere 10 percent of the amount by which the corporation had been unlawfully enriched. Could it be that these corporate men who were working to build weapons of mass destruction received special treatment because of the nature of their work?

I am now called upon to determine the amount of restitution that is to be required of the two individuals who have done damage to the property of Sperry. The financial information obtained by the probation officers indicates that neither of the defendants owes any money to anyone. While Ms. Katt has no assets, Mr. Laforge is comparatively well endowed. He owns a 1968 Volkswagen, a guitar, a sleeping bag, and $200 in cash.

The inexorable pressure which generates from those who are engaged in making a living and a profit from building military equipment and the pork barreling that goes on in the halls of Congress to obtain more such contracts for the individual state will in the ultimate consume itself in an atomic holocaust. These same factors exert a powerful pressure upon a judge in my position to go along with the theory that there is something sacred about a bomb and that those who raise their voices or their hands against it should be struck down as enemies of the people, no matter that in their hearts they feel and know that they are friends of the people.

Now conduct of this sort cannot be condoned under the guise of free speech. Neither should it be totally condemned as being subversive, traitorous, or treasonous in the category of espionage or some other bad things. I would here in this instance take the sting out of the bomb, attempt in some way to force the government to remove the halo with which it seems to embrace any device which can kill, and to place instead thereon a shroud, the shroud of death, destruction, mutilation, disease, and debilitation.

If there is an adverse reaction to this sentence, I will anxiously await the protestations of those who complain of my attempts to correct the imbalance that now exists in a system that operates in such a manner as to provide one type of justice for the rich and a lesser type for the poor. One standard for the mighty and another for the weak. And a system which finds its humanness and objectivity is sublimated to military madness and the worship of the bomb.

A judge sitting here as I do is not called upon to do that which is politically expedient or popular but is called upon to exercise his calm and deliberate judgment in a manner best suited to accomplish and accommodate and vindicate the rights of the people acting through its government and the rights of those people who are the subject matter of such actions. The most popular thing to do at this particular time would be to sentence them to a 10 year period of imprisonment, and some judges might be disposed to do just that. [Thereupon, sentence was imposed: Six months in prison, was suspended, six months on probation.]

I am also aware of the thrust of the argument which would say this would encourage others to do likewise.

If others do likewise, they must be dealt with at that time.

I am also impressed with the argument that this might in some way constitute a disparity of sentence, that you individuals have not been properly punished for your offense because some others might not be deterred from doing that.

I really wonder about the constitutionality of sentencing one person for a crime that may be committed by another person at another time and place.

It is also difficult for me to equate the sentence I here give you - for destroying $36,000 worth of property, because you have been charged — with those who stole $3,600,000 worth of property and were not charged, demoted, or in any way punished.

My conscience is clear. We will adjourn the Court.

Reprinted from Northern Sun News

Class of Nonviolence

Patriotism or Peace
By Leo Tolstoy

Strange is the egotism of private individuals, but the egotists of private life are not armed, do not consider it right either to prepare or use arms against their adversaries; the egotism of private individuals is under the control of the political power and of public opinion. A private person who has a gun in his hand takes away his neighbor's cow, or a desyatina[1] of his crop, will immediately be seized by a policeman and put into prison. Besides, such a man will be condemned by public opinion — he will be called a thief and robber. It is quite different with the states: they are all armed – there is no power over them, except the comical attempts at catching a bird by pouring some salt on its tail — attempts at establishing international congresses, which, apparently, will never be accepted by the powerful states (who are armed for the very purpose that they might not pay attention to any one), and, above all, public opinion, which rebukes every act of violence in a private individual, extols, raises to the virtue of patriotism every appropriation of what belongs to others, for the increase of the power of the country.

Open the newspapers for any period you may wish, and at any moment you will see the black spot — the cause of every possible war: now it is Korea, now the Pamir[2], now the lands in Africa, Now Abyssinia, now Turkey, now Venezuela, now the Transvaal. The work of the robbers does not stop for a moment, and here and there a small war, like an exchange of shots in the cordon, is going on all the time, and the real war will begin at any moment.

If an American wishes the preferential grandeur and well-being of America above all other nations, and the same is desired by his state by an Englishman, and a Russian, and a Turk, and a Dutchman, and an Abyssinian, and a citizen of Venezuela and of the Transvaal, and an Armenian, and a Pole, and a Bohemian, and all of them are convinced that these desires need not only not be concealed or repressed, but should be a matter of pride and be developed in themselves and in others; and if the greatness and wellbeing of one country or nation cannot be obtained except to the detriment of another nation, frequently of many countries and nations — how can war be avoided?

And so, not to have any war, it is not necessary to preach and pray to God about peace, to persuade the English-speaking nations that they ought to be friendly toward one another; to marry princes to princesses of other nations — but to destroy what produces war. But what produces war is the desire for the exclusive good for one's own nation – what is called patriotism. And so to abolish war, it is necessary to abolish patriotism, and to abolish patriotism, it is necessary first to become convinced that it is an evil, and that is hard to do. Tell people that war is bad, and they will laugh at you: who does not know that? Tell them that patriotism is bad, and the majority of people will agree with you, but with a small proviso: "Yes, bad patriotism is bad, but there is also another patriotism, the one we adhere to." But wherein this good patriotism consists of no one can explain. If good patriotism consists in not being acquisitive, as many say, it is nonetheless retentive; that is, men want to retain what was formerly acquired, that is, by violence and murder. But even if patriotism is not retentive, it is restorative – the patriotism of the vanquished and oppressed nations, the Armenians, the Poles, Bohemians, Irish, and so forth. This patriotism is almost the very worst, because it is the most enraged and demands the greatest degree of violence.

Patriotism cannot be good. Why do not people say that egotism can be good, though this may be asserted more easily, because egotism is a natural sentiment, with which a man is born, while patriotism is an unnatural sentiment, which is artificially inoculated in him?

It will be said: "Patriotism has united men in states and keeps up the unity of the states." But the men are already united in states — the work is all done: why should men now maintain an exclusive loyalty for their state, when this loyalty produces calamities for all states and nations? The same patriotism which produced the unification of men into states is now destroying those states. If there were but one patriotism — the patriotism of none but the English — it might be regarded as unificatory or beneficent, but when, as now, there are American, English, German, French, Russian patriotisms, all of them opposed to one another, patriotism no longer unites, but disunites. To say that, if patriotism was beneficent, by uniting men into states,, as was the case during its highest development in Greece and Rome, patriotism even now, after 1,800 years of Christian life, is just as beneficent, is the same as saying that, since ploughing was useful and beneficent for the field before the sowing, it will be useful now, after the crop has grown up.

It would be very well to retain patriotism in memory of the use which it once had, as people preserve and retain the ancient monuments of temples, as mausoleums stand, without causing any harm to man, while patriotism produces without cessation innumerable calamities.

What now causes the Armenians and the Turks to suffer and cut each others throats and act like wild beasts? Why do England and Russia, each of them concerned about her share of the inheritance from Turkey, lie in wait and not put a stop to the Armenian atrocities? Why do the Abyssinians and Italians fight one another? Why did a terrible war come very near breaking out on account of Venezuela and now on account of the Transvaal? And the Chino-Japanese War, and the Turkish, and the German, and the French wars? And the rage of subdued nations, the Armenians, the Poles, the Irish? And the preparation for war by all the nations? All that is the fruits of patriotism. Seas of blood have been shed for the sake of this sentiment, and more blood will be shed for its sake, if men do not free themselves from this outlived bit of antiquity.

C'est à prendre ou à laisser[3], as the French say. If patriotism is good, then Christianity, which gives peace, is an idle dream, and the sooner this teaching is eradicated, the better. But if Christianity really gives peace, and we really want peace, patriotism is a survival from barbarous times, which must not only be evoked and educated, as we do now, but which must be eradicated by all means, by preaching, persuasion, contempt and ridicule. If Christianity is the truth, and we wish to live in peace, we must but only have no sympathy for the power of our country, but must even rejoice in its weakening, and contribute to it.

Class of Nonviolence

A Russian must rejoice when Poland, the Baltic provinces, Finland, Armenia, are separated from Russia and made free; and an Englishman must similarly rejoice in relation to Ireland, Australia, India, and the other colonies and cooperate in it, because the greater the country, the more evil and cruel is its patriotism, and the greater is the amount of the suffering on which its power is based. And so, if we actually want to be what we profess, we must not, as we do now, wish for the increase of our country, but wish for its diminution and weakening, and contribute to it with all our means. And thus must we educate the younger generations: we must bring up the younger generations in such a way that, as it is now disgraceful for a young man to manifest his coarse egotism, for example, by eating everything up, without leaving anything for others, to push a weaker person down from the road, in order to pass by himself, to take away by force what another needs, it should be just as disgraceful to wish for the increase of his country's power; and as it now is considered stupid and ridiculous for a person to praise himself, it should be considered stupid to extol one's nations, as is now done in various lying patriotic histories, pictures, monuments, textbooks, articles. sermons, and stupid national hymns. But it must be understood that so long as we are going to extol patriotism and educate the younger generations in it, we shall have armaments, which ruin the physical and spiritual life of our nations, and wars, terrible, horrible wars, like those for which we are preparing ourselves, and into the circle of which we are introducing, corrupting them with our patriotism, the new, terrible fighters of the distant East.

In reply to a prince's question on how to increase his army, in order to conquer a southern tribe which did not submit to him, Confucius replied, "Destroy all thy army, and use the money, which thou art wasting now on the army, on the enlightenment of thy people and on the improvement of agriculture, and the southern tribe will drive away its prince and will submit to thy rule without war."

_____

[1] A desyatina is a Russian unit of land measurement, about 2.7 acres
[2] The Pamir is a mountainous region of central Asia, located mainly in Tajikistan and extending into NE Afghanistan and SW Xinjiang Uygur Autonomous Region, China; called the "roof of the world."
[3] Take it or leave it.

What Would You Do if?
By Joan Baez

Fred: OK. So you're a pacifist. What would you do if someone were, say, attacking your grandmother?

Joan: Attacking my poor old grandmother?

Fred: Yeah, you're in a room with your grandmother and there's a guy about to attack her and you're standing there. What would you do?

Joan: I'd yell, "Three cheers for Grandma!" and leave the room."

Fred: No, seriously. Say he had a gun and he was about to shoot her. Would you shoot him first?

Joan: Do I have a gun?

Fred: Yes

Joan: No. I'm a pacifist, I don't have a gun.

Fred: Well, I say you do.

Joan: All right. Am I a good shot?

Fred: Yes.

Joan: I'd shoot the gun out of his hand.

Fred: No, then you're not a good shot.

Joan: I'd be afraid to shoot. Might kill grandma.

Fred: Come on, OK, look. We'll take another example. Say, you're driving a truck. You're on a narrow road with a sheer cliff on your side. There's a little girl sitting in the middle of the road. You're going too fast to stop. What would you do?

Joan: I don't know. What would you do?

Fred: I'm asking you. You're the pacifist.

Joan: Yes, I know. All right, am I in control of the truck?

Fred: Yes

Joan: How about if I honk my horn so she can get out of the way?

Fred: She's too young to walk. And the horn doesn't work.

Joan: I swerve around to the left of her since she's not going anywhere.

Fred: No, there's been a landslide.

Joan: Oh. Well then, I would try to drive the truck over the cliff and save the little girl.

Silence

Fred: Well, say there's someone else in the truck with you. Then what?

Joan: What's my decision have to do with my being a pacifist?

Fred: There's two of you in the truck and only one little girl.

Joan: Someone once said if you have a choice between a real evil and a hypothetical evil, always take the real one.

Fred: Huh?

Joan:: I said, why are you so anxious to kill off all the pacifists?

Fred: I'm not. I just want to know what you'd do if...

Joan: If I was in a truck with a friend driving very fast on a one-lane road approaching a dangerous impasse where a ten-month old girl is sitting in the middle of the road with a landslide on one side of her and a sheer drop-off on the other.

Fred: That's right.

Joan: I would probably slam on the brakes, thus sending my friend through the windscreen, skid into the landslide, run over the little girl, sail off the cliff and plunge to my own death. No doubt Grandma's house would be at the bottom of the ravine and the truck would crash through her roof and blow up in her living room where she was finally being attacked for the first, and last, time.

Fred: You haven't answered my question. You're just trying to get out of it...

Joan: I'm really trying to say a couple of things. One is that no one knows what they'll do in a moment of crisis and hypothetical questions get hypothetical answers. I'm also hinting that you've made it impossible for me to come out of the situation without having killed one or more people. Then you say, 'Pacifism is a nice idea, but it won't work'. But that's not what bothers me.

Fred: What bothers you?

Joan: Well, you might not like it because it's not hypothetical. It's real. And it makes the assault on Grandma look like a garden party.

Fred: What's that?

Joan: I'm thinking about how we put people through a training process so they'll find out the really good, efficient ways of killing. Nothing incidental like trucks and landslides. Just the opposite, really. You know, how to growl and yell, kill and crawl and jump out of airplanes. Real organized stuff. Hell, you have to be able to run a bayonet through Grandma's middle.

Fred: That's something entirely different.

Joan: Sure. And don't you see it's much harder to look at, because its real, and it's going on right now? Look. A general sticks a pin into a map. A week later a bunch of young boys are sweating it out in a jungle somewhere, shooting each other's arms and legs off, crying, praying and losing control of their bowels. Doesn't it seem stupid to you?

Fred: Well, you're talking about war.

Joan: Yes, I know. Doesn't it seem stupid to you?

Fred: What do you do instead, then? Turn the other cheek, I suppose.

Joan: No. Love thine enemy but confront his evil. Love thine enemy. Thou shalt not kill.

Fred: Yeah, and look what happened to him.

Joan: He grew up.

Fred: They hung him on a damn cross is what happened to him. I don't want to get hung on a damn cross.

Joan: You won't.

Fred: Huh?

Joan: I said you don't get to choose how you're going to die. Or when. You can only decide how you are going to live. Now.

Fred: Well, I'm not going to go letting everybody step all over me, that's for sure.

Joan: Jesus said, "Resist not evil." The pacifist says just the opposite. He says to resist evil with all your heart and with all your mind and body until it has been overcome.

Fred: I don't get it.

Joan: Organized nonviolent resistance. Gandhi. He organized the Indians for nonviolent resistance and waged nonviolent war against the British until he'd freed India from the British Empire. Not bad for a first try, don't you think?

Fred: Yeah, fine, but he was dealing with the British, a civilized people. We're not.

Joan: Not a civilized people?

Fred: Not dealing with a civilized people. You just try some of that stuff on the Russians.

Joan: You mean the Chinese, don't you?

Fred: Yeah, the Chinese, try it on the Chinese.

Joan: Oh, dear. War was going on long before anybody dreamed up communism. It's just the latest justification for self-righteousness. The problem isn't communism. The problem is consensus. There's a consensus out there that it's OK to kill when your government decides who to kill. If you kill inside the country, you get in trouble. If you kill outside the country, right time, right season, latest enemy, you get a medal. There are about 130 nation-states, and each of them thinks it's a swell idea to bump off all the rest because he is more important. The pacifist thinks there is only one tribe. Three billion members. They come first. We think killing any member of the family is a dumb idea. We think there are more decent and intelligent ways of settling differences. And man had better start investigating these other possibilities because if he doesn't, then by mistake or by design, he will probably kill off the whole damn race.

Fred: It's human nature to kill. Something you can't change.

Joan: Is it? If it's natural to kill, why do men have to go into training to learn how? There's violence in human nature, but there's also decency, love, kindness. Man organizes, buys, sells, pushes violence. The nonviolent wants to organize the opposite side. That's all nonviolence is – organized love.

Fred: You're crazy.

Joan: No doubt. Would you care to tell me the rest of the world is sane? Tell me that violence has been a great success for the past five thousand years, that the world is in fine shape, that wars have brought peace, understanding, democracy, and freedom to humankind and that killing each other has created an atmosphere of trust and hope. That it's grand for one billion people to live off of the other two billion, or that even if it hadn't been smooth going all along, we are now at last beginning to see our way though to a better world for all, as soon as we get a few minor wars out of the way.

Fred: I'm doing OK

Joan: Consider it a lucky accident.

Fred: I believe I should defend America and all that she stands for. Don't you believe in self-defense?

Joan: No, that's how the mafia got started. A little band of people who got together to protect peasants. I'll take Gandhi's nonviolent resistance.

Fred: I still don't get the point of nonviolence.

Joan: The point of nonviolence is to build a floor, a strong new floor, beneath which we can no longer sink. A platform which stands a few feet above napalm, torture, exploitation, poison gas, nuclear bombs, the works. Give man a decent place to stand. He's been wallowing around in human blood and vomit and burnt flesh, screaming how it's going to bring peace to the world. He sticks his head out of the hole for a minute and sees a bunch of people gathering together and trying to build a structure above ground in the fresh air. 'Nice idea, but not very practical', he shouts and slides back into the hole. It was the same kind of thing when man found out the world was round. He fought for years to have it remain flat, with every proof on hand that it was not flat at all. It had no edge to drop off or sea monsters to swallow up his little ship in their gaping jaws.

Fred: How are you going to build this practical structure?

Joan: From the ground up. By studying, experimenting with every possible alternative to violence on every level. By learning how to say no to the nation-state, 'NO' to war taxes, 'NO' to military conscription, 'NO' to killing in general, 'YES' to co-operation, by starting new institutions which are based on the assumption that murder in any form is ruled out, by making and keeping in touch with nonviolent contacts all over the world, by engaging ourselves at every possible chance in dialogue with people, groups, to try to change the consensus that it's OK to kill.

Fred: It sounds real nice, but I just don't think it can work.

Joan: You are probably right. We probably don't have enough time. So far, we've been a glorious flop. The only thing that's been a worse flop than the organization of nonviolence has been the organization of violence.

Pray for Peace but Pay for War?
by Maurice F. McCrackin

Maurice F. McCrackin, born in 1905, was a Presbyterian pastor in Cincinnati, Ohio. In 1948 he stopped paying his federal income tax because a portion of the tax would be used for military affairs war preparations. He stopped filing his returns in 1957 because they aided the revenue department in collecting the taxes. When he was subpoenaed to appear in court with his financial records, he refused He was carried into the courtroom and sentenced to six months in jail. On his release, the Cincinnati Presbytery censured him and in 1960 suspended him from the ministry. This is his statement to the presbytery during his trial.

I do not think of the defense in this trial as a defense of me as a person, but rather the defense of a principle and that, the right of a Christian, yes, a Presbyterian Christian to follow what he believes to be God's will as it has been shown to him in Jesus Christ. In June 1945 I was offered the position of co-pastor of the West Cincinnati St. Barnabas Church. Since the church was in a racially inclusive neighborhood and because of my deep interest in church union and cooperation, I gladly accepted the opportunity to share in this venture undertaken by the Episcopal and Presbyterian denominations, and began work in August of the same summer. Two months later we opened a settlement house at what was the St. Barnabas Episcopal Church building. Before the federation of the two congregations Negroes were not welcome at either church, and so children and teenagers came by the hundreds to enjoy the activities at the new settlement house. Soon we organized a community council and tried to come to grips with community problems. Ties in church and settlement house were growing strong and meaningful. Camp Joy opened to children of all races and creeds, and with integrated camping and a racially mixed staff, children and teenaged young people grew in self-awareness and in respect and love for one another.

All the while our community work was expanding, cold war tensions were increasing. Nuclear bombs were fast being stockpiled and reports were heard of new and deadlier weapons about to be made. Fresh in my mind were the bombed cities of Hiroshima and Nagasaki. In the crowded, deprived areas of these two cities were people working as we were now working in Cincinnati to build a happier, healthier community. There were nurses, teachers, domestic workers, laborers, and secretaries. There were babies, children, young people, and adults living together, playing and working together, and praying together. The bomb fell and they, their institutions, their community organizations, all were destroyed.

It came to me that if churches, settlement houses, schools, if anything is to survive in Cincinnati or anywhere else, something must be done about the armaments race, a race which has always resulted in war. I preached against violence, against hatred, against wars, cold or hot. I preached about the dangers which the entire world faced and which had been made so vividly clear by renowned scientists. I was preaching, but what was I doing? We must build peace in our local communities; this we were doing but what about the international community? When I thought of Hiroshima and Nagasaki and of other cities in so-called enemy countries, which we were preparing to incinerate with even more deadly and devastating weapons, I said to myself, "I can no more give consent to the committing of this terrible atrocity against cities in Japan, Russia, or any other country than I would give my consent to such acts of barbaric cruelty being committed against my friends and neighbors surrounding the church and neighborhood house."

Long before, I had decided that I would never again register for the draft nor would I consent to being conscripted by the government in any capacity. Nevertheless each year around March 15 without protest I sent my tax payments to the government. By giving my money I was helping the government do what I so vigorously declared was wrong. I would never give my money to support a house of prostitution or the liquor industry, a gambling house or for the purchase and distribution of pornographic literature. Yet year after year I had unquestionably been giving my money to an evil infinitely greater than all of these put together, since it is from war's aftermath that nearly all social ills stem.

Income tax paid by the individual is essential to the continuance of the war machine. Over 50 percent of the military budget is paid for by individuals through their income tax payments and 75 to 80 percent of every dollar they pay via income tax goes for war purposes.

Again I examined what the principle of personal commitment to Jesus meant to me. Through the years I have tried to achieve a personal relationship with Jesus. This is the burden of the Christian gospel, that Jesus can be known personally and that he can bring a saving power into a man's life. For us Christians to know Jesus personally has reality only as we try earnestly to grow more like him "unto the measure of the stature of his fullness." If we follow Jesus afar off, if we praise his life and teachings but conclude that neither applies to our daily living, what are we doing but denying and rejecting him? Jesus speaks with authority and with love to every individual. "Follow me. Take up your cross. Love one another as I have loved you." What would Jesus want me to do in relation to war? What must I do if am his disciple? This was the conclusion I reached: If I can honestly say that Jesus would support conscription, throw a hand grenade, or with a flame thrower drive men out of caves, to become living torches—if I believe he would release the bomb over Hiroshima or Nagasaki, then I not only have the right to do these things as a Christian, I am even obligated to do them. But if, as a committed follower, I believe that Jesus would do none of these things, I have no choice but to refuse at whatever personal cost, to support war. This means that I will not serve in the armed forces nor will I voluntarily give my money to help make war possible.

Having had this awakening, I could no longer in good conscience continue full payment of my federal taxes. At the same time I did not want to withdraw my support from the civilian services which the government offers. For that reason I continued to pay the small percentage now allocated for civilian use. The amount which I had formerly given for war I now hoped to give to such causes as the American Friends Service Committee's program and to other works of mercy and reconciliation which help to remove the roots of war.

As time went on I realized, however, that this was not accomplishing its purpose because year after year the government ordered my bank to release money from my account to pay the tax I had held back. I then closed my checking account and by some method better known to the Internal Revenue Service than to me, it was discovered that I had money in a savings and loan company. Orders were given to this firm, under threat of prosecution, to surrender from my account the amount the government said I owed. I then realized suddenly how far government is now invading individual rights and privileges: money is given in trust to a firm to be kept in safety and the government coerces this firm's trustees into a violation of that trust. But even more evil than this invasion of rights is the violence done to the individual conscience in forcing him to give financial support to a thing he feels so deeply is wrong. I agree wholeheartedly with the affirmation of Presbytery made in February of 1958, that, "A Christian citizen is obligated to God to obey the law but when in conscience he finds the requirements of law to be in direct conflict with his obedience to God, he must obey God rather than man."

Disobedience to a civil law is an act against government, but obedience to a civil law that is evil is an act against God.

At this point it came to me with complete clarity that by so much as filing tax returns I was giving to the revenue department assistance in the violation of my own conscience, because the very information I had been giving on my tax forms was being used in finally making the collection. So from this point on, or until there is a radical change for the better in government spending I shall file no returns.

The nations seem unable to agree on any negotiated disarmament, and certainly there is little hope that in the foreseeable future any will do so unilaterally. At no time in human history, therefore, has there been such an acute necessity for individuals to disarm unilaterally, to behave as moral and responsible human beings, and to do what they know to be right, beginning now. Some have said that this is the age of the common man. However, if we are to survive, it must become the age of the uncommon man. Unilateral, personal disarmament means that we will accept only work which contributes to the peace, welfare, and uplift of mankind. One by one people are responsible for the most horrible crimes. These are not bad people; they are good people, many socially concerned, pillars of church and society. Yet, with little or no inward protest they respond to the state's demands to do all kinds of ghastly jobs—to perfect the H-bomb or the more terrible cobalt bomb, to work in laboratories to perfect still more deadly nerve gas or to help spawn insects which will be more deadly germ carriers. The state persuades these and others that they are not really responsible for what they are doing, that they are only small cogs in a big machine and if they have guilt it is so slight they shouldn't worry over it.

Leo Tolstoy described this evil process of rationalization in his book The Kingdom of God Is within You. He asks, "Is it possible that millions of men can go on calmly committing deeds which are so manifestly criminal, such as are the murders and tortures they commit, simply from fear of punishment? Surely these things would not exist were not the falsehood and brutality of their actions hidden from all classes of men by the system of political organization. When such deeds are committed, there are so many instigators, participants, and abettors that no single individual feels himself morally responsible. The rulers of the state always endeavor to involve the greatest number of citizens in the participation of the crimes which it is to their interest to have committed. Some demand it, some confirm it, some order it, and some execute it."

This evil chain of violence and death must be broken and it will be broken when enough individuals say to the state, "You may order me to do something I believe wrong but I will not execute your command. You may order me to kill, but I will not kill nor will I give my money to buy weapons that others may do so." There are other voices that I must obey. I must obey the voice of humanity which cries for peace and relief from the intolerable burden of armaments and conscription. I must obey the voice of conscience, made sensitive by the inner light of truth. I must obey the voice heard across the centuries, "Love your enemies, pray for those who despitefully use you and persecute you." In obedience to these voices lies the only path to brotherhood and peace. And these are the voices I must obey.

From Instead of Violence, Beacon Press, Boston 1963

A Vigil for Life While We Celebrate Death
by Colman McCarthy

Ten years ago this week, William Thomas, a practitioner of the First Amendment as well as a believer in it, took up residence on the sidewalk across from 1600 Pennsylvania Ave. Since then, he and others have formed an above-ground underground, a small collection of antiwar demonstrators who have been the closest neighbors to the country's last two pro-war presidents. They have turned Lafayette Park into Peace Park.

On this weekend as Washington's widest streets are commandeered by the Pentagon and military contractors to parade their hirelings and machines that did the slaughtering of at least 100,000 people in Iraq, Thomas will counter the mindless celebration of death with a vigil for life.

In front of the White House, he passes out pacifist literature, holds up antiwar signs, and keeps on being, in a decade of iron tenacity, the defiant citizen with whom Amos, Isaiah, St. Francis, Tom Paine, Eugene Debs, Emma Goldman, and other incorrigibles would link arms were they to return.

Like all of those connoisseurs of dissent, Thomas has paid heavily for his disaffections with warlords and their authority. He has endured more than 40 arrests, with about a dozen convictions for civil disobedience. His jail time has been mostly weekends, except for a 90-day stretch for unauthorized camping. The National Park Service has been dogged in its efforts to block Thomas from being a happy camper. Regulations sprout from NPS like springtime tulips in the White House flowerbed.

The doubting Thomas is a short and sturdily built man who was in the jewelry business until 1975 when he took to heart a biblical passage about placing total trust in God. With few such absolutists on the planet, an Episcopal priest, the Rev. J. Ellen Nunally, who is also an English professor at George Mason University, has devoted the past year to interviewing Thomas and his peace vigilers. In time, she will write a book, one that goes beyond the first impressions that this is a sidewalk commune of nomads to reveal the group to be motivated by authentic religious ideals and democratic instincts. Others have found this to be true, including a teacher from a public high school three blocks away who invites Thomas to come discuss civics with students.

As America's most visible antiwar group, and having the choicest real estate outside of the Rose Garden, Thomas and his weather-beaten friends are as accustomed to federal harassment as they are to being dismissed by the media as semi-loonies who, quaintly, prove that the First Amendment works: Tolerating a few sidewalk eccentrics verifies the superiority of the American system. The self-congratulation also allows the champions of the system to look away when prophets like Thomas show up with a suggestion or two on how governments could be truly humane if peacemaking were done in earnest.

The current suggestion from Peace Park is Proposition One, a proposed constitutional amendment that would require nuclear disarmament and create programs for converting weapons industries into peacetime industries. A Proposition One Committee has been formed to help organize state peace groups to get on voter initiative ballots.

The idea is visionary, revolutionary, and unwieldy, and has everything going against it except for one plus: The goal of Proposition One is what George Bush and Mikhail Gorbachev have been proclaiming since each took office. By putting the idea of disarmament to a vote, the Peace Park initiative is acting on the thought of Dwight Eisenhower: "I like to believe that people in the long run are going to do more to promote peace than are governments. Indeed, I think that people want peace so much that one of these days governments had better get out of their way and let them have it."

When that happens, William Thomas will pack up and give over his space in Peace Park to the squirrels, who had it first. He'll donate his sign, "Trust God and Disarm Everywhere," to the Smithsonian and vanish. "I don't favor national boundaries, armies, or governments—not because they're evil but because they aren't necessary," he said the other morning on bench near his sentry as Park Service mowers cut the lawn. "All that's necessary is a wholehearted belief In a God of love and life. The test of that wholeheartedness is the action it produces toward creating a peaceful world. "

As a major tourist attraction in Washington—free of charge, round the clock, accessible, and memorable—Peace Park and its keepers are a reminder this weekend that George Bush doesn't understand what's directly in front of his nose. On March 1st he said: "There is no antiwar movement."

From Washington Post, June 9, 1991

Questions for Lesson Seven

1. Write an essay entitled "Developing the attitude of a peacemaker."

2. Write an essay about your feelings and opinions concerning civil disobedience. Does going to jail for your disobedience really change anything?

3. Explain how the concept of satyagraha applies to Poland's resistance to the Soviet Union.

4. What do you think the concept of "turning the other cheek" means in the context of resisting violence and / or aggression.

5. What would you do if America was ever invaded by a hostile force?

Readings for Lesson Eight

Animals, My Brethren
by Edgar Kupfer-Koberwitz

Interview on Respect for Animals
by Isaac Bashevis Singer

A Vegetarian Sourcebook
by Keith Akers

Diet for a New America
by John Robbins

Diet for a Small Planet
by Frances Moore Lappé

'Terrorists' for Animal Rights
by Colman McCarthy

Animals, My Brethren
by Edgar Kupfer-Koberwitz

The following pages were written in the Concentration Camp Dachau, in the midst of all kinds of cruelties. They were furtively scrawled in a hospital barrack where I stayed during my illness, in a time when Death grasped day by day after us, when we lost twelve thousand within four and a half months.

Dear Friend:

You asked me why I do not eat meat and you are wondering at the reasons of my behavior. Perhaps you think I took a vow ~ some kind of penitence ~ denying me all the glorious pleasures of eating meat. You remember juicy steaks, succulent fishes, wonderfully tasted sauces, deliciously smoked ham and thousand a wonders prepared out of meat, charming thousands of human palates; certainly you will remember the delicacy of roasted chicken. Now, you see, I am refusing all these pleasures and you think that only penitence, or a solemn vow, a great sacrifice could deny me that manner of enjoying life, induce me to endure a great resignment.

You look astonished, you ask the question: "But why and what for?" And you are wondering that you nearly guessed the very reason. But if I am, now, trying to explain to you the very reason in one concise sentence, you will be astonished once more how far your guessing had been from my real motive. Listen to what I have to tell you:

- I refuse to eat animals because I cannot nourish myself by the sufferings and by the death of other creatures. I refuse to do so, because I suffered so painfully myself that I can feel the pains of others by recalling my own sufferings.
- I feel happy, nobody persecutes me; why should I persecute other beings or cause them to be persecuted?
- I feel happy, I am no prisoner, I am free; why should I cause other creatures to be made prisoners and thrown into jail?
- I feel happy, nobody harms me; why should I harm other creatures or have them harmed?
- I feel happy, nobody wounds me; nobody kills me; why should I wound or kill other creatures or cause them to be wounded or killed for my pleasure and convenience?
- Is it not only too natural that I do not inflict on other creatures the same thing which, I hope and fear, will never be inflicted on me? Would it not be most unfair to do such things for no other purpose than for enjoying a trifling physical pleasure at the expense of others' sufferings, others' deaths?

These creatures are smaller and more helpless than I am, but can you imagine a reasonable man of noble feelings who would like to base on such a difference a claim or right to abuse the weakness and the smallness of others? Don't you think that it is just the bigger, the stronger, the superior's duty to protect the weaker creatures instead of persecuting them, instead of killing them? "Noblesse oblige." I want to act in a noble way.

I recall the horrible epoch of inquisition and I am sorry to state that the time of tribunals for heretics has not yet passed by, that day by day, men used to cook in boiling water other creatures which are helplessly given in the hands of their torturers. I am horrified by the idea that such men are civilized people, no rough barbarians, no natives. But in spite of all, they are only primitively civilized, primitively adapted to their cultural environment. The average European, flowing over with highbrow ideas and beautiful speeches, commits all kinds of cruelties, smilingly, not because he is compelled to do so, but because he wants to do so. Not because he lacks the faculty to reflect upon and to realize all the dreadful things they are performing. Oh no! Only because they do not want to see the facts. Otherwise they would be troubled and worried in their pleasures.

It is quite natural what people are telling you. How could they do otherwise? I hear them telling about experiences, about utilities, and I know that they consider certain acts related to slaughtering as unavoidable. Perhaps they succeeded to win you over. I guess that from your letter.

Still, considering the necessities only, one might, perhaps, agree with such people. But is there really such a necessity? The thesis may be contested. Perhaps there exists still some kind of necessity for such persons who have not yet developed into full conscious personalities.

I am not preaching to them. I am writing this letter to you, to an already awakened individual who rationally controls his impulses, who feels responsible — internally and externally — of his acts, who knows that our supreme court is sitting in our conscience. There is no appellate jurisdiction against it.

Is there any necessity by which a fully self-conscious man can be induced to slaughter? In the affirmative, each individual may have the courage to do it by his own hands. It is, evidently, a miserable kind of cowardice to pay other people to perform the blood-stained job, from which the normal man refrains in horror and dismay. Such servants are given some farthings for their bloody work, and one buys from them the desired parts of the killed animal — if possible prepared in such a way that it does not any more recall the discomfortable circumstances, nor the animal, nor its being killed, nor the bloodshed. I think that men will be killed and tortured as long as animals are killed and tortured. So long there will be wars too. Because killing must be trained and perfected on smaller objects, morally and technically.

I see no reason to feel outraged by what others are doing, neither by the great nor by the smaller acts of violence and cruelty. But, I think, it is high time to feel outraged by all the small and great acts of violence and cruelty which we perform ourselves. And because it is much easier to win the smaller battles than the big ones, I think we should try to get over first our own trends towards smaller violence and cruelty, to avoid, or better, to overcome them once and for all. Then the day will come when it will be easy for us to fight and to overcome even the great cruelties. But we are still sleeping, all of us, in habitudes and inherited attitudes. They are like a fat, juicy sauce which helps us to swallow our own cruelties without tasting their bitterness.

I have not the intention to point out with my finger at this and that, at definite persons and definite situations. I think it is much more my duty to stir up my own conscience in smaller matters, to try to understand other people better, to get better and less selfish. Why should it be impossible then to act accordingly with regard to more important issues?

That is the point: I want to grow up into a better world where a higher law grants more happiness, in a new world where God's commandment reigns: You Shall Love Each Other.

Edgar Kupfer was imprisoned in Dachau concentration camp in 1940. His last 3 years in Dachau he obtained a clerical job in the concentration camp storeroom. This position allowed him to keep a secret diary on stolen scraps of papers and pieces of pencil. He would bury his writings and when Dachau was liberated on April 29, 1945 he collected them again. The "Dachau Diaries" were published in 1956. From his Dachau notes he wrote an essay on vegetarianism which was translated into "immigrant" English. A carbon copy of this 38 page essay is preserved with the original Dachau Diaries in the Special Collection of the Library of the University of Chicago. Theabove are the excerpts from this essay that were reprinted in the postscript of the book "Radical Vegetarianism" by Mark Mathew Braunstein (1981 Panjandrum Books, Los Angeles, CA).

Respect for Animals
interview with Isaac Bashevis Singer

Twice a winner of the National Book Award, Isaac Bashevis Singer was awarded the Nobel Prize for Literature in 1978. Singer's enormous popularity and stature in the United States is the more astonishing since his first language-the language in which he thinks and creates-is Yiddish. He once joked that his writing must be 150 percent better than it appears "because you lose 50 percent in the translation." Even though Singer speaks German and Polish and has a good command of English, he prefers to write in Yiddish because he feels that "it has vitamins that other languages haven't got." Consequently, he is the first writer to have received a Nobel Prize who writes in a language for which there is no country. Singer was born July 14th, 1904, in Radzymin, Poland. Both of his grandfathers were rabbis as was his father. It is difficult to imagine more unfavorable auspices for a young novelist than to be forced into exile from his native land at the age of 31 with a gift of eloquence in a language that was becoming extinct. Had anyone suggested in 1935 (the year of Singer's emigration to America) that a Polish refugee, writing in a language silenced by the Holocaust, would receive the Nobel Prize for Literature in 1978, Isaac Singer would have been the first to laugh.

How long have you been a vegetarian?
I've been a vegetarian for 14 years.

What do you usually eat in the course of a day?
I eat what I like. In the morning I have some skim milk and hardboiled eggs. For lunch I take a sandwich that consists of toast, sliced tomatoes, and cottage cheese. In the evenings, some vegetables. This is more or less how it goes every day.

Have you felt better since you became a vegetarian?
Since I didn't do it to feel better, I never measure it by that. I feel that I'm right. This is the main thing.

I once read that it was Spinoza's notion that man can do as he likes to animals which repelled you from eating meat.
Yes. I don't say that this passage made me a vegetarian, but I felt, when I read it, a great protest. I thought, if we can do to animals whatever we please, why can't another man come with a theory that we can do to human beings what we please? This did not make me a vegetarian. I was in my mind a vegetarian before-because when I read this I was revolted. And though I love Spinoza and always admired him (and I still do), I did not like this text.

Many of your own stories treat the subject of vegetarianism. Do you use vegetarian leitmotifs intentionally?
I would say that of course I never sit down to write a story with this intention, with a vegetarian tendency or morality. I wouldn't preach. I don't believe in messages. But

sometimes if you believe in something, it will come out. Whenever I mention animals, I feel there is a great, great injustice in the fact they are treated the way they are.

I've noticed that you use butchers and slaughtermen to represent evil.
Well, I'm inclined to do so. If a character's a ruffian, I would make him a butcher-although some of them are very nice people.

In the story Blood was it your intention to show that people who traffic in animal flesh have something rapacious about them?
What I wanted to show was that the desire for blood has an affinity with lust.
In **Blood**, the female character, Risha, first seduces the ritual slaughterer Reuben, then insists on killing the animals herself. She sets up as a nonkosher butcher, and, as though following a logical progression, finally becomes a. . .

She becomes a werewolf. Do humans who eat meat become predators?
In shedding blood there is always an element of lust.

At the beginning of the story, you mentioned that the Cabalists knew that blood and lust are related, and that's why the commandment "Thou shalt not commit adultery" immediately follows the injunction against killing.
Yes, but I feel so myself. There is always an element of sadism in lust and vice versa.

Do you feel that people who eat meat are just as reprehensible as the slaughterer?
The people who eat meat are not conscious of the actual slaughter. Those who do the hunting, the hunters, are, I would say, in the grip of a sexual passion. Those who eat meat share in the guilt, but since they're not conscious of the actual slaughter, they believe it is a natural thing. I would not want to accuse them of inadvertent slaughter. But they are not brought up to believe in compassion.

I would say that it would be better for humanity to stop eating meat and stop torturing these animals. I always say that if we don't stop treating these animals the way we do, we will never have any rest.
I think other people are bothered by meat-eating too, but they say to themselves: "What can I do!" They're afraid that if they stop eating meat they will die from hunger. I've been a vegetarian for so many years-thank God I'm still alive!

I've also noticed that in The Slaughterer, you say that the phylacteries . . .... are made of leather, yes. I'm always conscious of it. Even the Torah is made from hide. And I feel that this somehow is wrong. Then you say, or have the character in The Slaughter say, "Father in heaven, Thou art a slaughterer!"
Didn't we just have an earthquake in Turkey where thousands of innocent people died? We don't know His mysteries and motivations. But I sometimes feel like praying to a vegetarian god.

Do you feel that people who eat meat are evil?
Well, I wouldn't go so far. I don't want to say this about all the people who eat meat. There were many saints who ate meat, very many wonderful people. I don't want to say evil things

about people who eat meat. I only like to say that I'm against it. My vegetarianism is in fact a kind of protest against the laws of nature, because actually the animals would suffer whether we ate them or not. Whatever the case, I am for vegetarianism.

In previous interviews you have stated that like the Cabalists you feel that this is a fallen world, the worst of possible worlds.
This is what the Cabalists believe. I don't know all the worlds. All I can see is that this world is a terrible world.

Do you think meat-eating contributes to the triumph of evil throughout the world?
To me, it is an evil thing—slaughter is an evil thing.

Do you think the world might be improved if we stopped the slaughter?
I think so. At least we should try. I think, as a rule, a vegetarian is not a murderer, he is not a criminal. I believe that a man who becomes a vegetarian because he has compassion with animals is not going to kill people or be cruel to people. When one becomes a vegetarian it purifies the soul.

In an interview that you gave to Commentary in the mid-1960s, you mentioned that you were something of a scholar in spiritual matters.
Scholar? I wouldn't consider myself a scholar.

Well, do you think that animal souls also participate in the spiritual world?
Well, I have no doubt about it. As a matter of fact, I have a great love for animals that don't eat any meat.

Many of the great poets and philosophers of classical antiquity look back with nostalgia on a golden age in which war, murder, and crime were unknown, food was abundant, and everyone was vegetarian. Do you think that if people became vegetarian again they would become better people?
Yes. According to the Bible, it seems that God did not want people to eat meat. And, in many cases where people became very devout, or very pious, they stopped eating meat and drinking wine. Many vegetarians are anti-alcoholic, although I am not.

I think one loses desire for intoxicants when one becomes a vegetarian it purifies the body.
I think it purifies the soul.

Do you believe in the transmigration of souls?
There's no scientific evidence of it, but I personally am inclined to believe in it. According to the Cabalists, when people sin, they become animals in the next life, sometimes ferocious animals, like tigers and snakes. I wouldn't be surprised if it were true.

Do you believe in the actual manifestations of demons in the physical world?
I believe it—yes. I mean, I don't know what they are. I'm sure that if they exist, they are part of nature; but I feel that there are beings that we haven't yet discovered. Just as we discovered only about two hundred years ago the existence of microbes and bacteria, there is no reason

why we shouldn't one day discover some other beings. We do not know everything that goes on around us.

So you think there are malevolent spirits in the world today?
I think there may be such spirits or astral bodies-I don't know what to call them. Since I've never seen them or contacted them, everything I say is just guesswork. But I feel there may be entities of which we have no inkling. Just the same, they exist and influence our life just as bacteria and microbes did without our knowing it.

Do you think, on the other hand, that there are benevolent spirits?
Yes, I do. There is a great possibility of it.

Do you wear leather and articles of clothing made from animals?
I try not to, but I can never get the kind of shoes that are not, although I'm going to do something about it. What about you? Do you wear leather shoes?

No, I don't wear anything that could cost an animal his life.
Tell me the name of the place where I can get these shoes that you wear.
I can send you the name of a mail order shoe company where you can get them.
Do me a favor and please do.

I shall. There's a mail order firm in Patterson, New Jersey - The Haband Co. ~ which makes shoes of nothing but synthetic leather.
They're not to be gotten in stores?

You can get them, if you're willing to make a canvass of all the stores - which can be quite time-consuming - and insist upon shoes fashioned entirely from man-made materials.
I never wore furs, and I don't want to wear anything made from animals.

I just think that if one is vegetarian, one should be consistent.
You are absolutely right, 100 percent.

A Vegetarian Sourcebook
By Keith Akers

Animals do not want to be killed, of course, but in addition to being killed, they suffer a great deal of pain in the process of being turned into food. Of course, their slaughter itself causes a certain amount of pain (more or less, depending on the method of slaughter used). But the process by which the animals are raised in Western societies also causes suffering. Indeed, given the suffering of many animals' day-to-day life, slaughter itself is practically an act of mercy.

In most Western countries, animals are raised on "factory farms." The treatment animals receive in them is solely connected with price. While it is not necessary to be cruel to animals prior to their slaughter, it does save money.

There is no disagreement about the basic facts concerning the way animals are treated on these factory farms. The nature and types of pain endured by animals in the process of being raised on such farms have been detailed frequently before, most notably in Peter Singer's Animal Liberation. I will spare the reader too many of the grisly details, but will indicate the broad outlines of the issue Singer treats so well in his book.

Crowding is the worst problem. Indeed, it is the main cause of the high mortality rate amougt many factory farm animals. Chickens typically lose 10 percent or 15 percent of their population before they ever get to the slaughterhouse. Veal calves suffer a 10 percent mortality in their brief 15 weeks of confinement. It makes more economic sense to crowd the animals together and increase mortality than to pay the money necessary to maintain all of the animals in more humane conditions.

Chickens are probably the most abused animals. Near the end of its 8 or 9-week life, a chicken may have no more space than a sheet of notebook paper to stand on. Laying hens are crowded into cages so small that none can so much as stretch its wings. This inevitably leads to feather-pecking and cannibalism - the chickens attack and even eat each other. Obviously, such chickens are under a great deal of stress.

The manufacturer's response to this is de-beaking - cutting off most or all of the chicken's beak. Of course, this causes severe pain in the chickens, but prevents the cannibalism.

A similar problem arises when pigs are kept in confinement systems. Pigs, under the stress of the factory farm system, bite each other's tails. The solution, or course, is tail-docking, whereby the tail is largely removed.

About 75 percent of all cattle in the industrialized countries spend the last months of their lives in feedlots, where they are fattened for slaughter. Cattle usually have at least some degree of freedom for the first months of their lives, veal calves being the exception. Veal calves are kept in very small stalls, prevented even from turning around, and kept deliberately anemic. They are denied any roughage or iron. The purpose of this is to keep the flesh pale-looking. It has no effect on the nutritional value of the meat (except perhaps to make it less nutritious); it does not even alter the taste. The only effect this cruel diet has is to produce a pale-colored flesh.

Transportation of animals is frequently another traumatic event in the life of any animal destined for slaughter. Cattle may spend one or two days in a truck without any food, water, or heat - which can be terrifying, and even deadly, in winter time. It is not unusual for cattle to lose 9 percent of their body weight while being transported. About 24 hours or so before slaughter, all the animal's food and water is cut off - there is no point in feeding an animal food which won't be digested before it is killed.

The act of slaughter is not necessarily painful. In many slaughterhouses in the United States, animals must be stunned before having their throats slit. After being rendered unconscious, they are bled to death. The animals must experience awful terror in the minutes or hours before they are killed, smelling the blood of those who have gone before. But the moment of death itself need not be painful at all. Unfortunately, not all slaughterhouses utilize such stunning devices. It is probable, in such cases, that an animal bleeds to death while fully conscious.

The fact of death is almost impossible to minimize in most systems which produce animals for food. In our culture, the use of animals for food in any way usually means putting the animals to death. Even dairy cows and laying hens are likely to wind up in someone's soup once they cease producing. Efficient production of milk, eggs, or meat for humans invariably entails substantial suffering for the animals and - sooner or later - death. The ugly reality of modern factory farms is an open book, and for this reason I have not gone into detail. Peter Singer's comments are worth quoting at this point.

"Killing animals is in itself a troubling act. It has been said that if we had to kill our own meat we would all be vegetarians. There may be exceptions to that general rule, but it is true that most people prefer not to inquire into the killing of the animals they eat. Yet those who, by their purchases, require animals to be killed have no right be be shielded from this or any other aspect of the production of the meat they buy. If it is distasteful for humans to think about, what can it be like for the animals to experience it?"

Ethical Significance of these Facts

Among vegetarians there is certainly no consensus on what ethical system, philosophy, or religion one ought to have. Most ethical vegetarians, though, agree on these two points:

- Animals suffer real pain at the hands of meat producers, both from their horrible living conditions and, in some cases, from the way they are slaughtered; and in no case do animals want to die.
- Animals are our fellow creatures and are entitled to at least some of the same considerations that we extend to out (human) fellow creatures; specifically, not to suffer or be killed unnecessarily.

Very few have seriously attacked the first view, that animals suffer real pain or have real feelings. Some have questioned whether animals suffer quite as much pain as humans do, perhaps because animals (allegedly) cannot foresee events in the same way that humans do. Only one major philosopher, Descartes, is said to have held the extreme view that animals have no feelings whatsoever — that they are automations.

The second issue though, whether animals are our fellow creatures, entitled to those same considerations that we accord other human beings or even pets, is less obvious. This issue requires a more thorough examination.

Are Animals Our Fellow Creatures?

Most people recognize a set of living beings whom they acknowledge to be entitled to a certain amount of consideration of their part. The inhibitions against killing or mistreating one's own family or near relations may very well have a biological basis. Most human beings extend the idea of a "fellow creature" to other humans of their own race or nationality and often to all humans anywhere. The most logical ethical vegetarian position is that this idea would be extended to include animals as well as humans.

Animals are like us in many ways. They have the senses of sight, taste, touch, smell and hearing. They can communicate, though usually on a more rudimentary level than humans. They experience many of the same emotions that humans do, such as fear or excitement. So why shouldn't animals be considered our fellow creatures?

There are three frequently heard attacks on the idea that animals are our fellow creatures. These kinds of attacks can be summarized as follows:

- Killing for food is natural; "Animals kill other animals. Lions kill zebras, and spiders kill flies. Killing for food is part of nature; it can't be wrong for us to do something, which is natural.
- Animals are significantly different from people, so it's all right to kill animals: "We can only have equal considerations for those who are our equals. Animals are not our equals; they are weaker than we are, and they are not rational. Therefore they are not our fellow creatures, and it can't be wrong to eat them."
- To abstain from killing is absurd: "Plants are living creatures too. Perhaps plants have feelings. If one objects to killing, logically one ought to object to eating all living creatures, and thus ought not to eat plants either."

Let us examine these arguments one by one.

Is Killing for Food Natural?

The first argument, perhaps the most sophisticated, concedes that animals may be in some sense our fellow creatures and that animals suffer real pain. But because of the dictates of nature, it is sometimes all right to kill and eat our fellow creatures; or alternatively, it is all right to eat those of our fellow creatures which, as a species, are naturally food for us.

This is quite an admirable argument. It explains practically everything; why we do not eat each other, except under conditions of unusual stress; why we may kill certain other animals (they are in the order of nature, food for us); even why we should be kind to pets and try to help miscellaneous wildlife (they are not naturally our food). There are some problems with the idea that an order of nature determines which species are food for us, but an order against eating certain species may vary from culture to culture.

The main problem with this argument is that it does not justify the practice of meat-eating or animal husbandry as we know it today; it justifies hunting. The distinction between hunting and animal husbandry probably seems rather fine to the man in the street, or even to your typical rule-utilitarian moral philosopher. The distinction, however, is obvious to an ecologist. If one defends killing on the grounds that it occurs in nature, then one is defending the practice as it occurs in nature.

When one species of animal preys on another in nature, it only preys on a very small proportion of the total species population. Obviously, the predator species relies on its prey for it continued survival. Therefore, to wipe the prey species out through overhunting would be fatal. In practice, members of such predator species rely on such strategies as territoriality to restrict overhunting, and to insure the continued existence of its food supply. Moreover, only the weakest members of the prey species are the predator's victims; the feeble, the sick, the lame or the young accidentally separated from the fold. The life of the typical zebra is usually placid, even in lion country. This kind of violence is the exception in nature, not the rule.

As it exists in the wild, hunting is the preying upon of isolated members of any animal herd. Animal husbandry is the nearly complete annihilation of an animal herd. In nature, this kind of slaughter does not exist. The philosopher is free to argue that there is no moral difference between hunting and the slaughter, but he cannot invoke nature as a defense of this idea.

Why are hunters, not butchers, most frequently taken to task by the larger community for their killing of animals? Hunters usually react to such criticism by replying that if hunting is wrong, then meat-eating must be wrong as well. The hunter is certainly right on one point - the larger community is hypocritical to object to hunting when it consumes the flesh of domesticated animals. If any form of meat-eating is justified, it would be meat from hunted animals.

Is hunting wrong? A vegetarian could reply that killing is always wrong and that animals have a right to live. This would seem to have the odd consequence that it is not only wrong for humans to kill, but that it is wrong for lions to kill zebras, spiders to catch flies, and so on. If animals have a right not be killed, then they would seem to have a right not to be killed by any species, human or nonhuman.
There are two ways of replying to such an apparent paradox:

> • to draw a distinction between necessary and unnecessary killing. Humans have an alternative: they do not have to eat meat. A tiger or wolf, on the other hand, knows no other way. Killing can be justified if only it is necessary, and for humans it is not.
> • to accept the challenge, and to agree that the most desirable state of the world is one, in which all killing, even between nonhumans animals, has ceased. Such a world would, perhaps, be like that envisioned by Isaiah in which the wolf would lie down with the lamb...After humans become vegetarians, we can start to work on the wolves.

Class of Nonviolence

Are Animals Different from People?

The second argument justifying meat consumption is usually expressed as a sort of reverse social contract theory. Animals are different from people; there is an unbridgeable gulf between humans and animals, which relieves us of the responsibility of treating animals in the same way that we would treat humans.

David Hume argues that because of our great superiority to animals, we cannot regard them as deserving of any king of justice: "Our intercourse with them could be called society, which supposes a degree of equality, but absolute command on the one side, and servile obedience on the other. Whatever we covet, they must instantly resign: Our permission is the only tenure, by which they hold their possessions...This is plainly the situation of men, with regard to animals."

Society and justice, for Hume, presuppose equality. The problem with this theory is that it justifies too much. Hume himself admits in the next paragraph that civilized Europeans have sometimes, due to their "great superiority", thrown off all restraints of justice in dealing with "barbarous Indians" and that men, in some societies, have reduced women to a similar slavery. Thus, Hume's arguments appear to justify not only colonialism and sexual discrimination, but probably also racism, infanticide and basically anything one can get away with.

Thomas Aquinas provides a different version of the unbridgeable gulf theory. This time it is the human possession of reason, rather than superior force, that makes us so different from animals. Aquinas states that we have no obligations to animals because we can only have obligations to those with whom we can have fellowship. Animals, not being rational, cannot share in our fellowship. Thus, we do not have any duties of charity to animals.

There are two possible responses to this: that the ability to feel, not the ability to reason, is what is ethically relevant; or that animals are not all that different from humans, being more rational than is commonly supposed.

Both of these objections are expressed briefly and succinctly by Jeremy Bentham: "A full-grown horse or dog is beyond comparison a more rational, as well as a more conversable animal, than an infant of a day, or a week, or even a month old. But suppose the case were otherwise, what would it avail? The question is not 'Can they reason?', nor, 'Can they talk?' but 'Can they suffer?'"

The problem is that none of the differences between humans and animals seem to be ethically significant. Animals are just as intelligent and communicative as small children or even some mentally defective humans. If we do not eat small children and mentally defective humans, then what basis do we have for eating animals? Animals certainly have feelings, and are aware of their environment in many significant ways. So while animals may not have all the same qualities that humans do, there would seem to be no basis for totally excluding them from our consideration.

Equal Rights for Plants?

A third argument seeks to reduce ethical vegetarianism to absurdity. If vegetarians object to killing living creatures (it is argued), then logically they should object to killing plants and insects as well as animals. But this is absurd. Therefore, it can't be wrong to kill animals.

Fruitarians take the argument concerning plants quite seriously; they do not eat any food which causes injury or death to either animals or plants. This means, in their view, a diet of those fruits, nuts, and seeds which can be eaten without the destruction of the plant that bears their food. Finding a theoretically significant line between plants and animals, though, is not particularly difficult. Plants have no evolutionary need to feel pain, and completely lack a central nervous system. Nature does not create pain gratuitously but only when it enables the organism to survive. Animals, being mobile, would benefit from having a sense of pain. Plants would not.

Even if one does not want to become a fruitarian and believes that plants have feelings (against all evidence to the contrary), it does not follow that vegetarianism is absurd. We ought to destroy as few plants as possible. And by raising and eating an animal as food, many more plants are destroyed indirectly by the animal we eat than if we merely ate the plants directly.

What about insects? While there may be reason to kill insects, there is no reason to kill them for food. One distinguishes between the way meat animals are killed for food and the way insects are killed. Insects are killed only when they intrude upon human territory, posing a threat to the comfort, health, or well-being of humans. There is a difference between ridding oneself of intruders and going out of one's way to find and kill something which would otherwise be harmless.

These questions may have a certain fascination for philosophers, but most vegetarians are not bothered by them. For any vegetarian who is not a biological pacifist, there would not seem to be any particular difficulty in distinguishing ethically between insects and plants on one hand, and animals and humans on the other.

Diet for a New America
By John Robbins

As the sun dawns across North America every morning, the wave of slaughter begins. Each day in the United States nine million chickens, turkeys, pigs, calves and cows meet their deaths at human hands. In the time it takes you to have your lunch, the number of animals killed is equal to the entire population of San Francisco. In our "civilized" society, the slaughter of innocent animals is not only an accepted practice, it is an established ritual.

We do not usually see ourselves as members of a flesh-eating cult. But all the signs of a cult are there. Many of us are afraid to even consider other diet-style choices, afraid to leave the safety of the group, afraid when there is any evidence that might reveal that the god of animal protein isn't quite all it's cracked up to be. Members of the great American Steak Religion frequently become worried if their family or friends show any signs of disenchantment. A mother may be more worried if her son or daughter becomes a vegetarian than if they take up smoking.

We are deeply conditioned in our attitudes towards meat. We have been taught to believe that our very health depends on it. Many of us believe our social status depends on the quality of our meat and the frequency with which we eat it; and we take it for granted that only someone who "can't afford meat" would do without it. Males have been conditioned to associate meat with their masculinity and quite a few men believe their sexual potency and virility depend on eating meat. Many women have been taught that a "good woman" feeds her man meat.

Our cultural conditioning tells us we must eat meat and at the same time systemically overlooks the basic realities of meat production. We've been indoctrinated so thoroughly that it has become the ocean in which we swim. Our language is so disempowered by euphemisms and clichés, our shared experience so weakened by repression, our common sense so distorted by ignorance, that we can easily be held prisoner by a point of view beneath the threshold of our awareness.

Only yesterday I was in a market which proudly proclaimed their chickens were "fresh." And here all along I had thought they were selling "dead" chickens. I suggested to the manager that he might be able to clear up any confusion on the matter in the minds of his clientele by changing the sign to read "freshly killed chickens," but he didn't seem overly grateful for my suggestion.

Piercing the Veil

What, then is it like for someone if, for a moment, he somehow manages to pierce through this veil of repression? Well, it can be downright shocking and can stir up a great deal of confusion and disturbance. Henry S. Salt gives us an account of his experience in his book, Seventy Years Among Savages.

"…and then I found myself realizing, with an amazement which time has not diminished, that the "meat" which formed the staple of our diet, and which I was accustomed to regard like bread or fruit, or vegetables - as a mere commodity of the table—was in truth dead flesh the actual flesh and blood of oxen, sheep, and swine, and other animals that were slaughtered in vast numbers."

The meat business depends on our repressing the unpleasant awareness that we are devouring dead bodies. Thus we have refined names like "sweet-breads" for what really are the innards of baby lambs and calves. We have names like "Rocky Mountain Oysters" for something we might not find quite so appealing if we knew what they really were—pig's testicles.

Our very language becomes an instrument of denial. When we look at the body of a dead cow, we call it a "side of beef." When we look at the body of a dead pig, we call it "ham," or "pork." We have been systematically trained not to see anything from the point of view of the animal, or even from a point of view which includes the animal's existence. In Alexandra Tolstoy's book, Tolstoy, A Life of My Father, she tells of a time her aunt came to dinner, and her father chose to burst the bubble of repression by which she kept herself isolated from the truth about her diet:

"Auntie was fond of food and when she was offered only a vegetarian diet she was indignant, said she could not eat any old filth, and demanded that they give her meat, chicken. The next time she came to dinner she was astonished to find a live chicken tied to her chair and a large knife at her plate.

"'What's this?' asked Auntie.

"'You wanted chicken,' Tolstoy replied, scarcely restraining his laughter, 'No one of us willing to kill it. Therefore we prepared everything so that you could do it yourself.' Apparently, Auntie was appalled at the thought of killing the animal she wished to eat. Like most of us, she did not enjoy being reminded where meat actually comes from. Most of us are willing to eat the flesh of animals, but dislike the sight of their blood, and prefer to think of ourselves, not as killers, but as consumers.

It has often been said that if we had to kill the animals we eat, the number of vegetarians would rise astronomically. To keep us from thinking along such lines, the meat industry does everything it can to help us blank the matter out of our minds. As a result, most of us know very little about slaughterhouses. If we think about them at all, we probably assume and hope that the animals enjoy a quick and painless death.

"Meat-packing plants" as slaughterhouses are euphemistically called, are not exactly the most pleasant of working environments. Just being surrounded by death and killing takes an incredible toll on a human being.

The turnover rate among slaughterhouse workers is the highest of any occupation in the country. The Excel Corporation plant in Dodge City, Kansas, for example, had a turnover rate of 43 percent per month in 1980 - the equivalent of a complete turnover of its entire 500-person work force every two and a half months.

One meat producer described a typical meat-packing plant atmosphere:

"Earphone-type sound mufflers help mute the deadening cacophony of high-pressure steam used for cleaning, the clanging of steel on steel as carcasses move down the slaughter line, the whine of the hide and tallow removers, and the snarling of a chain saw used to split carcasses into sides of beef here on the killing-room floor.

"The killing room - is filled with animals, minus their hooves, heads, tails and skins, which dangle down from an overhead track and slowly make their way past the various stations of the various slaughterhouse workers like macabre pinots.

"The animals (have) their throats -slit, and then- with tongues hanging limply out of their mouths- their bodies are unceremoniously hooked behind the tendons of their rear legs and are swung upon into the air onto the overhead track, which moves them through the killing room like bags of clothes on a dry cleaner motorized rack. Once bled, their hooves are clipped off with a gigantic pair of hydraulic pincer. They are then beheaded, skinned--and finally eviscerated."

Amidst this carnage, workers in blood-spattered white coats and helmets are in constant notion, removing cattle legs with electric shears, skinning hides with whirring air knives, disemboweling animals with razor-bladed straight knives. The floors are slick with animal grease and the air is thick with stench.

It is a terribly difficult atmosphere in which to work. According to U.S. Labor Department statistics, the rate of injury in meatpacking houses is the highest of any occupation in the nation. Every year, over 30 percent of packing-house workers suffer on-the-job injuries requiring medical attention.

The same attitudes which determine policies in factory farms govern decisions in slaughterhouses, and these are not attitudes of compassion for the animals. A leading poultry producer discussed the philosophy underlying his endeavors in the trade journal Poultry World:

"I am in this business for what I can make out of it. If it pays me to do this or that, I do it and so far as I am concerned that is all there is to say about it."
The industry chooses the cheapest possible methods of killing. They do not purposefully choose to be brutal and sadistic. It just works out that way.

The "captive-bolt pistol" is one of the most effective methods of stunning cow, pigs, and other animals unconscious prior to killing them. Unfortunately, however, the cost of the charges used to fire the thing is enough to deter many slaughterhouses from using it. You must wonder how much money is saved thus, at the cost of forcing the animal to be fully conscious when killed. I've become somewhat accustomed to the industry's callousness, but I was still stunned to learn the savings amount to approximately a single penny an animal.

How They Taught Us

I am sitting in elementary school. The teacher is bringing out a nice-colored chart and telling all us kids how important it is to eat meat and drink our milk and get lots of protein. I'm listening to her, and looking at the chart which makes it all seem so simple. I believe my teacher, because I sense that she, herself, believes what she is saying. She is sincere. She is a grown-up. Besides, the chart is decorated and fun to look at. It must be true.

Protein, I hear, that's what's important. Protein. Lots of it. And you can only get good quality protein from meat and eggs and dairy products. That's why they make up two of the four "basic food groups" on the chart.

That day at lunch I feel like doing something good for myself and the world, so I spend the 10 cents I have left of my weekly allowance for another carton of milk.

Now I am an adult, and looking back, I know my teacher had all we could handle to keep control of the classroom and teach a few basics. When teaching aids were given to her that helped get the class's attention, and helped ease her burden, she was grateful. Not for a moment did it occur to her to wonder about the political dynamics that lead to the development of those aids. Neither she nor any of us little kids could have imagined that the pretty chart was actually the outcome of extensive political lobbying by the huge meat and dairy conglomerates. Nor could we have imagined the many millions of dollars which had been poured into the campaigns that produced those pretty chars. My teacher believed what she taught us, and never for a moment suspected was she being used to relay industrial propaganda.

Our innocent and captive little minds soaked it all up like sponges. And most of us, as planned, have been willing and unquestioning consumers of vast amounts of meat and dairy products ever since. Even those few of us who have come to experiment with vegetarian diet styles are often still haunted by the voices of our teachers and the lessons of those charts. When things aren't going well, a voice in the back of our minds whispers: "Maybe you aren't getting enough protein."

Step Right Up, Step Right Up

Of course, just because the concept of the "basic four" food groups was promoted by the National Egg Board, the National Dairy Council, and the National Livestock and Meat Board, doesn't mean it is necessarily false. Just because there were hucksters in our classrooms doesn't mean the hucksters lied.

But it does mean their motives were a little less pure than we thought, and their "concern" for our education a little more self-interested than we knew. It might cast a shadow upon the wisdom of unquestioningly accepting the "truths" we were taught. It might mean, for example, that we should consult sources of information less biased than the Egg Board, or the Meat Board, or the others who applied so much political and economic pressure to get those nice pretty charts to say what they wanted them to say.

Roger Williams, the biochemist and nutrient researcher who has probably contributed more to our understanding of biochemical individuality than any scientist alive, suggests that the range of protein needs among people may vary as much as fourfold. Interestingly, a fourfold range is just the span covered by the extremes of current scientific thinking. For if we top off the highest figures to make room for the extra protein needs of the most extreme cases, we have a spectrum ranging from two and a half percent at the low end up to ten percent at the top. Science tells us that the protein needs of the vast majority of people would be easily met within that range.

Nature, it seems, would agree totally. Human mother's milk provides five percent of its calories from protein. Nature seems to be telling us that little babies, whose bodies are growing the fastest they will ever grow in their life, and whose protein needs are therefore at a maximum, are best served by the very modest level of five percent protein.

What If We Need a Whole lot?

But what if we happen to be one of those people whose biochemical individualities are such that we need a whole lot of protein? What if we are at the high end of the spectrum? Don't we need to eat meat in order to get enough? And if not meat, don't we then need eggs or dairy products?

Even if fact, we were at the very top end of the spectrum in terms of our protein needs, needing to derive a full 10 percent of our calories from protein, unless we are trying to live only on fruits and sweet potatoes, vegetarian foodstuffs easily provide for our protein needs. If we ate only brown rice, and if our biochemical individualities required the maximum of protein, then, or course, we would fall a little short. But if we do nothing more than include beans or fresh vegetables to complement the rice, then our protein needs are easily and well satisfied without recourse to any animal products. This is true even in the most extreme case, where our protein needs are at the very highest end of the spectrum. If we ate nothing but wheat (which is 17 percent protein), or oatmeal (15 percent), or pumpkin (15 percent), we would easily have more than enough protein. If we ate nothing but cabbage (22 percent), we'd have over double the maximum we might need.

In fact, if we ate nothing but the lowly potato (11 percent protein) we would still be getting enough protein. This fact does not mean potatoes are a particularly high protein source. They are not. Almost all plant foods provide more. What it does show, however, is just how low our protein needs really are.

There have been occasions in which people have been forced to satisfy their entire nutritional needs with potatoes and water alone. I wouldn't recommend the idea to anyone, but under deprived circumstances it has been done. Individuals who have lived for lengthy periods under those conditions showed no sign whatsoever of protein deficiency, though other vitamin deficiencies have occurred.

You might think that with the growing wave of evidence indicating saturated fat and cholesterol as killers of more Americans than all the wars in our nation's history combined, the meat, dairy, and egg industries would be hard-pressed to maintain control over our food and nutrition policies. But the cards are stacked. They may not have interests of public health on their side, but their lobbying groups and political action committees are well financed, batttle-hardened veterans of political in-fighting. Opposing them are scientists and medical researchers whose skills don't lie in the political sphere, and who have little financial backing compared to what the industries provide their representatives. The fight is far from fair.

"As a rule, scientists and medical researchers make poor players in the complex game of special-interest politics, although they often think otherwise. They are not well endowed with the stamina, patience, and shrewdness that this game requires, and deep down they view it as an anti-intellectual activity beneath their scholarly dignity. Even when organized into illustrious professional groups they shrink from combat and bloodletting. This is more a reflection of the unsuitedness of their training and temperament to the political arena than is a mark of weakness of conviction."

On one side of the battlefield stands a formidable and experienced alliance of meat, egg, and dairy producers, with their purchased political and scientific allies. On the other side stands a relatively unorganized collection of independent medical researchers, underfinanced public interest and consumer groups, and the handful of political leaders who are willing to endure the sizable risk of an unpopular stance.

In this battle, the industries who sell us foods high in saturated fats and cholesterol have produced multimillion-dollar public relation campaigns, telling us brightly of the "incredible, edible egg," saying that beef is "nutrition you can sink your teeth into," and reassuring us the "milk does a body good." They do not mention that these foods clog our arteries, and promote heart disease and strokes.

Of course no advertising mentions the disadvantages of the products it promotes. But time and time again these industries have drawn the ire of consumer groups, the courts, and medical researchers for their flagrant disregard of fact.

Stillpoint Publishing, Walpole, NH

Diet for a Small Planet
By Frances Moore Lappé

How did you get interested in food? How did you come to write Diet for a Small Planet? Countless times I have been asked these questions. Invariably I am frustrated with my answers. I never really get to explain. So, here it is. This is my chance.

I am a classic child of the 1960s. I graduated from a small Quaker college in 1966, a year of extreme anguish for many, and certainly for me: the war in Vietnam, the civil rights movement, the War on Poverty. That year was the turning point.

While I had supported the U.S. position on the Vietnam War for years, finally I became too uncomfortable merely accepting the government's word. I set out to discover the facts for myself. Why were we fighting? I read everything I could find on U.S. government policy in Vietnam. Within a few weeks, my world began to turn upside down. I was in shock. I functioned, but in a daze. I had grown up believing my government represented me—my basic ideals. Now I was learning that "my" government was not mine at all.

From that state of shock grew feelings of extreme desperation. Our country seemed in such a terrible state that something had to be done, now, today, or all hope seemed lost. I wanted to work with those who were suffering the most, so I did what people like Tom Hayden suggested. For two years, 1967 and 1968, I worked as a community organizer in Philadelphia with a national nonprofit organization of welfare recipients—the Welfare Rights Organization. Our goal was to ensure that welfare recipients got what they were entitled to by law.

Then, in the spring of 1969, I made the most important decision of my life (next to the decision to have children, that is): I vowed not to do anything to try to "change the world" until I understood why I had chosen one path instead of another, until I understood how my actions could attack the roots of needless suffering.

The first struggle for me and for so many of my friends has been to reconcile our vision of the future with the compromises we must make every day just to survive in our society. If we attempt to be totally "consistent," eschewing all links between ourselves and the exploitative aspects of our culture, we drive ourselves—and those close to us—nuts! I still remember my annoyance as a friend, sitting with me in a restaurant in the late 1960s, scornfully picked the tiny bits of ham out of her omelet.

Who wants to be around someone so righteous that they make you feel guilty all the time? But while self-righteousness is not very effective in influencing people, this does not mean we should not try to make our personal choices consistent with out political vision. Indeed, this is exactly where we have to begin.

If the solution to needless hunger lies in the redistribution of decision-making power, we must become part of the redistribution. That means exercising to the fullest our power to make choices in our daily life. It means working with other people to force the few who have more power to share it with the majority. It also means preparing ourselves to share responsibility with others in areas that we now leave to unaccountable "experts" and politicians.

All this implies taking ourselves seriously, which for years I found difficult. In part, taking ourselves seriously means taking responsibility for how our individual life choices either sustain our challenge the antidemocratic nature of our society.

What do we eat? What we eat links us to every aspect of the economic order. Do we allow ourselves to be victimized by that structure, or do we choose a diet that the earth can sustain and that can best sustain our own bodies?

Where do we shop? Do we support the handful of supermarket chains that are tightening their grip over food? In more than a quarter of all U.S. cities, four chains control at least 60 percent of all sales. That tight control means monopoly power and monopoly prices. In 1974 Americans were overcharged $660 million due to concentration of control by supermarket chains alone. Or do we support the growth of a more democratic alternative, the mushrooming network of consumer- and worker-managed retail food cooperatives, which already have more than three million patrons? Their consumers have much greater influence over what is sold and where the products come from.

In school, how do we study? Are we studying to please the professor, or to hone our knowledge to heighten our own power? Are we studying toward a narrow career path, or to prepare ourselves for a life of change?

How do we try to learn about the world? Only through the mass media, whose interpretations and choice of stories reinforce the status quo? Or do we seek alternative sources of information that discuss the lessons which we might learn from our counterparts here and abroad?

Where do we work? One of the greatest tragedies of our economic system is that few people are able to earn a livelihood and still feel that they are making a meaningful contribution to society. So many jobs produce either weapons of destruction or frivolous nonessentials. Therefore, our struggle is first to find a livelihood that reflects our vision of the world. If that is not possible, then we can do what more and more people are doing—find the least destructive job that pays, and then devote our creative energies to unpaid work. (Some of the volunteers at our institute have chosen this path.) But just as important are these questions:

How do we work? Are we challenging the arbitrary hierarchies that we were taught to accept? Are we struggling to create structures in which responsibilities are shared and accountability is broadened—so that we are accountable not just to one boss but to one another and to ourselves?

Do we work alone (as I tried to do for too many years)? Or do we join with others to learn how to share decision-making power and to experience the excitement of collaborative work? (All the projects I have undertaken in the last six years have involved teamwork, and I'm convinced that the whole is greater than the sum of our individual contributions.)

How do we choose our friends? Do we surround ourselves with people who reinforce our habits and assumptions, or do we seek out people who challenge us?

Class of Nonviolence

Obviously these are only some of the questions that we must ask ourselves as we become part of the redistribution of power. Every choice we make that consciously aligns our daily life with our vision of a better future makes us more powerful people. We feel less victimized. As we gain confidence in ourselves, the more convincing we are to other people.

The less victimized we are by forces outside us, the freer we become. For freedom is not the capacity to do whatever we please; freedom is the capacity to make intelligent choices. This implies knowledge of the consequences of our actions. And that is what this book is all about—gaining the knowledge we need to make choices based upon awareness of the consequences of those choices.

Overcoming Hopelessness: Taking Risks

According to a 1980 Gallup Poll, Americans are more "hope-less" than the people in any other country polled except Britain and India. Fully 56 percent of Americans queried believed the coming year would be worse than the past year. These findings come as no surprise. Hopelessness is a growing American malady. Increasingly, Americans feel alienated from "their" government—witness the lowest voter turnout since 1948 in the Reagan-Carter contest. Americans increasingly perceive that their government operates in the interests of a privileged minority.

This hopelessness is born of the feelings of powerlessness I have been talking about. Consciously working to make our lives more consistent is the first step in attacking the powerlessness that generates despair—but only the first step.

Taking more responsibility for ourselves—and for the impact of our choices in the world—we start changing ourselves. This is the key to overcoming hopelessness. Unless we experience ourselves changing, can we really believe that illiterate peasants in the Philippines, El Salvador, or Chile can change? (After all, they face much greater obstacles and much stronger messages telling them of their own incapacity.)

If the belief that "the world" can change depends on changing ourselves, how do we start? I believe there is only way—we must take risks. There is no change without risk. The change, we must push ourselves to do what we thought we were incapable of doing.

What Do We Risk?

We risk being controversial. Personally, I hate being controversial! I hate it when people attack my views—or, worse, attack me. I remember burning inside when a well-known university president tried to dismiss my views on U.S. support for the Marcos dictatorship in the Philippines. "What does she know?" he said. "She's just a cookbook writer." I was outraged when a speaker sympathetic to agribusiness who shared the platform with me several years ago in Minneapolis tried to dismiss my positions by suggesting that I was getting personally wealthy from Diet for a Small Planet royalties and therefore was a hypocrite. (Royalties have allowed me to work full-time on food and hunger issues, and have helped pay the bills at the Institute for Food and Development Policy. The money I earned from speeches goes directly to the institute.) I grew up wanting everyone to like me (preferably, to love me!), but to change myself and to try to change the world, I have to accept that many people will not like me.

We risk being lonely. Maybe this is even harder. Changing yourself often means taking independent positions that those closest to you cannot accept. For me, this meant deciding I no longer wanted to be married. At the prospect of being on my own, I experienced the greatest pain and terror I had ever felt. I can't deny that I do feel lonely sometimes, but I came to realize that many of the most important things I wanted to do, I could only do alone. Yes, I do work in a team. I enjoy our meetings, making plans and reacting to each other's work. But when it comes right down to getting the words on the page, it is me and the typewriter. I came to learn also that there is a reward for being alone in order to do what I believe in: I feel connected to others who share my vision, not only to others at the institute but to a growing network of people throughout the world.

We risk being wrong. Taking controversial positions is hard enough, but how do we deal with our fear of being wrong? Part of the answer for me was discovering that those learned academics and government officials—whom I believed—are wrong. They may be mostly correct in their statistics, but how useful are statistics if their questions are the wrong questions? Those "experts" intimidate so many of us and use their grasp of trivial detail to avoid asking the important questions. (In Rome in 1974, all the experts were asking, "How can we increase food production?" But I had already learned that many counties were increasing food production faster than their population grew and yet had more hunger than ever.)

In learning not to fear being wrong, I had to accept that to ask the important questions is to ask big questions—and this inevitably entails crossing many disciplines. If you have read our book Food First, you know what I mean. The material spans dozens of disciplines, from anthropology to climatology to nutrition to economics. When you ask big questions, it is impossible to be an "expert" in everything that you study. But instead of being paralyzed by that realization, I try to keep in mind the advice of a wise friend. "If you ask a big question you may get something wrong," Marty Strange told me. "But if you ask a small question—as most narrow academics do—it doesn't matter if you're wrong. Nobody cares!" My positions have changed as I have learned. In process, I have become more convinced that acting out of sheer emotion, even genuine compassion, is not enough. If we are serious about committing our lives to positive social change, we must always be learning, and accepting the logical consequences of what we learn as a basis for what we do.

Yes, we must be able to risk—risk being controversial, risk being lonely, risk being wrong. Only through risk-taking do we gain the strength we need to take responsibility—and to be part of the redistribution of political and economic power essential for a solution to needless hunger.

But How Do We Learn to Take Risks?

Few people change alone. As I have already suggested, we must choose friends and colleagues who will push us to what we thought we could not do. But we must select friends who will "catch" us, too, when we push ourselves too far and need to be supported. Wherever we are, we must not be content to work alone. Only if we experience the possibility and the rewards of shared decision-making in our own lives—in our families, our schools, our community groups, our workplaces—will we believe in the possibility of more just sharing of decision-making in our government and economic structures.

Second, we must learn to associate risk with joy as well as pain. Despite my parents' struggle against racism and McCarthyism through the Unitarian church they founded, the cultural messages were so strong that I grew up believing that the "good life" we all are seeking would be a life without risk-taking. This was my "sailboat" image of the good life. First you work to acquire your sailboat (husband, kids, etc.), then you set your sails, and go off into the sunset. Of course, I assumed that you might have to adjust the sails now and then. But, short of hurricanes, I thought of life as a continuous and relatively riskless journey.

Well, at the age of 37 my view of the good life is different. I discovered that a life without risk is missing the ingredient—joy. If we never risk being afraid, failing, being lonely, we will never experience that joy that comes only from learning that we can change ourselves. Third, we can gain inspiration from our counter-parts around the world whose lives entail risks much greater than ours. But this requires our seeking out alternative news sources, because the mass media rarely show us the courageous struggles of ordinary people. Learning about our counterparts around the world, we'll come to realize that we do not have to start the train moving. It is already moving. In every country where peole are suffering, there is resistance. Those who believe in the possibility of genuine democracy are building new forms of human organization. The question for each of us is, how can we board that train, and how can we remove the mighty obstacles in its way?

But none of what I have presented here makes much sense unless we develop a perspective longer than our lifetimes. Glenn, a volunteer at the institute, joked with us before he moved to the East Coast. "For a while I considered getting into your line of work—you know, trying to change the world—but I decided against it" he told us. "The problem is that you can go for weeks and not see any change!" We laughed. Glenn was right. It took hundreds and hundreds of years to create the web of assumptions and the unchallenged institutions of exploitation and privilege that people take for granted today. It will take a very long time to create new structures based on different values. But rather than belittling our task, this realization—seeing ourselves as part of a historical process longer than our lifetimes—can be a source of courage. Years ago I read an interview with I.F. Stone, the journalist who warned Americans about U.S. involvement in Vietnam long before antiwar sentiment became popular. He was asked, "How can you keep working so hard when no one is listening to you?" His answer: "I think that if you expect to see the final results of your work, you simply have not asked a big enough question." I've used Stone's answer in several books and probably too many speeches! For me it sums up an attitude we all must cultivate. I call it the "long-haul perspective."

A book on how our eating relates us to a system that destroys our food resources and deprives many of their right to food would seem, on the surface, to carry a message of guilt and self-denial. But not this book!

I don't think the solution to the tragedy of needless hunger lies in either guilt of self-denial. It lies rather in our own liberation. If we do not understand the world, we are bound to be its victims. But we do not have to be. We can come to see the tragedy of needless hunger as a tool for understanding.

We can discover that our personal and social liberation lies not in freedom from responsibility but in our growing capacity to take on greater responsibility.

"Terrorists" For Animal Rights
by Colman McCarthy

Police at the United States Capitol put the nation at risk last Sunday. They allowed an estimated 24,000 terrorists to gather for an afternoon rally on the west lawn of the Capitol. The group was an international assembly of citizens working for animal rights, labeled "terrorists" three days before by Louis Sullivan, secretary of health and human services. Sullivan, a physician who argues with a broadax more that a scalpel, said the "animal right terrorists" coming to the rally were "on the wrong side of morality." On the right side, Sullivan places—besides himself—medical researchers whose lethal experiments on hundreds of millions of animals have been carried out, until lately, with few constraints beyond amiable peer review, if that.

Sullivan's smear is part of an emerging counteroffensive being waged by those agencies or businesses whose grants and profits are animal-based. The secretary mouthed publicly what many researchers in lab coats have been grumbling among themselves for some time: animal right advocates are anti-science fanatics, while we are selfless pursuers of human advancement.

On hand for Sullivan's terrorism speech were several appreciative research organizations as well as some nonmedical slaughterers and tormentors of animals who also see themselves toiling away on behalf of humankind: the American Meat Institute, the National Cattlemen's Association, the National Pork Producers Council, the National Turkey Federation, and the National Broiler Council. A worry arises: If organized protests have lowered fur sales, can meat be next?

In medical research alone, large numbers are involved. The Department of Agriculture reported in 1988 that 140,471 dogs, 42,271 cats, 51,641 primates, 431,457 guinea pigs, 331,945 hamsters, 459,254 rabbits and 178,249 "wild animals" were used experimentally. That figure of 1.6 million animals, which excludes mice and rats, is an annual roll a small fraction of the estimated 10 million creatures killed daily for food in the United States.

Until the 1970s both commercialists and medical researchers killing animals had little reason to be on the defensive. Meat was not only macho but was promoted as necessary for health, and the only people alarmed at animal experimentation were a few antivivisectionists, usually in England.

The 1970s and '80s saw a flow of books and articles on factory farming, a surge of animal rights and vegetarian magazines, and new animal welfare legislation to protect creatures from carriage horses in Central Park to parrots imported from Central America. In 1980 People for the Ethical Treatment of Animals had a membership of six. Now it's 300,000. In the same decade, the Human Society of the United States grew from 160,000 to 963,000 members.

Sullivan's labeling these citizens "terrorists" on the "wrong side of morality" is a squeal of panic desperation. If he had more concern for the health of the public than the health of the medical research and meat industries, he would have skipped the polarizing invective. On animal testing, Sullivan may share the prevailing research opinion that human beings can ethically subject animals to pain that would never be sanctioned for people. But why isn't he raising questions on either the practicality or effectiveness of animal testing? Was it medically necessary for the U.S. Army to pay $2.1 million to Louisiana State University to shoot 700 cats in the head to learn that the animals had post-trauma breathing problems. Was it medically effective to force primates to inhale tobacco smoke to learn that it caused lung cancer?

These are the equivalents of the Pentagon needing $600 toilet seats to defend the free world. University and medical researchers have been as artful as military contractors in enriching themselves with grants to discover the miracle vaccine always just one more animal experiment away. Or two more. Or three more.

The barbarity of using animals in painful tests aside, which is where Sullivan and friends prefer it, the objection of People for the Ethical Treatment of Animals stands: "Despite the decades of animal research, no one has been cured of heart disease, multiple sclerosis, spina bifida, muscular dystrophy, diabetes, or cancer of the colon, breast, or uterus." Clean drinking water, food, and already available medicine can prevent nearly all the 60,000 disease-induced deaths that Oxfam reports are occurring daily in the Third World.

Louis Sullivan can keep on with his axings, but too many citizens are being educated on both the ethics and uselessness of killing animals for human benefit, greed, or pleasure. Changes, brought on by animal rights advocates, have come without commercial devastations. Revlon, Avon, and Mary Kay have recently stopped animal testing. Each had been routinely inflicting their chemicals on animals. Revlon now advertises its products as "cruelty-free."

It was terrorism, all right, behind this conversion, the fearful terror of losing money. Revlon lives. So do some animals.

Class of Nonviolence

Questions for Lesson Eight

1. Read about a contemporary environmental activist. Write about that person. In what ways was he or she effective in confronting environmental violence?

2. Do vegetarians carry things too far? After all, the life of plants is taken to feed them; what is different from that and taking an animal's life to sustain us?

3. Do animals have rights? Explain.

4. How do you envision your relationship with the rest of nature? Do other elements of Nature exist primarily for our use? Read the essays of Gary Snyder, The Practice of the Wild.

5. Carson McCullers wrote that, "before you can love a person you have to start with simpler things and gradually build your skills - start with a rock, a cloud, a tree." Is this too simplistic a notion?

TEACHING PEACE?

Class of Nonviolence: 48 Readings, by Colman McCarthy

University Essays for the Class of Nonviolence: 77 Readings, by Colman McCarthy

Facilitator's Manual for the Class of Nonviolence by Susan Ives; foreword by Colman McCarthy

Peace is Our Birthright: *the p.e.a.c.e. process and interfaith community development* by Ann E. Helmke and Rosalyn Falcón Collier, with a foreword by Arun Gandhi

Hajj Journal by Narjis Pierre, with an introduction & photographs by Ali Moshirsadri

Insights on the Journey: *Trauma, Healing and Wholeness.* Anthology of Women's writing compiled by Maureen Leach, OSF

Working It Out! *Managing and Mediating Everyday Conflicts* by Rosalyn Falcón Collier

Death Sentences: 34 Classic Short Stories about the Death Penalty Susan Ives (editor) with a foreword by Jay Brandon

End of the Line: Five Short Novels about the Death Penalty, Susan Ives (editor)

Detour to Death Row by David Atwood, founder, Texas Coalition to Abolish the Death Penalty

Capital Ideas: 150 Classic Writers on the Death Penalty, from the Code of Hammurabi to Clarence Darrow, Susan Ives (editor)

Visualize Whirled Peas: Vegan Cooking from the San Antonio peaceCENTER, Susan Ives

Shall We Ever Rise? A Holy Walk Lenten collages by Rosalyn Falcón Collier and Ann E. Helmke

Cerca de la Cerca: Near the Border Fence. Photographs by María Teresa Fernández

Time-tested information written from decades of grassroots experience, designed for all who seek peace, teach peace, demonstrate peace and celebrate peace.

San Antonio, Texas **peaceCenter**

1443 S. St. Mary's, San Antonio, TX 78210 210.224.HOPE pcebooks@yahoo.com

www.salsa.net/peace/ebooks

Ask us about bulk purchase discounts for bookstores, classes and community groups

Made in the USA
Charleston, SC
15 September 2012